ESSAYS IN ECONOMIC DYNAMICS

By the same author

ELEMENTARY ECONOMICS FROM THE HIGHER STANDPOINT
ESSAYS IN LINEAR ECONOMIC STRUCTURES (*forthcoming*)

ESSAYS IN ECONOMIC DYNAMICS

R. M. Goodwin

First published 1982 by
THE MACMILLAN PRESS LTD
London and Basingstoke
Companies and representatives throughout the world

ISBN 0 333 29094 1

Printed in Hong Kong

Contents

Preface

These essays, together with a separate forthcoming volume devoted to linear disaggregation, represent those of my writings that seem worth preserving. Arranged in chronological order, they embody a long, rather desultory preoccupation with ways of re-formulating economic problems in a more illuminating fashion. The first paper, though rather dated because of institutional change, is retained partly for its own worth and partly because of the current vogue of monetarism. Originally I was taught that the misbehaviour of the economy stemmed from the banking system, so that if it were only properly controlled, all would be well — a doctrine that is again popular with both academics and politicians. My doctoral study of the British monetary system gave strong grounds for doubting this, both because of the tenuous connection between the control parameters and actual spending of money, and because of the ways in which producers can circumvent attempts at control.

Disillusion with monetary management was re-enforced by my growing interest in cycle theory. It all stemmed from Jacob Marschak's superb seminar in Oxford, during which we studied a survey by Tinbergen of business cycle theory. This convinced me once and for all that it was not only possible but likely that the 'real' behaviour of the economy could and would be wave-like, quite without help from the banks. This, plus the impact of the *General Theory*, accounts for the predominance of essays on cycles.

The particular direction my work took can best be understood in terms of my personal history. At the time Keynes's book was nearing publication, I was a pupil of Harrod: he was undertaking to fill a glaring gap in the *General Theory* by a book on the trade cycle phrased in terms of the accelerator and the multiplier. I was, and still am, much impressed by that largely forgotten book, but I felt that its intuition far outran its analytic expertise. I told him that Tinbergen, reviewing the book in a German periodical, had pointed out that the accelerator plus multiplier gave a first order differential equation and hence could only produce exponential growth not cycles. Harrod seems to have been convinced by this, for two years later he produced his famous article on growth.

Nonetheless, in spite of the fatal impact of the criticism, I continued to feel that Harrod and not Tinbergen had the sounder view of capitalist dynamics, but that he lacked the technical equipment necessary to formulate and solve the problem. Consequently I continued to mull over the issue; illumination, however, had to wait for a spell of teaching physics at Harvard during the war. There I met and sat at the feet of Philippe Le Corbeiller, a mathematician who had specialised in the theory of oscillators. He told me that electronics engineers had originally analysed their cycle generators by assuming that the first order parameter was zero in a linear second order equation. This approach, whilst giving some correct results, had proved to be quite inadequate: it was replaced by the far richer and more productive assumption of certain crucial non-linearities, yielding stable limit cycles of a great variety of wave forms. I realised that this had been the burden of Frisch's criticism of Kalecki's original cycle model: it was a case of what would now be called structural instability, though the concept was then unknown. In my view Frisch's resolution (in the Cassel Festschrift) was not very helpful. Non-linearities gave the more fruitful answer, an answer which also largely eluded Kalecki.

For a number of years I worked exclusively on the problem of reformulating business cycle theory in a way which would conform to the well-known facts of the history of capitalism and yet be capable of rigorous analytic treatment. In my view at least three requirements had to be met. Growth had to be envisaged in terms of the impact of innovations and not in the repetitive form of the accelerator (this from Schumpeter whose influence on me was greater than any of my other teachers). Secondly, the accelerator, basic to cycle theory, had to be conceived in a more flexible form. (Being much impressed by Norbert Wiener's generalisation of the engineering concept of negative feedback control, I incorporated it into the accelerator.) Finally, these things had to be combined in such a way as to describe a system that would have a stable equilibrium motion, the dynamical analogue of a stable equilibrium point. In a sense the culmination of some thirty years fitful preoccupation with Harrod's problem may be found in the essay 'A Growth Cycle', where I tried to arrange an indissoluble union of growth and cycle, instead of the usual marriage of convenience. It had long been clear to me that most of the inadequacies of cycle models stemmed from the failure to incorporate growth: likewise every economist knows, but ignores, the fact that growth proceeds in spurts. By adapting an analysis of Volterra I was able to construct a model in which neither would exist without the other, and at the same time to bring Marx back into a picture from which he should never have been absent.

In conceptualising the problem of the irregular growth of capitalism, I came early on to the conclusion that the right way to visualise the process was of an elastic system bumping repeatedly against a rising 'ceiling'. Consequently I was critical of the use of a 'floor' along with a 'ceiling' in various models, because a rising trend of investment is not a datum but a part of the system. The basic, single, given, short-run non-linearity is full employment, whether of capacity or of labour. In pursuit of this conception, I formulated a one-sided oscillatory economic model, which, I was told by Le Corbeiller, represented a hitherto unknown class of oscillator. A paper by Professor Le Corbeiller explaining the theory is included as an Appendix. Though the exposition is in physical–mathematical terms, economists should not ignore it, in view of its potential importance. All cycle models have more or less difficulties in explaining the lower turning point and any use of exogenous investment is suspect. The various cycle essays in this volume are all to some extent concerned with this problem. Only with the use of the Volterra–Lotka model did I feel at last close to a sound formulation, because it is based on the Phillips curve, which is simply the expression of the consequences of full employment. However, though in essence satisfying, that model still yields a conservative system (a closed curve in phase space) which, as Le Corbeiller had taught me, is no proper way to explain the persistence of cycles. In fact by the introduction of a single, appropriately formulated, non-linearity, the model can be rendered structurally stable *and* yield a single, stable limit cycle, along the lines adumbrated in the Le Corbeiller paper.

Capitalism has both stable and unstable aspects: the Malthusian Catastrophe paper is an exercise in structural, as distinct from dynamical, instability. Under certain circumstances a small parametric change can set a system on a totally different course with far reaching consequences. This is an important aspect of phase space analysis: it permits qualitative as opposed to quantitative analysis. How important this is for economics can be grasped from the simple fact that there is not in the whole of economics one single reliable number available for use in analysis or control. I would expect qualitative state space analysis to play an increasing role in the future. The essay on optimal growth arose from my experience in working on the second five-year plan in India. Everyone wanted to accelerate growth but no one seemed to know in principle how much, how fast and for how long. In working out a simple answer, I found I was re-tracing Ramsey's steps.

Schumpeter's great admiration for Walras always seemed somewhat excessive in view of the latter's neglect of dynamics. Iteration appeared to me to be the natural way to remedy this defect in Walras and the essay presented here is the result. The piece on dynamical coupling was an attempt to face some of the complications of disaggregation and to suggest ways of dealing with them. The remaining essay represents an attempt to reconcile Keynesian liquidity preference with more conventional theories of interest.

It is evident how much I have been influenced by my teachers, and I have found great satisfaction in teaching others in turn. If this collection enables me to reach some others, I shall be very pleased.

Peterhouse, September 1979 R. M. Goodwin

Acknowledgements

The author and publishers are grateful to the following, in whose books and journals the essays in this book first appeared: Bulletin of Economic Research for the article 'The Problem of Trend and Cycle' from *Yorkshire Bulletin*, vol. 5, no. 2, September 1953; Cambridge University Press for the articles 'The Multiplier as Matrix' (1949), 'Does the Matrix' (1950) and 'The Optimal Growth Path' (1961) from *Economic Journal*, and 'A Growth Cycle' from C. H. Feinstein (ed.), *Socialism, Capitalism and Economic Growth*; *Capital and Class* (the journal of the Conference of Socialist Economists) for 'Capitalism's Golden Rule' from *Bulletin of the Conference of Socialist Economists*, vol. 2, no. 2, 1972; the Econometric Society for the articles 'Dynamical Coupling with Especial Reference to Markets Having Production Lags' from *Econometrica*, vol. 15, no. 3, July 1947, and 'The Non-Linear Accelerator and the Persistence of Business Cycles' from *Econometrica*, vol. 19, no. 1, January 1951; North-Holland Publishing Company, Amsterdam, for the articles from the *Review of Economic Statistics*, 1943 and 1950; W. W. Norton for extracts from the articles 'Econometrics in Business-Cycle Analysis' from Alvin H. Hansen, *Business Cycles and National Income* (1951, 1979), and 'Secular and Cyclical Aspects' from L. A. Metzler (ed.), *Income, Employment and Public Policy: Essays in Honor of Alvin H. Hansen* (1948, 1976); Oxford University Press for the article 'The Supply of Bank Money' from *Oxford Economic Papers*, 5, 1941; Nuova Casa Editrice Licinio Capelli SpA, Bologna, for an extract from *Metroeconomica*, April 1951, vol. III, fascicolo I; and the *Scandinavian Journal of Economics* for the article 'Wicksell and the Malthusian Catastrophe' from vol. 80, no. 2, 1978.

1. The Supply of Bank Money in England and Wales, 1920–1938

OXFORD ECONOMIC PAPERS, 1941

This paper attempts by an analysis of the available statistics to make some estimate of the forces governing the supply of bank money in England and Wales. The latter in turn presumably controls the total supply of money. The general difficulty in drawing any conclusions from the study of time series, especially for relatively short periods, is operative here and makes results tentative. Yet the problem is rendered easier by the fact that frequently the controlling factors are not cyclical and hence are not especially liable to inter-correlation.

The statistics are taken from easily available published material and hence are not reproduced here. At most only simple changes have been made to render them continuous and to put them in more useful form. All the data refer to the London clearing banks, which, excluding the National Bank, have 92.7 per cent of the deposits of the area. For total deposits the published monthly averages of the ten clearing banks have been used. These have been extended from February 1921 back to January 1920 by the use of the material in the Macmillan Committee *Report.*[1] The deposits of the District Bank have been excluded after 1936. The series for current and deposit accounts are those published by the B.E.S.S.[2] and exclude the Irish branches of the National Bank. Current accounts have been corrected for seasonal variation, and have an estimated correction for the inclusion of the District Bank after 1936 and the Irish branches in 1938. The assets of the ten banks are given until 1936, those of both the ten and the eleven for 1936, and those of the eleven after 1936. The true cash reserves of the clearing banks are taken as the sum of their till money and 'Bankers' Deposits' with the Bank of England. Except for month to month comparison the figures used refer to a three-months' moving average of the series corrected for seasonal variation. The ratio is obtained by dividing the uncorrected banks' cash by total deposits, but except for month to month comparison the figures used are a three-months' moving average of this series.

The employment series is that of the Ministry of Labour for the estimated total number of persons, 16–64, at work. The figures used are those of Messrs Brown and Shackle as corrected for seasonal variations by Wald's method.[3] They have been extended from 1923 back to 1920 by use of the *Economist* Index of Employment. Lack of adequate statistics makes this index somewhat untrustworthy, but it is presumably accurate enough for the limited use made of it here.

The calculation of all seasonals has been by the link relative method. Curves drawn on scatter diagrams have been done by inspection because any gain from more exact methods seemed scarcely worth the trouble.

The figures for the notes and coin in the hands of the public are those published in the B.E.S.S., but with an estimated correction for the till money of non-clearing banks, and they have been scaled down to England and Wales. This is done on the assumption that the public's cash is distributed over the British Isles in proportion to the population of the various parts.

1. The Determination of Banks' Cash

If there is a closed banking system connected with the outside world only through a gold standard, and carrying a part of its cash reserves in a central bank which has customers other than the system banks, then changes in aggregate banks' cash must necessarily be the algebraic sum (signs correctly given) of

(1) Net inflow or outflow of notes and coin to or from the banks,
(2) Net import or export of gold,
(3) Changes in the central bank's holding of securities, and
(4) Changes in the amount of deposits by the central banks' other customers.

The change in the public's cash with opposite sign should equal the inflow or outflow of notes, since there was no change in the total amount of notes and coin outstanding except through the banks. The changes in the gold stock of the Bank of England, when the gold standard was operative, gave the net import or export of gold and similarly the other two items were obtainable from the Bank statements. Unfortunately the changes in these factors do not add up to the changes in banks' cash in the period 1925–31. For example, from 1925 to 1929 the Bank of England's holding of securities dropped by £30m;[4] and this was offset by a decrease in the public's cash of £5m, a decrease in the deposits of other customers of £3m, and an increase in stocks of gold of £1m. These changes would be expected to mean a drop of £21m in banks' cash, whereas in fact it fell by only £8m. Such discrepancies are found both in the short and in the long run and whether yearly or monthly data are used. This may be because of errors of estimate in some of the series or because the clearing banks do not constitute a closed system.

The cash reserve of the clearing banks is not a stable quantity in the short-run; it exhibits violent unsustained fluctuations, as can be seen from an inspection of FIGURES 1.5 and 1.6, which give the unsmoothed series for six years. These fluctuations are partially seasonal, and hence foreseen; but they also contain an erratic element. This comes largely from the size of public deposits, the variations in which must necessarily mean an equal inverse variation, neglecting the other constituents, in banks' cash. Given the volume and character of the payments it must make, the Treasury has only been able to keep the fluctuations down to the present magnitude by exercising care in its short-term borrowing.

The variations in public deposits are not primarily seasonal, but nonetheless banks' cash shows a definite seasonal pattern. This is given in FIGURE 1.1 in £ millions. If the banks kept rigidly to a fixed ratio, this would mean really violent fluctuations. Deposits would tend to be, for example, some £160m higher in January than in November.

In FIGURE 1.1 are given the average seasonal variations in £ millions of various factors controlling banks' cash.[5] These were calculated by applying to the average for the whole period the percentage seasonal variations. This will not give a completely accurate picture of the seasonal influences: it assumes one unchanging seasonal pattern; and it associates the 'normal' for each month with the average for the period.

Two broad facts stand out from a study of FIGURE 1.1. The banks' cash is more stable than the series controlling it. This evidently is the result of the fact that the Bank of England loan portfolio varies inversely with the public's cash. This, especially since the negative correlation is so close, is presumably the result of a definite policy of the Bank of England to soften the seasonal fluctuation in reserves. Since the exigencies of the foreign exchange market allow sufficient freedom for a partial cure, there is no obvious reason why there should not be a complete removal of the seasonal.[6]

The second striking thing is that the gold stock and public deposits are only minor factors in the seasonal perturbations. Here we have the

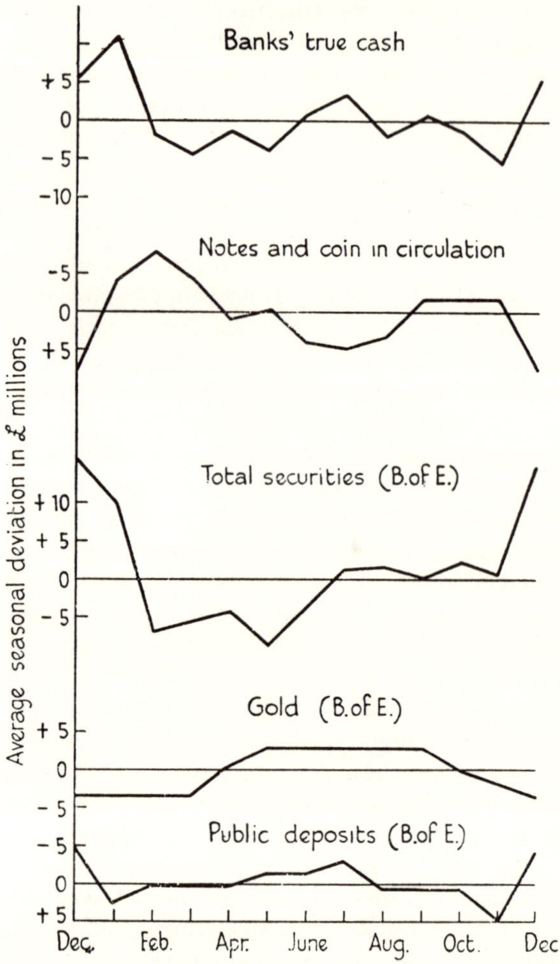

FIGURE 1.1 Factors affecting seasonal variations in banks' cash

present shape and magnitude of the famous 'autumnal drain'. In the first estimates of this shown in TABLE 1.1, Palgrave, using crude methods, derived an index of seasonal movements from 1845–1900.

In so far as these estimates give a correct picture, it is possible to say that broadly the variation has not changed, although it is much simpler now. There has been, however, a reduction by half in the percentage intensity of fluctuation. The level of public deposits shows only small

TABLE 1.1 Average Seasonal Movement of Bank of England Gold Stock

	Dec.	*Jan.*	*Feb.*	*Mar.*	*Apr.*	*May*	*June*	*July*	*Aug.*	*Sept.*	*Oct.*	*Nov.*	*Dec.*
1845–1900	96	97	99	101	99	98	104	105	103	103	98	95	96
1925–1931	98	98	98	98	100	102	102	102	102	102	100	99	98

Source: R. H. Inglis Palgrave, *Bank Rate and the Money Market* (London: 1903) p. 71.

seasonal variation and that is unreliable since the averages used were not highly typical in spite of the fact that the determination of the seasonal should be especially easy and reliable since there is no secular or cyclical factor.

The character of the seasonal pattern of Bank of England securities evidently is largely determined by that of the public's cash. Their remarkably close inverse movements indicate that the Bank definitely acts in part to counterbalance the periodic inflow and outflow of cash. The effect of these efforts curiously enough is more than to iron out the fluctuation, with the result that the movement of banks' cash is more like that of securities than that of the public's cash. Since the amount of securities is determined by policy, it is possible to place on it the immediate responsibility for the seasonal variation in reserves, although it may be that because of other limitations or practical difficulties no different result is attainable.

If the ratio were freely variable in response to recurrent seasonal ups and downs in reserves, then deposits would be unaffected and the whole subject would be of no interest except to bankers. On the other hand, were the ratio given independently of the level of reserves, then deposits would have the same average percentage seasonal deviations as banks' cash. As can be seen in FIGURE 1.2, something in between these two happens. If the ratio had the same percentage seasonal deviations as those in reserves, then it would have absorbed the seasonal in cash. But if it had no seasonal, or one entirely different, then the seasonal variations in deposits would have been determined by other factors, presumably the demand for loans. Actually the pattern for the ratio is similar to that for banks' cash, but definitely less violent. This means the variations in cash tend in part to be absorbed. The bulk of the seasonal in deposits occurs in current accounts, and we see that its pattern is broadly similar to that of banks' cash. The fact that it is not identical is an indication of the influence of other factors besides the cash reserves.[7]

The seasonal in the supply of money gives us perhaps the best opportunity of studying the relation between money and the interest

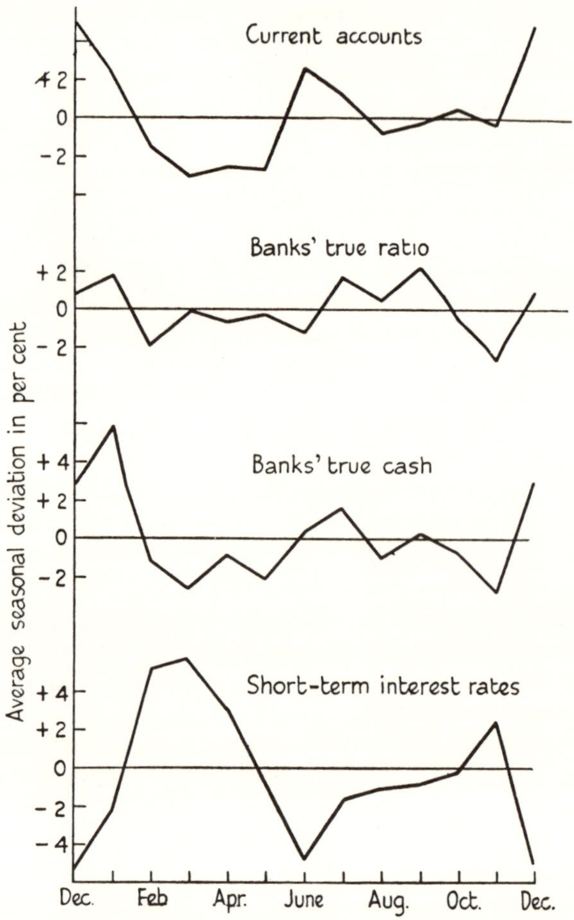

FIGURE 1.2 Some seasonal variations

rate. The short-term rate appears to be the relevant one, and as a measure of this a simple average of day-to-day and three-months bill rates may be taken. Over the period 1920–9 short rates have a well-defined seasonal which is given in FIGURE 1.2. They have a clear negative correlation with the level of current accounts, and this is shown in the form of a scatter diagram in FIGURE 1.3. Given the crudity of the data used for interest and the fact that the seasonals are necessarily rough approximations and often untypical averages, this relation is fairly linear. If we assume that the liquidity demand schedule did not change

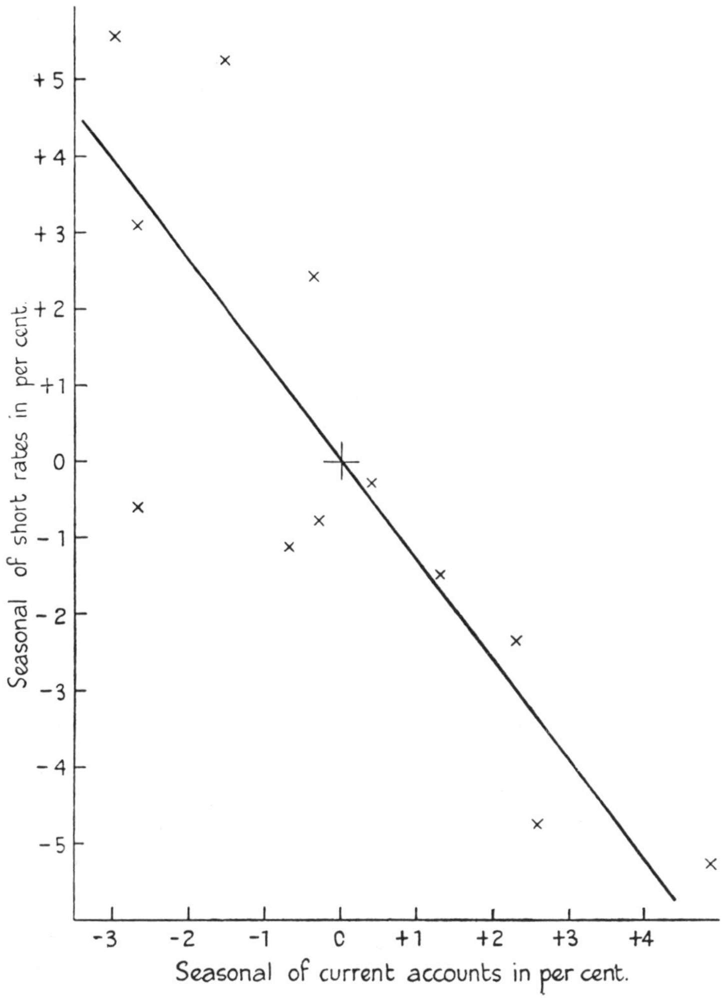

FIGURE 1.3 Seasonal variations in interest rates and current accounts

either seasonally or over longer periods, then an estimate is easily made for the interest elasticity of demand for current accounts in this period. These points would be most consistent with a constant elasticity of around 0.7 within the range of observation. There are, of course, grave difficulties in determining any static relation from historical data, but this method avoids the worst dangers of meaningless cyclical or secular inter-correlations. There is no strong evidence of any regular change in the seasonals, which lends support to the validity of the hypothesis of an unchanging relation. The relation is a demand curve only to the extent that all the observed variation comes from shifts in the supply, or the supply schedule, of money, but we have seen that this is largely the case. It is not the Keynesian liquidity function, since short-term rates presumably affect only money held for the transactions motive. The Keynes function is concerned with a different kind of thing and is certain to be subject to change over time. It is of some interest that the seasonal of the yield on consols does not show for this period any clear tendency to a negative correlation with current accounts, although his hypothesis appears to require it.

2. Window-Dressing

Banks' published statements of their cash and its ratio to deposits differ from their true cash and ratio by an amount commonly referred to as window-dressing. Since the publication of the Macmillan Committee's *Report* it has been possible to make an accurate estimate of banks' true cash. By subtracting this from the published figure it is possible to estimate window-dressing either in banks' cash or in the ratio. In 1927 this made a difference between the true and the untrue ratio of 0.015 (the reserve claimed being 11.5 per cent of deposits as against an actual one of 10).

Window-dressing serves the purpose of making banks appear more liquid than they are, but in addition it serves another purpose not generally recognised. As has been pointed out above, the banks face a highly unstable reserve, both from seasonal and erratic sources. If they kept a constant ratio, they would enforce violent and frequent variations in the supply of deposits, or if they allowed the ratio to vary freely they might be subject to criticism and possibly some lack of confidence. Actually they achieve some of the benefits of both worlds by allowing large fluctuations in the amount of window-dressing and thereby keeping the published ratio much more stable than the true ratio. In FIGURE 1.4 is given for the six sample years 1921–3 and 1931–3, the relation between the increments in the true ratio and the increments in the amount of window-dressing of the ratio (the difference between the two). The relation is remarkably close, especially in view of the fact that if all connection between true and untrue ratios is not to be lost they must sometimes vary equally. Fitting a straight line by inspection we find that a change of 0.0010 in the true ratio tended to be associated with (and, we

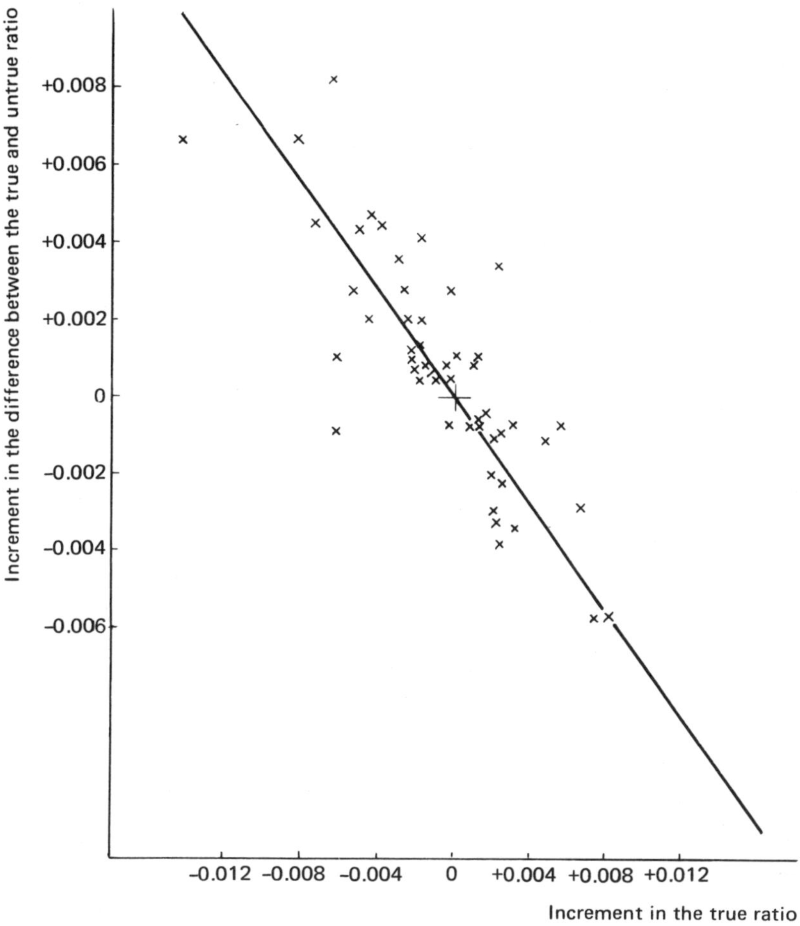

FIGURE 1.4 Changes in window-dressing, 1921–3 and 1931–3

may fairly safely add, caused) a change in the opposite direction of 0.0007 in window-dressing. This method of estimation gives the result that a change in the untrue ratio tends to be only one-third that in the true ratio.

This phenomenon of resistance to change in the untrue ratio is not confined to monthly movements but extends over much longer periods. The case of 1921–3 is instructive. Banks' true cash fell rapidly; untrue cash fell, but by no means as much, because of a progressive increase in window-dressing *over a period of two years.* Deposits were reduced, but by enough only to keep the untrue, not the true, ratio constant. Average yearly window-dressing has by no means been constant, having nearly doubled from 1921 to 1927 and having been reduced from £26.5 m in 1929 to £12 m in 1934. These variations are neither negligible nor accidental, but are related to the whole monetary development. They were such as to introduce greater stability in the published ratio than in the true one, for from 1921 to 1927 the true ratio fell by 0.0084, whereas the untrue one was allowed to drop only by 0.0011. From 1931 to 1934 a rise of 0.0154 in the true ratio was accompanied by a rise in the untrue ratio of only 0.0092. From 1921 to 1938 for annual averages the coefficient of variation (100 times the standard deviation divided by the mean) was 5.50 for the true ratio and 4.84 for the untrue one.

These facts about the variability in window-dressing are of some importance. Until 1931 the Bank of England had knowledge of month to month movements of only banks' untrue cash.[8] This means that it had no certain knowledge of or control over short-run developments. Since Bank of England policy seems largely to have been concerned with short-run problems, this was a serious limitation. On the other hand, however, a highly desirable freedom was allowed the banks to keep a semblance of a constant ratio without forcing violent seasonal and erratic variations in the supply of deposits.

It is difficult to see any such justification for the longer-run variations in window-dressing. These have operated in such a way as to give to the ratio an apparent stability much greater than is actually the case. A stable ratio is basic to nearly all recent theory and practice of monetary control. Window-dressing is one of the elements that help to weaken the validity of this assumption. One cannot help but think that it is a mistaken impression, got from a study of the untrue ratio, that has led theorists to an uncritical acceptance of this assumption. Central bank operations designed to produce a given effect on the level of deposits must be larger because of window-dressing, but how much larger is a variable factor not determined alone by the size of the operation nor by the previous level of banks' cash. The 'automatic' effects of gold flow or the public's holding of cash will also be influenced by this.

3. The Ratio

Let

N = notes and coin in circulation,
B = banks' cash,

D = total deposits,
$C = N + B$,

$\alpha = \frac{N}{D}$ and

$\beta = \frac{B}{D}$ = the ratio.

Neglecting the distinction between types of deposits, we may write for the amount of money:

$$D + N = \left(\frac{1+\alpha}{\alpha+\beta}\right)C.$$

The two parameters α and β determine the amount of money resulting from any given C, and if they are constant then C is the sole determinant. Since α and β are not constant, it is desirable to study them separately. In this section we shall study the relation between B and D. Such a formal simplification has good empirical grounds because changes in C ordinarily come through B, and because it is generally agreed that N depends on D either directly or through prices, wages, etc. We have studied the proximate determination of banks' cash and this in turn is the determination of the amount of bank money if the ratio, β, is given independently.[9]

The assumption that the ratio does not vary—or rather varies only slowly and not as a result of the state of trade[10] or the level of reserves—became widely accepted by monetary theorists. Mr Keynes, for example, says: 'We shall find that the ratio varies with different types of bank, and that it has been changed, for various reasons, from time to time. But at any given time banks stick closely to their established ratio and, as the figures to be given below show, such fluctuations as there are exhibit no correlation with the state of trade.'[11] And it is upon this foundation that most theories of variations in the quantity of money are built, and it is fundamental to all theories of central bank control. Since the banks cannot in England influence the amount of banks' cash except temporarily, this would mean that the banks themselves do not influence the quantity of money and hence presumably could not be of much importance in the business cycle. Opposed to this point of view are those, like Professor Hayek, who believe that the banks play an important role by allowing cyclical variations in the quantity of money through alternate weakening and strengthening of the ratio.[12]

The dependence on a constant—at any one time at least—ratio has become so common that it is easy to forget its limitations. It rests on no better grounds than the belief, not very well substantiated, that the banks did keep the ratio stable. In recent years the American banks have allowed violent fluctuation, and as will be shown, considerable variation occurred in England and Wales. The actual ratio kept by the clearing banks is partly an irrational survival from the earlier days of smaller size banks and could be lower than it is. It is true that any lowering of its ratio by a particular bank might bring some lack of confidence on the part of the public. Yet one suspects that this is no longer important because there has not been a failure for so long. A high ratio was once an absolute necessity for a bank, but now it is not, and given this fact it has tended downward and probably will so continue. This, however, is not likely, as Mr Keynes appears to suggest, to occur steadily over time, but rather in a definite relation both to changes in the cash base and to the phase of the business cycle. The pressure on bankers to reduce the ratio will be greatest and the dangers of loss of confidence least in the upswing, and the reverse will be true in the downswing.

Furthermore, the 'safe' ratio cannot be independent of the liquidity of the banks' other assets, and this undoubtedly is subject to change. How much, if any, effect this has on the ratio is difficult to determine. It is fairly certain that the amount of the most liquid funds available for replenishing possible sudden losses of cash does influence the ratio in a few extreme cases. This will be shown below.

If the ratio is not constant, then the quantity of bank money is determined by other factors as well as banks' cash. This really presents two very different problems. If the ratio varies: (i) as a function of time (changing bank practice) but independently of the state of trade, and/or (ii) as a function of changes in banks' cash, and/or (iii) erratically but still independently of any non-monetary factors, then complexities are introduced into the determination (or partial indeterminacy) of the supply of bank money, but it is still determined by the banking system in the broadest sense. In this case we may agree with Mr Keynes that 'the quantity of money is not determined by the public'.[13] But, on the other hand, if the ratio varies also as a function of the state of trade or other economic factors, or if the changes in practice of the banks show correlation with these factors, then this has more difficult and more important consequences for theory. In any theory of general equilibrium money is introduced as an arbitrary parameter, arbitrary, that is, with respect to the other variables in the system, and this is the most prominent feature of the quantity theory of money. This is not valid if the state of trade affects the supply of money.

It has already been pointed out that the ratio shows considerable month to month variations, and this was found to be related to the instability of banks' cash. More important is its behaviour over longer periods. For the study of this it is useful to smooth the curves somewhat to eliminate the large unmaintained changes. In FIGURE 1.5 are given a three-months' moving average of banks' cash with estimated correction for seasonal, a three-months' moving average of the ratio, and total deposits.

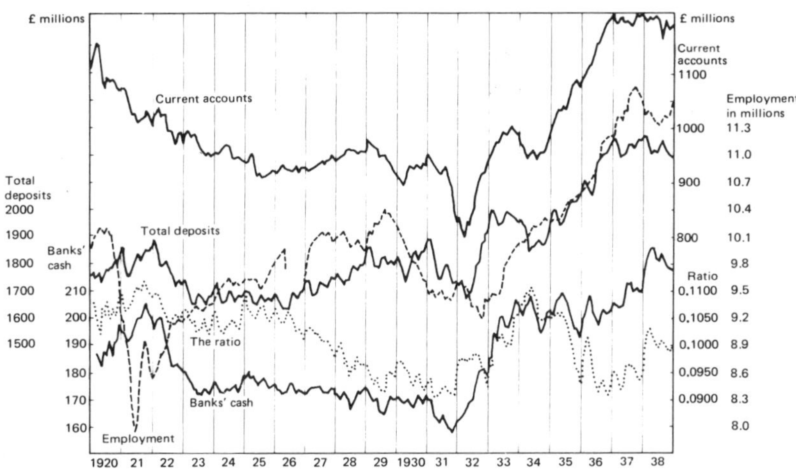

FIGURE 1.5 Factors affecting total deposits, 1920–38

From this figure it is evident that the ratio is by no means constant. From 0.112 in September 1921 it fell to 0.102 in May 1923 and to 0.090 by September 1931. From there it rose again to 0.109 in February 1934, and by October 1936 it had fallen to 0.090. Nor were these changes accidental or inexplicable; they were closely related to the major variations in banks' cash and the state of trade. Also continuous change over time was not a predominant factor. Some indication of the importance of these changes is given by the fact that a variation from 0.100 to 0.090 will mean elevenfold in place of tenfold expansion or contraction, and one from 0.100 to 0.110 will reduce it to ninefold. Though the ratio does appear, at first glance, to have considerable stability, the apparent degree of stability is deceptive. The significance of small variations in the ratio is brought out by considering the ratio of a given *increment* in banks' cash to the *increment* in total deposits associated with it, i.e. the marginal instead of the average ratio. From September 1921 to September 1931 a fall in banks' cash of £47m brought a drop in deposits of only £103m, which gives a marginal ratio of 0.456. From then to February 1934 an increase of £46m resulted in one in deposits of only £155m, the marginal ratio being 0.297. This should demonstrate plainly the error involved in saying that because the ratio does not vary much from 0.100, a change in banks' cash will bring roughly ten times that change in deposits. Yet our only interest is in increments. It is necessary to add that to say that a given increment in banks' cash was associated with a change in deposits three times as large, is not to say it caused that change. It may well be that as a result of the change in reserves, deposits were higher or lower than they would have been otherwise by ten times the amount of the increment in reserves. But this is, then, to say that the amount of deposits depends on other things beside the level of banks' cash, and to admit the impossibility of uniquely estimating even approximately the change in deposits which will be associated with any given change in reserves.

It is not difficult to imagine that many and complex elements enter into the relation actually existing between banks' cash and deposits. To gain the best insight possible into this it would be desirable to study in some detail the major changes in the period, but considerations of space prevent it. From FIGURE 1.5 it is easily seen that broadly the ratio is positively correlated with banks' cash, similarly to the short-run movements already discussed. This is unlikely to be a meaningless correlation because there are good reasons to expect it and because the movements are by no means uniquely related to the trade cycle nor do they show the same trends, if any. Therefore the correlation is highly likely to indicate a direct influence rather than an indirect and non-necessary one operating somehow through the total economic system. The relation between the ratio and the cash reserve does not always hold nor is it uniform. This can be in part explained by introducing the state of trade as governing the shifts in the demand for loans from the banks. As the best measure of this the estimated number of persons in employment is used.[14] The state of trade should give some indication of, for example, the ease or difficulty (and the loss or gain) which the banks experience in attempting to reduce the level of deposits. The fact that the banks take the initiative in the lending in all cases except advances does not seriously weaken the influence of this factor, which will manifest itself through changes in the rate of interest which can be obtained on bills or securities.

Inability or unwillingness to continue expanding the amount of money cannot have been a factor in bringing the post-war boom to an end. Resistance to expansion of deposits in the ensuing downswing is clearly to be explained in the state of demand for loans. What expansion did occur can be largely attributed to the rise in Government short-term borrowing. The long, slow improvement in the state of trade to 1929 brought a rise in deposits and loans in spite of the Bank of England's policy of allowing the banks' reserves to decline. A careful study of the more complete data now available conclusively demonstrates that this decline in the ratio was not entirely the result of the Midland Bank's change of practice as was believed by Mr Keynes.[15] The decline in reserves from June 1929 to September 1931 was not resisted at all, again evidently because of the state of trade.

After September 1931 came the enormous expansion in banks' cash, presumably as the consequence of a monetary policy in line with the Macmillan Committee *Report*. By April 1933 reserves had risen £42m, bringing an increase of £213m in deposits with the marginal ratio as 0.193. The quantitative significance of such a marginal ratio can be brought out by the fact that the level of deposits would have been £2210m instead of £1925m if the marginal ratio had been equal to the average ratio of 0.090. The explanation of this resistance to expansion is clearly the fact that the state of trade, although it had ceased to become worse, had shown no marked improvement. Employment had touched bottom, but had not gained much.

On the other hand, by October 1936 banks' cash had risen by only £1m more than in 1933, but deposits had been expanded to £2201m. This secondary expansion of deposits came not as a result of a change in banks' cash, but presumably because of a rapid and vigorous upsurge in the state of trade into almost boom conditions. After October 1936 there came again a heavy increase in banks' cash which exerted no upward pressure on deposits, as a result of the ending of the upswing.

The assumption that the average and marginal ratios remain roughly equal would be more tenable if the conditions of perfect competition were realised in the banking business. If numbers were so large that no one bank could by itself influence the rates of interest, and if no action were based on anything but direct gain for that bank alone, then, subject to liquidity considerations, the banks would always lend so long as they had any cash above their customary ratio and so long as the rates of interest (cost and risk deducted) were above zero. In these conditions the amount of expansion in deposits which is possible would depend on the interest elasticity of demand for loans.[16] In the short run this demand is presumably rather inelastic, although much more so in some phases of the cycle than in others. If this is so, then a considerable increase in banks' cash would lead to the appropriate expansion in loans and deposits, to heavy losses by the banks and, if carried far enough, even to suspension of operation. A decrease in reserves would depend for its effect on how rigidly the bankers kept to their supposedly necessary minimum ratio.

This difficult situation is mitigated by the functioning of the factors Mr Keynes calls liquidity preference. The banks may bring about some increase in total borrowing by forcing rates down, but in times of greater inelasticity, for the most part, they merely supplant other lenders, who then hold their money idle. The latter is the result of the peculiar fact that in our society lending and the provision of money are joined together, which gives some possibility for varying the quantity of money through the banking system, independently of the state of trade. But it should be noticed that what freedom there is results from variations in idle money, which is of no importance for the functional aspect of money, i.e. its relation to prices and quantities. What is usually desired is not a mere change in what has been defined as money, but rather a change in what money is supposed to do, but which this money will not do.

People who lend at short-term have little reason to prefer holding cash and hence are difficult to supplant. This is one reason why the short-term rates of interest tend so easily to fall close to a zero net rate, whereas longer term rates resist the tendency. This significant fact is usually passed over by blanket references to changes in the complex of rates.

This lessens but does not remove the inelasticity of demand for bank loans. Faced with such inelasticity, the banks have had strong incentives not to act competitively. Given an increase in cash reserves in the middle of a depression, as in 1932, what should they do? They cannot buy advances to customers, but, if competitive, they could and would lower rates in hopes of getting new business either from rivals or new borrowing. More especially they can simply go into the market and buy bonds and bills, and whatever the rate, this apparently will always be better than holding cash. If both can be bought liquidity will not be impaired.[17]

Any net positive rate (quoted rate less cost of lending and risk of default) on sufficiently short-dated securities will always be preferable to holding cash for banks as for anyone else. Long-term bonds might at first sight appear to be the ideal thing for banks to go into because any expansion does not affect the rate on previous loans of that type, as is the case with all their other assets. This is, however, balanced by the fact that for banks as for private investors there is a speculative factor involved in the purchase of bonds. By their nature banks are unwilling to undertake considerable risks. Furthermore, even were this not so, they would find, like any other rational investor, at one point, that the probabilities of loss offset those of gain plus the interest payments. These facts are a complication and make it difficult to say in any particular case how important respectively the market imperfections and the speculative risks are in determining bank actions. Liquidity in its correct sense does not enter in here.

Whether there ever were competitive conditions is difficult to know, but certainly they do not exist now. Before the Macmillan Committee the bankers made it clear that they play a passive role in the making of advances. The rate is ½ to 1 per cent above bank rate with an 'agreed' minimum of 4 to 5 per cent. As in all such administered prices, there is unquestionably some flexibility for each particular loan, but, broadly speaking, any safe loan asked for at the set price is granted. As can be seen from a study of bank assets, the result is a regular cyclical pattern quite independent of the many vagaries of the level of deposits. If banks behaved in a similar way towards all assets, then the quantity of money would be cyclical and largely independent of banks' cash in the short run.

It remains possible for the banks to allow their cash reserves to govern the level of deposits, if they are willing freely to buy and sell investments and bills regardless of the rates involved. The difference should not be overemphasised since it is of no matter whether they operate on the price, as in the case of advances, or the quantities, as in the case of bills and investments. A real difference is the greater elasticity in the demand for bond loans (regarded only from the banks' point of view) due to the possibility of supplanting other lenders. Also there may be variations in the amount of Treasury short-term borrowing independently of the state of trade.[18]

From September to September 1920–1 a £14m rise in banks' cash brought one in deposits of only £41m. This was made possible by an expansion in the holding of bills more than sufficient to counteract the heavy fall in advances. The explanation of the failure to expand more fully is presumably to be found in the fact that the bill rate fell from 6.78 to 4.09 per cent. It is of great importance to note that even this amount of expansion was only possible without a drastic fall in rates because of the increase in Government borrowing.[19] In 1930 the level of deposits did not follow the steadily worsening state of trade, and this again can be traced largely to the relatively large amount of Government borrowing which allowed a big rise in bills without a disastrous fall in rates. This time, unlike 1921, investments were purchased too.

Once the gold standard was abandoned the easy money policy was undertaken. The extent to which banks acted upon individualistic competitive grounds may be in some degree tested. The aim was by increasing the quantity of money and lowering interest rates to help to bring a revival of business activity and help the conversion. But such an operation on a large scale is based on the assumption that banks will calmly co-operate in diminishing their earning power. Actually the banks expanded their deposits by approximately one-half of what a constant ratio would have dictated. This was accomplished by enormous purchases of bills and investments, but concurrently and fairly evidently as a result, advances fell precipitously. Interest rates dropped enormously, which put the banks in a difficult situation. The *Economist* Banking Supplement of 8 October 1932 estimated by a complicated system of averages that the banks had by this action reduced net revenue sufficiently to destroy all their aggregate profits. This appears to have been an extreme estimate, since published profits for the year 1932 were only 10 per cent below 1931.[20] By drastic action and limitation in the size of the expansion the banks were able to avoid any considerable direct loss in revenue. They were assisted in this by the large expansion in Government short-term borrowing in connection with conversion operations. Had they expanded by twice the amount they would have faced serious loss. All this, however, only estimates the immediate effect. To trace the total impact is certainly impossible because it cannot be isolated from the many other developments. Yet one cannot ignore the arresting fact that the upswing of 1933, 1934 and 1935 took place without any increase in advances, which is in startling contrast to 1923, 1924 and 1925. By 1937 employment and output were far higher than in 1929, but advances had only reached their previous height. In this circumstance it is fairly obvious that the banks had manœuvred themselves into a large exchange of their most lucrative asset for less lucrative ones. These facts must considerably impress bankers and make them reconsider their policies. Where there are only a few large banks it is open to serious question whether in such circumstances self-interest can be relied on to bring any desired expansion or contraction in the volume of deposits, while the degree and the timing of the change will certainly not be solely determined by banks' cash.

Within the broad sweep of events since 1931 there occurred two peculiarities which must be accounted for. From July 1933 to March 1934 deposits fell by £142m. This was doubly remarkable because banks' cash rose by £8m and because the upswing of the cycle was vigorously under way by this time. The explanation is to be found in the

Government's policy of converting short- into long-term borrowing. The result was that even with drastic curtailment of the size of their holding of bills the banks faced a falling bill rate which at one point in August came down to $\frac{1}{4}$ per cent. They then took the non-competitive action of agreeing not to buy bills below certain rates.

This forced the banks into a difficult position. Their actual distribution of assets is always a compromise between the profitableness of advances and investments, and the liquidity of cash, bills, and money at call and short notice. For the aggregate of banks[21] it is a danger sign when the sum of these latter three falls below 30 per cent of deposits. Bills and short money form a source of replenishment for cash and to a limited extent may be substituted for it. Had the banks replaced the falling bill holdings with investments they would have forced this percentage well below 30 by the beginning of 1934. After 1934 the banks were able to buy an increased amount of bills at their agreed-on rates and expansion of deposits was possible.

From November 1936 to the same month in 1938 banks' cash rose by £16m, whereas deposits dropped by £41m. So violent an inverse movement cannot be explained alone by the mild worsening of the state of trade from the middle of 1937 to the middle of 1938. A part of the explanation is clearly contained in the fact that the percentage of liquid assets to deposits was only twice above 30 in 1937–8. This meant that since the banks were able to buy, at their agreed rates, less and less bills, they were forced to sell investments, instead of purchasing them, as would have been necessary to maintain a constant ratio. The fact that the banks sacrificed their liquidity requirements as much as they did is probably related to the relatively favourable state of trade.

The result of this study is more negative than positive. The level of banks' cash does not control the amount of deposits; it is only the most important among several elements. It is not feasible by means of multiple correlation analysis to determine exactly what elements do enter in and their relative influence. There is no numerical measure of the broad factor of the state of trade. The Employment series constitutes only the best available rough approximation. The banks' reactions to this depend on many indefinite, changeable, and certainly unmeasurable things, such as the degree of competition, bankers' feelings about the present and their estimates of the future. There would be no assurance that any of the relations thus determined would remain unchanged in the future. Finally, the number of factors which should be included would make it unmanageable and the results unreliable.

Many errors in economic theorising have come from applying to short periods what would only hold for long ones. The amount of banks' cash, in conjunction with certain secular changes in bank practices, may well determine uniquely the level of deposits over long periods: in fact it is difficult to see why this should not be so. *As between two boom times* there is no reason to dispute Mr Keynes's point that banks should always buy assets as long as they have any more than their customary liquidity requirement in cash. Yet the evidence conclusively demonstrates that it is not permissible to proceed from this to the conclusion that this happens regardless of the phase of the business cycle. Within one business cycle deposits show a remarkable independence of the level of cash reserves, but over a longer period this may not be so. Although two complete cycles occur during this time, no final judgement is possible as to the long-period behaviour of the ratio because it is not possible to say whether there is an independently given secular trend in the ratio. Consequently a special type of lag appears, not a simple one nor a 'distributed' lag, but one dependent on the phase of the cycle. A change in banks' cash may take much longer to have its full effect in one phase than in another.

As an example we may take the theory of the automatic operation of the gold standard under modern conditions. For its functioning it requires a fairly rapid effect on prices, otherwise all a country's gold will be gone. Yet how quickly a change in banks' cash will change proportionately the supply of money cannot be determined without reference to the phase of the cycle, and similarly for the effect of any change in the amount of money on prices. This helps to explain why the gold standard has always proved difficult to maintain in practice.

The shorter the period the more tenuous appears to be the Bank of England's control over the level of deposits. In any case a much larger change in banks' cash is required than would be indicated on the assumption that the marginal is equal to the average ratio. The amount of expansion or contraction necessary to achieve a given end will depend on the state of trade and may depend on government borrowing. Furthermore, there may be limits to expansion, if not contraction, beyond which no amount of change in reserves will carry deposits. This will depend on the effect of the expansion on interest rates and the effect of these in turn on the banks' policies. Especially noteworthy was the cancellation of advances in 1932. The significance of this can be brought out by imagining a situation in which the banks keep rates on advances constant. As a result for every investment they buy they lose an advance, with no net increase in deposits regardless of the magnitude of the increase in their cash.

Evidently Mr Keynes's dictum that 'the quantity of money is not determined by the public'[22] is unacceptable. At least, for the only period about which we have full knowledge, the banks of England and Wales have shown themselves remarkably amenable to influence by the public. This is, it is true, the result of the demand for loans, not for money, but they are intimately related, and in any case it is the public and not the banking system which is taking the decisions in question. These act both through the amount of loans made at given rates of interest and also through the rates of interest. Hence the supply of money is in part subject to the rates of interest and hence cannot be taken as given in the study of liquidity preference schedules. Graphically considered, Mr Keynes regards the supply schedule of money as vertical at any one moment, whereas it appears to be considerably less steep than this; how much less cannot be determined in general.

Any discussion of the influence of the public, independently of the banking system, on the supply of money must include the problem of the division of total deposits between current and deposit accounts. Since no distinction is made for reserve purposes, the determination of total deposits still leaves undetermined the actual supply of active bank money. Transfer to or from deposit accounts could conceivably bring in the neighbourhood of 100 per cent variation in the supply of active money without affecting the banks' cash reserve position or their total lending.

Unfortunately the distinction between deposit and current accounts is not clear, nor is the meaning of any such distinction certain. Broadly speaking, deposit accounts are not used for transactions. This follows from the basis used by the Macmillan Committee: 'There is no universally recognised line of division between the two, but as far as possible current accounts are taken as sums payable on demand and deposit accounts as sums payable after date or notice.'[23] There is no way of telling whether any of the current accounts are just as idle as deposit accounts, but there is some evidence that this is so part of the time at least. In some respects deposit accounts are money because they serve as a store of value and as a source which may be used to supplement active accounts. Nevertheless they are not money for the purposes of carrying out current transactions.

The proportion of current to deposit accounts does, in fact, show some tendency to vary in sympathy with the business cycle, showing a shift to current accounts in the upswing and away from current accounts in the downswing. As has been often mentioned, there was after World War I a secular trend in the growth of deposit accounts as a result of restoring their level, which was depleted by war borrowing. Allowance must be made for this. From FIGURE 1.6 it can be seen that this proportion experienced its most rapid fall from the first quarter of 1920 to the second quarter of 1921 in co-ordination with the violent downswing. From 1921 to 1923 it actually rose and after that continued its downward trend, but less steeply than before. From about the beginning of 1929 to the first quarter in 1932 the proportion fell more rapidly than before, with the exception of a brief upturn. From then to 1937 it rose fairly steadily. The correlation is not good, but this may be in part connected with the difficulty in separating the evidently strong trend. At best, however, the proportion can only give some indication. To take an extreme example, let us suppose that the amount of current accounts is uniquely determined by the level of business activity. Then deposit accounts will be the difference between this and total deposits and the proportion of one to the other may show any sort of uncyclical behaviour depending on the level of total deposits.

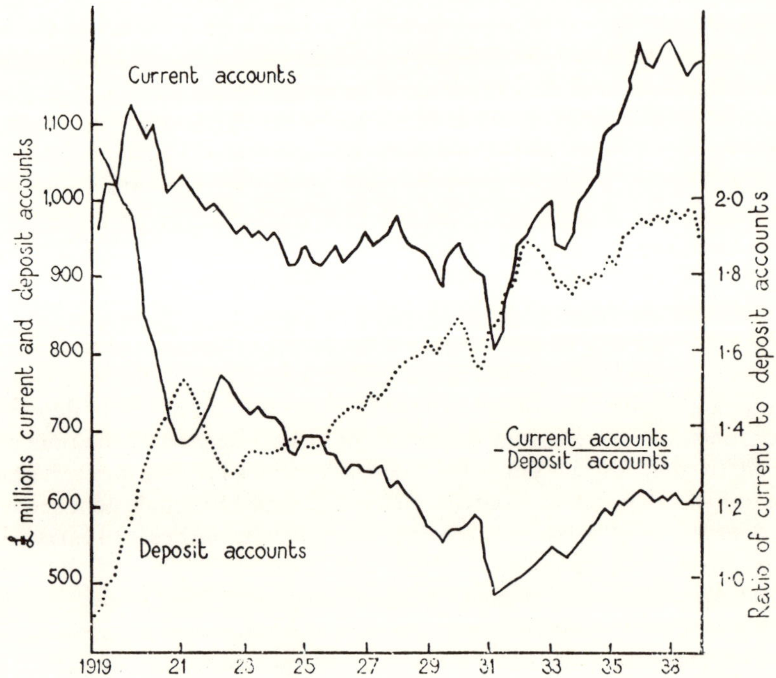

FIGURE 1.6 Current and deposit accounts, quarterly, 1919–38

Actually, on several occasions current accounts show a much closer relation to the state of trade than do total deposits. From FIGURE 1.5 it is easy to see that, although in 1920–1 the considerable expansion in banks' cash did produce a less than proportionate expansion in total deposits, the result had little significance. From March 1920 current accounts declined rapidly to the end of 1921. The amount of potentially active money appears to have been the result of cyclical forces quite independently of the amount of cash reserves or of total deposits. The surprising thing is that the decline continued until the middle of 1925, but this is perhaps explained by the heavy fall in prices, the level of transactions (clearings) not having begun to rise until 1924.

Total deposits did not show much tendency to decline with the cycle from 1929. Current accounts declined much more markedly, the fall being 18.3 per cent from February 1929 to February 1932, as compared with 8.6 per cent in total deposits. The inexplicable thing is that current accounts shared in the rise of total deposits in 1930. The development here failed to repeat the experience of 1920–1. After 1932 the great expansion in deposits was predominantly one in current accounts, and this too meant a close relation with the rise in business activity. The result was that from February 1932 to November 1936 current accounts rose by 53 against 33.2 per cent for total deposits.

There can, I think, be no doubt that this distinction between the two kinds of accounts makes the supply of money even more variable independently of the amount of banks' cash. The difficulty lies in the problem of how and under what conditions the deposits are distributed between the two. The whole matter has not been adequately discussed nor have the bases for a solution been laid down.

One thing, at least, is fairly certain: the rate of interest paid on deposit accounts enters into the determination of the result. The rates paid in country banks apparently vary according to place, and they do not follow the bank rate. Apparently they were around 2½ per cent until after 1932, when they were gradually reduced to 1½. The London deposit rate alone is easily available, being ordinarily 2 per cent below bank rate. This rate refers only to a part of deposit accounts, but against this limitation should be placed the fact that it is that part which is probably the most sensitive to any changes. In both 1920 and 1929 current accounts began seriously to decline some months before employment fell. This may be the result of business actions related to the coming events. But it also may be the effect of the existing high rate on deposit accounts leading to a transfer. The violent fall from 5 to 1 per cent in 1921–3 is presumably related to the rise in the proportion of current to deposit accounts at that time. After that the rising deposit rate assisted in the continued fall and later mild rise in current accounts. Particularly plain is the usefulness of the fall in the London rate from 4½ to 1 per cent in explaining the sudden end to the decline in current accounts in 1930–1.

Throughout 1931 there was a cancellation of deposits. In the first part this came largely in deposit accounts, but later when the London rate was raised to 4 per cent, they actually increased while current accounts dropped precipitously. Finally, the extremely low rates on both London and country deposits after 1932 are an important element in explaining why the bulk of the expansion after that came in current accounts. Not only were the rates low, but the banks resorted to direct control by refusing any large new deposit accounts.

The rate on deposit accounts obviously does not by itself control the distribution of deposits between the two kinds. Yet these facts tend to demonstrate that it is one important element in that distribution. Since the practice is to let bank rate determine the London deposit rate, this gives the Bank of England a considerable influence over the supply of money, in a way which has been neglected. The facts point to the conclusion that current accounts are not a simple function of the volume of transactions. This may mean either that current accounts may be 'idle' or that the requirement for transactions is not a fixed amount at any one time, but rather a schedule depending on the relevant interest rates; or it may mean both. The other short-term rates necessarily move between bank rate and the London deposit rate.

Broadly speaking, the operation of the banking system has been in part in accordance with the line of thought held by the Banking School in nineteenth-century controversies. Such operation has not been accepted as desirable by most economists on the grounds of conclusions drawn from the quantity equation. These conclusions are of doubtful validity when applied to short-run, cyclical phenomena, because they rest on the bad assumption that any amount of money will always be spent with roughly the same rapidity as in the past.

The banks do, to a certain extent, maintain the quantity of money independently of the state of trade. But such stabilisation may be more apparent than real if the effect is merely to increase or diminish the amount of idle deposits, whether as current or deposit accounts. The net result may simply be that the banks exchange more liquid assets for less, or vice versa, the interest rates varying sufficiently to bring about the public's acquiescence in it. Especially in the short run the supply of money cannot be separated from the spending of it.

4. Total Cash and Total Money

Thus far the notes and coin in circulation have been taken as given, but it is certain they depend to some extent at least on the level of deposits. Therefore any complete analysis of the supply of money must consider this.

Let

$$\rho = \frac{1+\alpha}{\alpha+\beta},$$

then

$$N + D = \rho C,$$

where C is the total cash available both to the public and the banks.[24] The parameter ρ is the one that is ultimately the interesting one. If N is always proportionate to D, then C and the ratio, β, determine the amount of money. If N is always proportionate to the D of a fixed time interval previous, there is created the possibility of endogenous oscillation in the amount of money, as suggested by Mr Hawtrey. In neither of these cases does the proportion α appear to be constant in this period. From year to year the changes in the public's cash are by no means even in the same direction as those in deposits, to say nothing of being proportionate. For the two major movements of deposits in the period, the marginal α shows some tendency to approach its average value, which for 1921–38 was 0.141. Using annual averages, the marginal α for 1921–2 was 0.730, but for 1921–4 was 0.191; for 1931–2 it was 0.260, and for 1931–3 0.050, but for 1931–7 it was 0.185. The movements of public's cash do not reflect any of the lesser movements of deposits, neither rising to 1929 nor declining after. Little better results are obtained if current accounts are used instead of total deposits. Also, this suffers from the difficulty that there is no reason to expect banks' cash to control current accounts, although in fact they do so as closely as they do total deposits.

The parameter α is not controlled by slowly changing institutional factors, as has been widely believed. Evidently, as with β, this parameter is influenced by many things, including the general economic development.

For 1921–38 the average value of β is 0.0998 and of α 0.141, which yields the value of ρ as 4.74. This means that the amount of money in England and Wales averaged 4.74 times the total cash base. This does not mean that any increase or decrease in the cash base will bring a fivefold change in the amount of money. It is impossible to state in purely monetary terms what will happen because it depends on other things as well. The only situation in which ρ would be more stable than α and β would be one in which α and β varied inversely. There is no reason to expect this and no marked evidence that it occurred.

TABLE 1.2

Period	Marginal ρ
1921–2	1.8
1921–3	3.5
1921–4	3.7
1921–5	3.6
1921–6	3.5
1931–2	1.7
1931–3	4.5
1931–4	2.3
1931–5	3.9
1931–6	4.9
1931–7	4.1
1931–8	4.1

For large changes in C, and given sufficient time, the marginal value of ρ does tend to be closer to its average value. Calculating the marginal value of ρ from the increments to deposits and to the total cash base for the periods indicated, we have the results shown in TABLE 1.2. For the longer periods ρ tends to be more stable and hence more useful, but scarcely stable enough to give any confidence that it could be used for prediction.

NOTES

1. I shall refer throughout to the *Report of the Committee on Finance and Industry* by this better-known title.
2. *Bank of England Statistical Summary.*
3. *Oxford Economic Papers*, May 1939.
4. Most of the monetary data used will be in millions and this will be indicated by an 'm'.
5. Public deposits and securities are inverted. Movements up or down for all the factors will tend to be associated with equal movements in direction and magnitude of banks' cash.
6. It is not surprising that there should be imperfect action, since until 1931 the Bank of England *did not know* the level of cash reserves of banks. Only in

June and December could they get a correct figure. Cf. Macmillan Committee, *Evidence*, vol. I, p. 14.

7. These differences may be in part the results of errors resulting from the imperfect method of estimating seasonal deviations.
8. Macmillan Committee, *Evidence*, vol. I, p. 14.
9. Unless otherwise specified all references are to banks' true cash and the true ratio.
10. This expression is used in the same sense as Mr Keynes used it, i.e. roughly the general level of economic activity.
11. *Treatise on Money*, U.S. 1st ed., vol II (New York: Harcourt Brace, 1930) p. 53.
12. This might come without variations in the ratio, if banks' cash had a cyclical pattern, but there is no reason to expect this except for the relation to public's cash and this did not happen in the two cycles studied here. The only other possibility is the central bank, but it is hard to see why it should provide periodic variations.
13. *General Theory*, U.K. 1st ed. (London: Macmillan, 1936) p. 174.
14. This is only used to indicate the state of trade in a crude way; it can at least reveal the phase of the business cycle. The years before 1923 are poor estimates, but good enough for the purpose.
15. *Treatise*, vol. II, p. 57.
16. The term 'loans', here as elsewhere in the paper, is used to include all types of earning assets.
17. Gilt-edge securities are highly liquid, in the sense of being readily marketable.
18. Money at call and short notice does not show much variation and may be neglected.
19. Macmillan *Report*, Appendix I.
20. Other income-earning activities were involved, so that this is not conclusive.
21. The percentage varies among banks according to the type of business they do.
22. *The General Theory*, p. 174.
23. *Report*, Appendix I, p. 283.
24. See above, p. 11.

2. Keynesian and Other Interest Theories

REVIEW OF ECONOMIC STATISTICS, 1943

In spite of many attempts, it is difficult to feel that a satisfactory reconciliation of the Keynesian and the more traditional interest theories has been attained. Yet, I believe, both theories are necessary. Can anyone really hold, for example, that the older theories give a satisfactory explanation of the extraordinary course of interest rates in recent years, or of their contrasting behaviour in the two World Wars? On the other hand, the newer analysis fails to find any place for the body of doctrine associated with the names of Böhm-Bawerk, Wicksell, Fisher, Schumpeter and others, and it does not, I think, fill in the gap thus left.[1] When there are no speculative hoards, the Keynesian theory breaks down.

For further discussion I offer the following possible method of reconciling the two types of theory in such a manner as not to deny any considerable part of either. If the loan market be regarded explicitly as a highly speculative one, in which it is very easy to carry stocks, then the Keynesian theory becomes not a contradiction of but a completion of traditional theory. Furthermore, the method that I propose, instead of being new and special to monetary theory, can be treated with the more usual concepts of value theory.

The beginning student, at some point in his indoctrination, is suddenly told that it is often not current supply (or rather production) and demand which control prices in many markets; on the contrary, it is the expectations of various people about the future of prices — something which at first sight is quite different. Yet modern value theory integrates these apparently disparate approaches satisfactorily. Capital theory, though in essence related to the passage of time, not unnaturally was first elaborated with the tools of static analysis. It is not, therefore, surprising that the introduction of dynamic elements should make more difference in capital theory than in other branches of theory. In this light the innovations of Lord Keynes are seen to add to, not supplant, the older capital analysis; in some sense they are matters of detail, yet peculiarly important detail, especially for concrete, short-run or cyclical analysis.

Let us now consider some of the ways in which the approach I suggest can be used. We may regard loans as a commodity bought and sold in the capital market, the stock or carry-over of which is idle money.[2] They must necessarily be regarded as monetary transactions, which form they ordinarily take in our society. Such a procedure does not conflict essentially with the study of the 'real' factors.[3] This commodity has several obvious peculiarities, which need cause no difficulty if kept in mind.

Let us first deal in some detail with an artificially simple, though significant, situation, after which the restrictions may be relaxed. Suppose that all lending is done through perpetual bonds which are riskless in the sense that there is no danger of non-payment of principal or interest. There are no short-term loans and no re-sales of bonds. Uncertainty is not a necessary factor in this situation, and since it is difficult to deal with, we shall at first omit it. In any speculative market, arbitrage over time presents interesting problems. It has an essential asymmetry: present supply can be carried forward but future output cannot be made available now. The central fact is that if any stock is to be held, expected prices (to the time of intended liquidation) must rise over the current price by the carrying cost of the commodity. If prices are expected to fall and if no stocks of the good exist, there is no effect on the cash price. If stocks exist, they will be liquidated entirely, or to the extent which brings the cash price below some or all expected prices by the proper amount.

We may take it as approximately true that in modern conditions money may be held idle without incurring any expenses. Therefore, the effective carrying cost of holding a stock of money idle is the loss of interest. In general, the holding of stocks requires that for some point of time in the future (indicated by the subscript and measured in any time unit)

$$P_n \geqq P_0(1 + \epsilon)^n,$$

where P is price and ϵ is the unit carrying cost for one period expressed as a per cent of value. In the case of loans, the rate of interest, R, is both price and carrying cost. For one year we get the result, enunciated by Lord Keynes,

$$R_1 \geqq R_0 + R_0^2.$$

Approximately the same result can be deduced from the rationale of investors' actions in the bond market. If the annual interest payment on any perpetual bond is a, then the present value and market price is given by G in

$$G_i = \frac{a}{R_i}.$$

If R_n is foreseen exactly, or expected with a probability of 1, what value will make it worthwhile to hold cash until year n? Ignoring compound interest, if $G_0 - G_n$ is respectively greater than, equal to, or less than na, there is a gain in holding cash, lending and hoarding are indifferent, or lending is preferable. By substitution and rearrangement, we obtain from

$$G_0 - G_n = na$$

the equation

$$\frac{R_n - nR_0R_n}{R_0} - 1 = 0.$$

If the terms are separated to determine how expected change in the rate is related to the present rate, the result becomes

$$R_n - R_0 = \frac{nR_0{}^2}{(1 - nR_0)}.$$

For one year this can become

$$R_1 = R_0 + R_0{}^2(1 + R_0 + R_0{}^2 + \ldots),$$

so that if we neglect the higher order terms we secure the same result as that derived from the necessary price relations in any speculative market.

In a study of the investment market, disregard of compound interest is unwise. Therefore, if we assume the compounding to be done at R_0 rather than at the current market rate,[4] we have in place of na,

$$a + a(1 + R_0) + a(1 + R_0)^2 + \ldots + a(1 + R_0)^{n-1}.$$

Its sum is

$$\frac{a[(1 + R_0)^n - 1]}{(1 + R_0) - 1};$$

$$\therefore \frac{a}{R_0} - \frac{a}{R_n} = a\left(\frac{(1 + R_0)^n - 1}{R_0}\right).$$

From this we get

$$R_n - R_0 = \frac{R_0(1+R_0)^n - R_0}{2-(1+R_0)^n}.$$

The rise in interest rate which will just induce a lender to hold cash is a function of the current rate and of the length of time before the necessary rise will occur. The higher the current rate, the greater the rise must be; and similarly, the greater the length of time until the expected rise, the greater that rise must be. A more definite notion of this interesting relation can be obtained from FIGURE 2.1. The present rate is measured along the horizontal axis, and the expected rise, along the vertical axis. Any present rate and expected rise can be plotted as a point. The line on which the point lies will indicate the maximum number of years that it will be worthwhile to hold cash idle. Thus, if in 1935 an investor in England could get 4 per cent on consols, and if he believed that public policy was designed to keep the rate there, and if he expected that a war would come in 1939 and would thwart that policy, with the rate rising to nearly 5 per cent, then he should hold idle cash. If, on the other hand, he expected that the war would come in 1940 (and that the rate would not rise above 5 per cent in the course of that year and subsequent years), then he should invest in 1935.

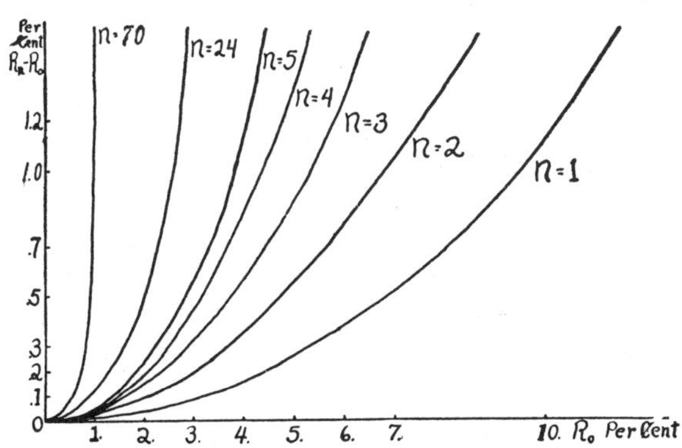

FIGURE 2.1 Speculative hoards and the interest rate

With a 3 per cent rate in 1935, a war-time rate of only 3.57 per cent or more would have induced him to hold cash until 1940; and had the rate been 1 per cent, an expectation of a rate of more than 1.05 would have led to the same result. These considerations lead to Lord Keynes's highly original point about the obstacles to the existence of a low rate of interest. The convergence of all these curves upon zero for a zero rate of interest gives a vivid and complete picture of his theory. At a zero rate no one would lend if any rise was expected ever to occur. If we take 6 per cent as the highest likely yield, a wait for it up to sixty-one years, cash in hand, at a current rate of 1 per cent, would be worthwhile. For other current rates up to 5 per cent, the limits are twenty-six, fourteen, seven and three years. At a high rate of interest the inducement to withhold lending would be weak. For a current rate of 10 per cent, the necessary expected rise would be to 15 or more per cent within three years, and to 25 or more per cent within five years. Not the absolute rate alone makes the difference, but rather the necessary expected change. No tendency for the liquidity preference curve to 'flatten out' at any particular low rate is essential. Rather, such a flattening out is increasingly likely to occur as a zero rate is approached. If interest rates are expected to remain unchanged or to decline, then a man is as much a fool to hold useless cash at 1 per cent as at 10 per cent. Any connection between levels and expectations is not necessary even though it may occur frequently. Possibly, because of a certain tendency to stability in the long-term bond rate, the more it rises above some average level, the greater the number of people who expect a fall (and hence do not hold cash); and the more it falls below an average level, the greater the number who expect a rise (and hence do hold cash).

In terms of this analysis there is no relation between money and the interest rate; there is a relation only between money and the present rate together with expected rates. Such a relation is more complicated and difficult to use than the original Keynesian formulation, but it is, I believe, more satisfactory. If expected rates do not change in response to changes in current rates, then the two approaches become the same. The view that people do have such stable expectations is supported by considerable evidence. Yet, obviously, estimates of the future may be revised, and thus the rate of interest may change without a change in the amount of money (and in transactions) or a change in the amount of money may bring none in the rate of interest. For example, at first an increase in idle money may lead to a decline in rates on the assumption of a future return to the old level. This confidence may, however, be undermined as the rate remains down, thus necessitating a further decline in the rate without any increase in idle money. Or again a shift to the opinion of even higher future rates will lead to a rise in the current rate although the amount of idle money remains unchanged. In an unpublished study I have attempted to show that there is some evidence that both types of movement occurred in England after 1932.

The addition of an expected rate of interest to the Keynesian system contributes one new element and no new equation, so that unless the rate is given independently the values of the variables become indeterminate. If the expected rate depends in a definite way on the current rate, then the number of equations and unknowns are equal; but whether or not this yields a determinate equilibrium depends on the type of 'elasticity of expectations'. If a change in the current rate brings a change in the expected rate just large enough to compensate for it (as required by the formula discussed above), then the current rate is not determined by the quantity of idle money; i.e. it is in neutral equilibrium, with any value satisfying. If the expected rate changes more than enough, then no current rate will satisfy the equations and no equilibrium is possible. On the other hand, if the expected rate changes less than enough (which is perhaps the only likely case), there will be one equilibrium; but under this condition the current rate will show wider fluctuations, as a result of given changes in idle money, than would be the case if the expected rate were unchanged.

Where the relevant expected rate, *ER*, is not independent of the current rate, there may be no stable equilibrium. In general with an increase in idle money it will be approximately true that, if with some time lag $\frac{\Delta ER}{\Delta R} > 1$, there will be explosive decline in *R*; if $\frac{\Delta ER}{\Delta R} = 1$, continuous decline at a constant rate; and if $\frac{\Delta ER}{\Delta R} < 1$, decline approaching a limit. The fact that the rate of interest does not appear to behave in this way is some argument against the first two hypotheses; but the argument is not conclusive because there may be other factors. The condition may possibly exist over a limited range.

A decrease in idle money will force the current rate up if the *ER*s remain the same. But if the *ER*s move upward, then a further rise will occur in R_0, and so on. Whether or not the rise will approach a limit, depends on the same conditions as in a fall.

Movements of expectations inverse to those of R_0 need not be ruled out. If people are conscious of a business cycle, a continued rise will lead, at some point, to a decline in *ER*s of the rather near future (and conversely at the bottom of the cycle). As a result, a decrease in idle money in boom times might lead to a decrease in R_0; and an increase in the slump, to an increase in R_0. These movements are the reverse of those which Lord Keynes considered, and yet they are plainly possible. In fact, the long-term interest rate does not behave in a way to suggest that the liquidity preference schedule, as he describes it, holds without exception. Likewise, autonomous shifts in expectations which will alter R_0 without any change in idle money should be taken into consideration, although nothing in general can be said about such shifts.

With certainty and universal agreement about expected interest rates, it appears that there would be stable equilibrium only if no idle funds existed. For if idle funds were available for holding, and if R_0 were below a certain level (the same level for all bondholders), everyone would offer his bonds for sale. No one would buy, and hence G_0 would fall and R_0 rise until it was above the critical point. Yet if R_0 were to be above the critical point, no one would care to hold money idle; those who did have money would try to buy; but with no sellers, G_0 would rise until R_0 dropped below the critical point.[5]

That different people may have certain but inconsistent views about the future is logically possible, and may happen. In such cases, there will be an equilibrium. Each investor will have definite expectations, and given his situation with regard to brokerage costs, R_0 will be such that any market rate below it will lead the investor to sell all his bonds and hold cash.[6] If we array and sum these demands for cash, we get a demand curve for idle money in terms of the current rate of interest. With a given stock of idle money, the rate of interest is determined.

In two remaining senses, the 'money' market differs from the more usual speculative ones. First, 'real' goods for loan cannot be transferred to the future, as wheat very definitely can, and therefore a complicated additional analysis is required to find the 'real' results of holding money for speculative purposes. Secondly, wheat speculators, taking account of present and expected prices, determine in a concrete way the amount of the wheat carry-over; but the same is not true of the speculative hoarder. The loan carry-over, idle money, is determined independently of the individual or group of speculators (if the banks be excluded), who must adjust, by competitive bidding, present and future interest rates so that they will be consistent with the loan carry-over. The reasoning involved is essentially of the same type as that employed in traditional monetary theory and should be no more objectionable. Money holders, acting as if they took prices as given, determine how much money(active) they shall hold. Nonetheless, theorists have always maintained that the money supply is given and that prices are determined. Analogously, the individual operator takes the present and expected rates as given and decides how much money he will hold idle. Yet, in fact, the banking system determines the total quantity of money, which, subtracting the requirements of active trade, fixes the total quantity of idle money that must be held, and thus determines the interest rate.

At this point we must note a curious peculiarity of the capital market, i.e. that some of the operators, the banks, have an important influence on the available supply of speculative stocks. When an expansive programme is undertaken, a part of it often results in an increase in bank reserves, which, it is expected, will lead banks to buy bonds and to lower the interest rate. But why should banks buy bonds when they are considered a bad investment by some of the best market opinion (those who trade bonds for cash)? The problem may be put as follows: If all investors, banks included, had the same estimates of the future of interest rates, then no rationally actuated banks would force an expansion of money by buying bonds. Where opinions differ, banks which are of the same opinion as those individuals who would be supplanted as bondholders will leave the added reserves unused.[7] If, on the other hand, the banks' opinion differs from that of the individuals, the reserves will be used — at least until the interest rate shifts enough to change the banks from intra- to extra-marginal buyers. Therefore we have not only a theory of the determination of the current rate of interest, but also one of the determination, in part, of the stock of idle money and unused reserves. The supply of idle money is not a given quantity, but rather a rising supply schedule depending on the rate of interest and the speculative views of the banks.[8] There is an important difference between the actions of banks and of the public. If excess reserves are considered as idle money, the purchase of a bond by a bank means an increase in idle money of something less than 100 per cent, while a similar action by an ordinary investor means no increase at all.

Limitation of space prevents a complete discussion of the problems created by the possibility of shifting into and out of bonds. Obviously, however, if the future is foreseen, all actions can be reduced to pairs, the present and the nearest date at which a shift is desirable. Therefore, an elaboration of the above analysis can be used. Also, brokerage costs must be considered, but they need cause no difficulty.

Where the possibility of making loans of different maturities exists, the theoretical apparatus must be extended.[9] Long-term loans may be made by repeated short-term lending. Likewise, by going in and out again of the long-term market, a type of short-term loan may be made. Expecting higher rates, a speculator may go 'long' either by holding cash or by making short-term loans; expecting lower rates, he may go 'short' by continuous short-term borrowing or by long-term lending.[10] All these courses of action will naturally be influenced to some extent by brokerage costs. Until recently, economists were inclined to say that, with allowance for cost, risk of non-payment, etc., long-term and short-term rates would tend toward equality. That there is no such tendency is due to the speculative nature of the loan market. There will be rates such that those at the margin cannot expect to do any better by shifting, but this will not mean equality of rates.

Anything less than a perpetual bond allows re-contract and hence adjustment to any change in rates. Therefore, the shorter the loan, the less the risk, i.e. the risk of earning more or less than could have been earned by lending at a later date. The shortness of the loan enters into the picture only in the sense that it limits the amount of change likely and the duration of the change until re-contract.[11] Loss as well as gain can result from short-term lending. Two distinct elements affect the result—change and uncertainty. The fact that long-term lending can be undertaken by successive short-term loans means that if future short-term rates are expected with certainty to rise by certain amounts, the current long-term rate for any period must be higher by an amount sufficient to make the two net expected returns equal. For the same reason, where a decline is expected a long-term rate must be less than a short-term rate. Where reliance must be placed on guesses, the long-term rate must be such as to balance at the margin the estimated chances of loss against those of gain, compared with successive short-term loans. The necessity of taking account of uncertainty does not alter the fact that, where rises are expected, people would prefer to lend at short-term with equal rates; and where declines are anticipated, they would prefer to lend at long-term. In each case, the rates must be adjusted so as to equalise supply and demand for each category of loans. In view of these facts, it is difficult to see why Professor Hicks concludes without qualification that '. . . if no extra return is offered for long lending, most people (and institutions) would prefer to lend short. . . .'[12]

Clearly, short-term rates may be above long-term rates, and, in fact, they often have been. Yet such behaviour is in conflict with Lord Keynes's blanket assertion that interest is the reward for parting with liquidity. Short-term loans are more liquid than long-term ones in any common usage of the term liquid, and therefore they should always have lower rates than long-term loans. The use of the general concept of liquidity, though helpful and illuminating, can produce contradictions like the above. The whole relation of interest and money has been analysed here without the use of the word liquidity or the concept as such. Treating the problem as one of speculation gives more satisfactory results. The increasing approximation of loans to money as the term grows shorter can easily be explained by the lessening speculative risk from interest rate changes, which will be true, however, only when rates are expected to rise. This case is the only one with which we are concerned, for it is necessarily a condition for the carrying of stocks of idle money.

Wherever the question is one of waiting for a higher interest rate on long-term loans, the cost is not the rate of interest but the difference between the long- and the short-term rate. This conclusion follows only if short-term lending is as good as holding cash; and, as we have pointed out, the shorter the loan, the more nearly is the conclusion true. Therefore, the gap between long-term rates and very short-term ones is as significant for the speculative position as is the long-term rate itself. An important qualification is that a considerable market in short-term loans must be easily available to the investor. Thus, considering the loan market as a speculative one yields not only a workable theory of the rate of interest, but also a theory of the organic composition and evolution of the structure of interest rates.

The preceding analysis may appear unrealistic because, in order to make it precise, certainty of expectations was introduced. Yet in fact it is not so unreal, because all that it requires is certainty that a rate will be above or below a particular value. A person may have only the vaguest notion of what the rate of interest will be five years from now, yet feel certain that it will be at least three-quarters of a per cent higher than it is now.

Professor Hicks and others have used a kind of frequency probability curve in representing the uncertain expectations of people. This method offers considerable analytical advantages in dealing with a highly intractable problem, but it does not, I believe, have any sound foundation. As Professor Knight pointed out long ago, business decisions usually cannot be based on *a priori* or statistical probability.[13] The method might have some basis for dealing with expected variations in the yield per unit of input in agriculture, but surely not in expected bond prices. Although the probability curve is presumed to be rather symmetrical about the most probable value, it has nothing to do with the law of large numbers. It expresses mere vagueness and lack of knowledge. Whether one takes a subjective or an objective approach to the nature of probability, expectational probability is subjective in a different sense, for it conforms to nothing either past or present in the external world. It has essentially little to do with the body of doctrine known as probability theory.

People's expectations are for the most part uncertain, yet they will (and often must) act on them. Some price is low enough to induce the holding of stocks. If a future rate of interest is expected with certainty, a present rate below a certain level will induce the holding of cash. If some doubt is entertained about the expected rate, then the present rate must be still lower by an amount sufficient to induce cash holding; this is the speculative element as distinguished from arbitrage. The greater the doubt, the lower must be the present rate (or the greater the potential gain) to lead to the holding of cash. The nature of the process by which these decisions are reached still resists any general, detailed analysis, perhaps precisely because the process has no rational content. We may take it as a good rule that the greater the probability of gain (or the greater the gain of a given probability), the more a person will risk on it. Therefore, to the extent that expectations are independent of current price, the lower is the present rate, in given circumstances, the more cash will investors desire to hold.[14] This strengthens the proposition that there is a declining demand curve for idle money in terms of the current rate of interest.

Precise expectations are not necessary. In the wheat market, for example, traders are willing to make precise estimates only for the very near future. Yet an unusually large crop, by forcing a considerable price decline, can ordinarily get a part of itself absorbed as stocks. So also with money: the rate of interest can fall as far as is necessary, and yet no matter how unsure people are, the point will be reached where they will believe that the rate is bound to go up sooner or later. The further it falls, the less is the anticipated rise. Where the point lies for different people is rather arbitrary since the grounds for rational estimate are small. And above all, the expectations can and do change easily and, perhaps, independently of any other economic conditions. Very likely, estimates because of their indefiniteness often cover rather long periods. There is a kind of compound probability. The prices at succeeding dates are not mutually exclusive events, and, though not completely independent, may occur under situations that are essentially different. If at least a 20 per cent rise is expected within the next five years, and if it does not come in the first year, the game is still not lost.

NOTES

1. Professor Schumpeter can, of course, be included in this group only at a cost of some theoretical strain. He cannot, however, be classified with Lord Keynes, in spite of the fact that both take the monetary approach to interest problems. For Professor Schumpeter's own brief remarks, cf. his *Business Cycles* (New York: 1939), vol. I, p. 127 and vol. II, p. 608.
2. It is obvious that this is in some senses an arbitrary convention. Idle money is not the same thing as a loan.
3. Cf. Schumpeter, *Business Cycles*, vol. I, p. 129.

4. The error from this assumption will be small.
5. These are hypothetical, not actual, movements in time.
6. Where there is uncertainty, the lower is the market rate, the larger will be *the proportion* of total resources which each individual will put into cash. This complication is easily introduced here, as in analogous, other value problems.
7. If the banks are uncertain about expected rates, they will leave some portion of their added reserves unused.
8. This assumes as given the supply of reserves and the quantity of short-term and commercial loans of the banks.
9. Although corporation bonds and stocks should be included, too, they will be ignored here because of the difficulties involved. In addition to all the interest problems discussed already, there are those coming from the uncertainty about future dividends.
10. Both here and elsewhere in this essay I am indebted to J. B. Williams, *Theory of Investment Value* (Cambridge, Mass.: 1938).
11. Another way to look at it is that the greater the proximity of repayment at face value, the greater the limitation on the effect of rate changes on market price, as well as the less the probable change in the rate within the period.
12. J. R. Hicks, *Value and Capital* (Oxford, 1939), p. 146.
13. Frank H. Knight, *Risk, Uncertainty and Profit* (Boston and New York: 1921) esp. pp. 223–32.
14. The principle is subject to a qualification: '. . . more generally, a player should not enter a game, no matter how brilliant the prospects, if the expectations of loss be too large a proportion of his fortune'. J. L. Coolidge, *An Introduction to Mathematical Probability* (Oxford: 1925) p. 30.

3. Dynamical Coupling with Especial Reference to Markets Having Production Lags

ECONOMETRICA, 1947

There is widespread agreement that it is necessary to introduce into economics both dynamical relations and general interdependence. This is not a counsel of perfection or a manifestation of the desire for theoretical elegance and completeness. The most concrete, practical analysis is often vitiated by restrictive assumptions which ignore or 'eliminate' the elements of change and of interconnectedness. When two sectors of an economy are interdependent in some way (coupled, we may say), and when we have another than the null or trivial solution of no change, then it is quite inadmissible to discuss the one sector assuming the other unchanged. For, if the one does not remain constant, the other cannot either, by virtue of the coupling. Therefore to allow one sector to vary and keep the other constant would be to hold contradictory assumptions.

What we should say is that each sector depends on all the others, but then the problem becomes really unmanageable. To see this, one need only reflect on the relative sterility of general equilibrium theory in statics, and add on the special difficulties of dynamical analysis. The question then arises: can we legitimately break down this monolithic problem in such a way as to get answers that are not seriously wrong. Actually progress in the understanding of any subject comes through successful abstraction, i.e. finding out what can be ignored and what cannot.

There is a pervasive asymmetry in economic interdependence, which is of fundamental importance in reducing the difficulties of analysis. In most cases an industry will not be important to the whole economy, but the converse will be so. Thus the state of the pork industry, prosperous or depressed, will not make much difference to the national income, but the latter will vitally affect the former. This condition tends to hold even in detail, for it will infrequently be the case that industry *A* purchases a considerable portion of the output of *B*, and in turn sells a marked proportion of its own output to *B*. The finer we make our subdivisions the more true this will be. The important thing is that while we must consider the influence of *B* on *A*, we need not consider the return effect of *A* on *B* and hence on *A*, etc. The problem of coupling, or simultaneous dynamical equations, goes over into the much simpler one of forced motion, or inhomogeneity. Because of its essential asymmetry, we might call it unilateral coupling. The quantitative importance of the return effect will fix the degree of error in making a partial analysis. Where it is large we are not justified in breaking up the problem into simpler ones.

Unilateral coupling is a partial dynamics analogous to partial statics and should be able to enjoy some of the advantages of the latter type of theory while avoiding some, at least, of its defects. If the assumptions are stated explicitly, it should be possible to avoid making errors in problems where they do not apply. A large industry that cannot be satisfactorily subdivided, as in the building trades, would not fulfil the conditions. The level of activity in such a case does make a significant difference to the balance of the economy. Or again, if we subdivide the economy not according to market or industry, but along some other lines, such as consumption, investment, raw materials, durable goods, etc., they very likely cannot be isolated. Even the smallness of the sector will not guarantee unilateral coupling, for as we eliminate interdependence through expenditures by more minute subdivision, we may have tighter coupling, through price, with allied goods, either competing or complementary.

After stating somewhat more precisely in Section I the conditions for unilateral coupling, in Section II I shall consider, assuming the conditions satisfied, the behaviour of markets characterised by a production lag (the cobweb theorem). This is perhaps the oldest, empirically most successful, and simplest of dynamical hypotheses. Yet it has remained too close to partial statics. There is some evidence to show that the behaviour of many markets may be fairly well explained by considering national income and one or two other prices as well as its own price. In Section III the effect of shifting supply and demand curves is shown to be irregular oscillations, which are maintained in spite of the realistic assumption of a stable market. Both of these results are in accord with what we know of such cycles. The cobweb theorem is based on naive expectations that are continually disappointed. Hence the question naturally arises: why has not this experience led to somewhat more sophisticated expectations, and if so, would this destroy the cycle? Somewhat surprisingly it turns out (Section IV) that it is not so. The theorem is obviously an example of partial analysis in that it includes the market's own price to the exclusion of all others. In Section V it is shown that we may include one or a few other dynamical markets which mutually interact. The stability of both markets is decreased by the coupling; their phase relations (lead or lag) are entirely arbitrary though there will be a tendency for them to swing together. Two markets with the same production lag will not have their periods altered by coupling, but if they have different lags, their periods are scrambled in a complicated way so that both have longer periods and different ones from the uncoupled state. Also, both cease to be simply periodic, i.e. they have an ever-changing wave shape, even in the absence of outside disturbance. Finally, we may study the case of two mutually coupled markets, which are, however, unilaterally connected with the balance of the economy. Of particular interest is the possibility of an exaggerated or resonant response to special periodic constituents in the behaviour of the balance of the economy. This will impart to these sectors a systematic, individual character markedly different from the rest of the economy.

I. Unilateral Coupling

If an economy be divided into two sectors, the condition for unilateral coupling is obvious. Consider a system represented by a dynamical matrix with x_1 and x_2 representing sector outputs, D the differential operator, $a(D)$ a polynomial in D with constant coefficients, and $\psi_1(t)$ and $\psi_2(t)$ unexplained functions of time which are the demand for outputs not explicable by the outputs and their derivatives. Then the system is represented by

$$\begin{bmatrix} a_{11}(D) & a_{12}(D) \\ a_{21}(D) & a_{22}(D) \end{bmatrix} \begin{Bmatrix} x_1 \\ x_2 \end{Bmatrix} - \begin{Bmatrix} \psi_1(t) \\ \psi_2(t) \end{Bmatrix} = \begin{Bmatrix} 0 \\ 0 \end{Bmatrix},$$

and the condition is that either a_{12} or a_{21} must be zero, but, of course, both must not be zero since that would mean no interdependence and no difficulty. If a_{12} is zero then payments from Sector 1 do not depend on sales to the balance of the economy, as might be the case with a public works or relief authority. The more likely situation is that a_{21} is zero, which would mean that payments by Sector 1 do not depend on its output (and derivatives). Actually the requirement that one $a(D)$ be zero is unnecessarily severe. What is meant is that $a(D)$ be such that treating it as zero will not introduce an error in our answer greater than some tolerable limit. In practice it may be difficult to set a limit and to decide whether a given problem lies within it, but the principle is clear. For simplicity I shall speak of the various $a(D)$s being zero with the understanding that this means that they have a negligible effect on the result.

If we subdivide the economy into more than two sectors, the condition for unilateral coupling is not quite so obvious. Given the system

$$\begin{bmatrix} a_{11} & a_{12} & \dots & a_{1n} \\ a_{21} & a_{22} & \dots & a_{2n} \\ \cdot & \cdot & \dots & \cdot \\ a_{n1} & a_{n2} & \dots & a_{nn} \end{bmatrix} \begin{Bmatrix} x_1 \\ x_2 \\ \cdot \\ x_n \end{Bmatrix} = \begin{Bmatrix} \psi_1 \\ \psi_2 \\ \cdot \\ \psi_n \end{Bmatrix} = \begin{Bmatrix} 0 \\ 0 \\ \cdot \\ 0 \end{Bmatrix}, \tag{1}$$

let us suppose that by shifting rows and columns we have brought the sector under consideration into leading position. Partitioning off column 1 and row 1, we have

$$\left[\begin{array}{c|c} a_{11} & B \\ \hline A & C \end{array}\right] \begin{Bmatrix} x_1 \\ X \end{Bmatrix} - \begin{Bmatrix} \psi_1 \\ \Psi \end{Bmatrix} = \begin{Bmatrix} 0 \\ 0 \end{Bmatrix}. \tag{2}$$

From this we get

$$a_{11}x_1 + BX - \psi_1 = 0, \tag{3}$$

and

$$Ax_1 + CX - \Psi = 0. \tag{4}$$

If we may drop the first term in (4) and assert

$$CX - \Psi \approx 0, \tag{5}$$

then we are justified in making the highly advantageous simplification of partially isolating one industry or sector. Although it is less likely, B may be zero, permitting the study of x_1 separately in (3). Then (4) would tell us how the payments would influence the balance of the economy.

Assuming A zero, we may, if it is feasible, solve for X and substitute in (3), obtaining approximately the true behaviour of x_1. We might even iterate once or twice, putting our approximate solution into (4) as a given function. If, however, we can solve $n-1$ dynamical equations, we can probably solve n, and therefore there would really be no point in concerning ourselves with partial dynamics. But in fact the state of development in calculating machines and in economic statistics is not such as to have yielded any such perfect result. Consequently it is desirable, when possible, to analyse the structure and behaviour patterns of particular industries. Without solving equations (5) we possess a great fund of both qualitative and quantitative information about the actual observed solutions. These results may be fed into equation (3) to find the reactions of the industry to the various types of movement in the rest of the economy. It should be noted that B is a row matrix and X a column one and hence we need not take aggregates, but may be able to restrict or call attention to the particular effects of the one or two sectors which are the major markets of Sector 1. Likewise we may study, at least qualitatively, the response of a sector to a trend, a forty-month cycle, a major business cycle, an irregular cycle, and so on through the known types of economic motion.

The condition that A or B must be zero is more stringent than required; it is sufficient but not necessary. It is not difficult to see this intuitively. Industry 1 may be small but yet buy, say, 40 per cent of the output of industry 10, which will also be small, if we have subdivided the industries somewhat evenly. Therefore each element in A is not zero (negligible) although industry 10 may still not have any influence, direct or through other industries, on industry 1. There would be unilateral coupling although neither A nor B is zero. If we partition the dynamical matrix in the following way,

$$\left[\begin{array}{c:c:c} A & B & C \\ \hdashline L & a_{jj} & F \\ \hdashline K & H & G \end{array}\right], \tag{6}$$

having shifted rows and columns until all the non-zero column elements are in B, then necessary and sufficient conditions for unilateral coupling are that H, K and L shall be zero.[1] These guarantee that those sectors influenced by Sector j will not exercise any significant return effect. It may be difficult to establish the fact that a sector fulfils these conditions, so that in practice we may have to fall back on the intuition that a small enough sector of the economy will almost certainly qualify.

There are, I think, two points that should be always kept in mind. If we were conceptually to make a complete and satisfactory analysis of the economy sector by sector, we should still not have explained its operation; e.g. why it has cycles of such and such a duration. Secondly, no matter how finely we subdivide, though the economy will become insensitive to one sector, it will not cease to dominate the sector through expenditures. Yet as we reduce our difficulties in this direction, we may often increase them in another, i.e. through prices. The finer the classification the greater will be the element of competition or complementarity between goods. Thus, as we descend the scale from food to meat, to pork, we are likely to find increasing sensitivity to price. For example as between pork and lamb we cannot expect to find unilateral coupling through price. In Section V I shall attempt to indicate by example how such questions may be approached.

II. The Cobweb Theorem

The cobweb theorem is typically and essentially partial dynamics, since both supply and demand depend on price in the commodity's own market. Its considerable success in explaining actual phenomena is a remarkable demonstration of how even such a drastic simplification may be satisfactory. If in addition we take account of overall shifts in demand and also of the price of the one or two other goods most closely related, we may hope to improve the completeness and accuracy of explanation. From a static point of view, Staehle has shown how completely we may account for demand, in a number of cases, by using own price, one other price, and aggregate income.[2] The results are good, and convincing, because they are simple and in accord with what market theory would lead us to expect.

Throughout I shall assume continuous marketing and production planning. The more usual examples of annual planting or particular breeding times are special cases; which can be obtained by allowing the variable time to take on only the discrete values indicated by the particular market. Also I shall consider only linear supply and demand relations with the hope that within the effective range of variation the curves are approximately straight lines.

Consider a competitive market for a single commodity with demand at time t given by

$$D-\alpha p(t)+\eta(t), \tag{7}$$

and supply by

$$-S+\beta p(t-\theta)+\psi(t-\theta), \tag{8}$$

where D, α, S, β and θ are positive constants and p is price. The slope of the supply and demand curves are respectively $-1/\alpha$ and $1/\beta$, while θ is the time required from the decision to produce until the good appears on the market. The functions $\eta(t)$ and $\psi(t-\theta)$ represent any shifts in the two curves due to influences 'outside' of the market primarily as a result of changes in income or the general level of activity. By taking α and β as constant, it is implied that changes in the curves, here straight lines, are only shifts. If supply is equal to demand[3] we have

$$\alpha p(t) + \beta p(t - \theta) = \phi(t) + D + S, \tag{9}$$

where $\phi(t)$ is $\eta(t) - \psi(t - \theta)$ and represents the difference between the shifts in the demand and in the supply curves. D and S serve only to determine an unchanging level about which the price moves, so that if we consider only deviations from this level, we may set them equal to zero. If there is a trend of mild degree, the S and D will change slowly with time and then we will have deviations from a trend.

It is always assumed that decisions to produce lead to the same output at a later date, but this is not true, especially in agriculture, where the output of most crops is heavily affected by the weather. Thus acreage may consistently be controlled by prices, but yield per acre will have a non-systematic or random character. In industry, strikes or material shortages may make the output deviate from the intended one. Since $\phi(t)$ is absolutely unrestricted, we may include in it the result of all these uncontrollable factors. Ezekiel has shown that for potatoes it is likely that this kind of disturbance has been the maintainer of the oscillation, which otherwise would have died down.[4] For simplicity in what follows, I shall speak only of shifts, but $\phi(t)$ is to be understood as including these other elements as well.

The general solution of (9) is to be found by setting $\phi(t)$ equal to zero. In Section III I shall take up particular solutions for any given ϕ. It is also convenient to measure time in unit lag periods so that $\theta = 1$, and to let $a = \beta/\alpha$. Then

$$p(t) + ap(t - 1) = 0, \tag{9a}$$

which has solutions of the type

$$p(t) = P\lambda^t, \tag{10}$$

where the Ps are to be determined by initial conditions and the λs by the structure of the market. For a non-trivial solution,

$$\lambda = -a, \tag{11}$$

or, as is more convenient for our purposes,

$$\lambda = |a| e^{i(\epsilon + 2n\pi)}, \quad n = 0, \pm 1, \pm 2, \ldots. \tag{11a}$$

Should a be negative (e.g. supply and demand curves both downward or both upward sloping, or multiplier analysis with a lag), then $\epsilon = 0$, and the general solution is

$$p = e^{ln|a|t}\{P_0 + P_1 e^{i2\pi t} + P_{-1}e^{-i2\pi t} + P_2 e^{i4\pi t} + \ldots\}. \tag{12}$$

The maximum period is 1, which merely expresses the fact that the behaviour over an initial lag period is arbitrary so far as market structure is concerned. Any given shape will be repeated, and in the absence of outside disturbance, will be repeated indefinitely as the price subsides to its equilibrium value or explodes beyond the range of linearity.

The normal situation, which we assume here, is for the demand curve to be negatively sloped and the supply curve to be positively inclined. Then λ is negative real and $\epsilon = \pi$, so that the solution becomes

$$p = e^{ln|a|t}\{P_0 e^{i\pi t} + P_{-1}e^{-i\pi t} + P_1 e^{i3\pi t} + P_{-2}e^{-i3\pi t} + \ldots\}. \tag{13}$$

By pairing complex conjugate terms, and reintroducing our original symbols, we may write the solution in purely real terms:

$$p = e^{(ln\beta/\alpha)t/\theta}\sum_{k=0}^{k=\infty}\left\{A_k \cos\frac{2k+1}{\theta}t + B_k \sin\frac{2k+1}{\theta}t\right\}. \tag{13a}$$

The arbitrary constants A_k and B_k may be determined by Fourier analysis from the behaviour of price over any one lag period. The infinity of solutions results from the assumption of continuous input and sale. If all producers make decisions and market but once each period, there is only one solution.

Barring shifts in the curves, we thus get the well-known results of the theorem, a period of oscillation of twice the lag θ. The first half of one vibration will have an arbitrary shape, but the second half must be its mirror image reflected about the time axis (except for damping). The swings increase in amplitude if β/α is greater than one; they remain constant if β/α is unity; and they decrease in violence if it is less than one.

III. Shifting Supply and Demand Curves

If there is a single shift that is maintained for some time, the solution is quite simple, especially if the market has a tendency to decreasing fluctuation, i.e. is dynamically stable. For a single shift which persists, Φ, the price is given by

$$p(t) = \frac{\Phi}{\alpha} - \frac{\beta}{\alpha}p(t-\theta)$$

and

$$p(t-\theta) = \frac{\Phi}{\alpha} - \frac{\beta}{\alpha} p(t-2\theta).$$

By thus recurring, we get

$$p(t) = \frac{\Phi}{\alpha}\left\{1 - \left(\frac{\beta}{\alpha}\right) + \left(\frac{\beta}{\alpha}\right)^2 - \left(\frac{\beta}{\alpha}\right)^3 + \ldots + \left(-\frac{\beta}{\alpha}\right)^\tau\right\}, \tag{14}$$

where τ represents the largest integral number of lag units, θ, elapsed from the time $t = 0$ when Φ occurred to the time t. If this was long ago, and if $\beta/\alpha < 1$, then the final result is

$$p(t) = \frac{\Phi}{\alpha+\beta}, \text{ approximately.}$$

This is shown graphically in FIGURE 3.1, with $\alpha = 0.80$, $\beta = 0.52$ and $\Phi = 6.4$.

As is easily seen, the oscillation quickly dies down because of the positive damping. There are only two other possibilities. There is the unlikely case of equal slopes to the supply and demand curves, neutral equilibrium with undiminishing swings. Or it could explode into ever-increasing amplitudes. The dynamically stable case leads to cycle suicide, the neutral could be expected only rarely, and the unstable case leads to absurd results. Therefore the simple cobweb theorem is not adequate to explain the continued existence of commodity cycles.

One possible way out of this difficulty was demonstrated by Leontief.[5] As the amplitude grows or declines, the price will surely strike a region in which the curves are not straight lines. Then barring unusual shapes, he showed that a point of neutral equilibrium will be reached, where the cycle will remain or to which it will return if disturbed. Thus he demonstrated for non-linear difference equations of this type a limit cycle analogous to the famous Poincaré limit cycle in non-linear differential equations—a conception fundamental to the theory of oscillators.

There is, of course, a basis for using straight-line curves, the reason being that only in this case can any really complete analysis be carried out. Over a certain range any curve may be approximated by a straight line, and if the range is large enough, considerable advantages accrue. But for stationary curves there is not much value to the cobweb theorem if we make this approximation. The moment, however, we drop the assumption of fixed curves, the difficulty disappears. Why this is so can be seen

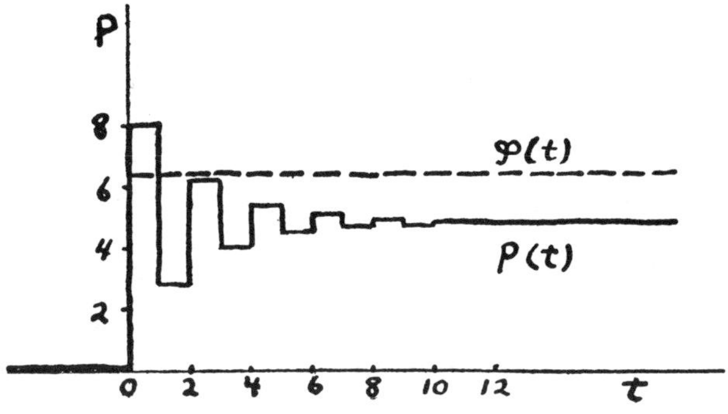

FIGURE 3.1

from FIGURE 3.1. There one shift excites an oscillation which gradually damps down. Then if one imagines many shifts following one another, the result is a maintained oscillation, since as the old ones are dying out new ones are continually being excited. Therefore if we have a dynamically stable market mechanism, its cycle will not disappear so long as it is disturbed from 'outside', i.e. from changes, whether cyclical, random or other, in income, weather, etc.

By this method we may study the results of any series of shifts whatsoever. Any arbitrary $\phi(t)$ may be approximated as closely as desired by considering it as made up of a series of short intervals during each of which it is a constant about equal to the average of the true values of ϕ. By the same argument as before,

$$p(t) = \frac{1}{\alpha}\left\{\phi(t) - \left(\frac{\beta}{\alpha}\right)\phi(t-\theta) + \left(\frac{\beta}{\alpha}\right)^2 \phi(t-2\theta) - \dots\right\}. \tag{15}$$

In FIGURE 3.2 is given an example of the results from an approximation to a continuously shifting difference between supply and demand curves, the short time interval being taken as one-quarter of the lag. The values of α and β are the same as before.

Although the price fluctuation left to itself would quickly die out (note the extreme right end of the curve), it is evident from this example that so long as there is change, the cycle is kept alive, at times becoming milder, at times more violent, depending on the extent and shape of the changes. The oscillation is not only maintained but distorted, and this irregularity is also in accord with reality. Neither characteristic is contained in the simple cobweb theorem. In the absence of outside disturbance the period would be 8 time units, whereas here we find for the major swings from

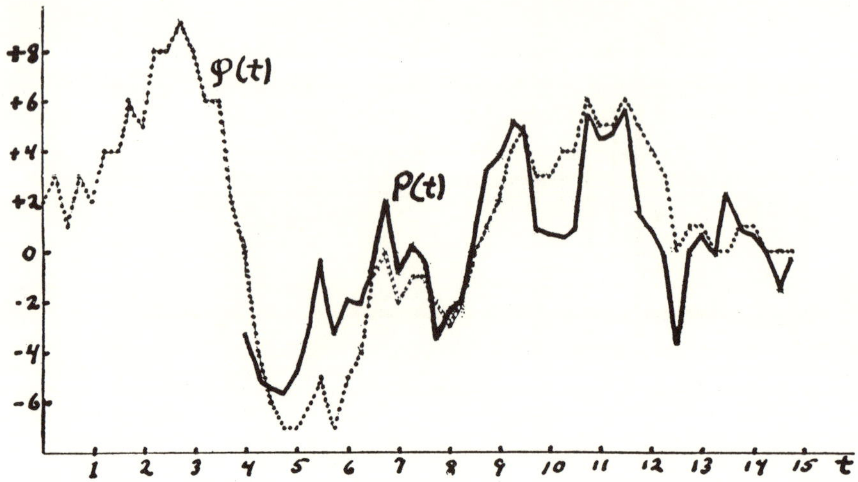

FIGURE 3.2

crest to crest, 5, 19, 9, and 8 units, or from trough to trough, 4, 8, 9, 10, 8 units.

If there is instability with $\beta/\alpha > 1$, then any disturbances only increase the rate at which it explodes. In this case it is necessary to fall back on Leontief's argument that it will explode until it reaches a damped region, and will come to a dynamically neutral equilibrium at the dividing point between the two regions. We may guess that continuing disturbances will push it into the damped region, but for non-linear relations this would be hard to demonstrate. Even neutral dynamical equilibrium becomes inadmissible for constantly shifting curves. Each new shift adds to the amplitude of swing and there is no subtraction, so that the amplitude will increase without limit. Since markets are subject to continual change, we are driven to assume at some point or other a damping element.

IV. The Consequences of Expectations

The producer in a market with a commodity cycle is always tending to get the worst of it; he has little to sell when prices are high and much when they are low (naturally, since that is what makes them low). For these and other reasons producers may cease to take current prices as expected prices, especially if the duration of the cycle is short. In addition there is the important problem of public policy: is there any other simple type of expectation that would lead to destruction of the cycle?

Expectations present a difficult task for economic analysis because there are so many possibilities and little information about their actual behaviour. Both expediency and realism suggest the investigation of a very simple type. Let us consider the case in which the price is expected by all producers to change in the next production period by a constant fraction of the change in the last one. Calling this fraction ρ and expected price ex p, we have

$$\begin{aligned} \text{ex}\, p(t) &= p(t-\theta)+\rho\Delta p(t-\theta) \\ &= (1+\rho)p(t-\theta)-\rho p(t-2\theta). \end{aligned}$$

The supply at time t is determined by

$$-S+\beta\, \text{ex}\, p(t),$$

so that (8) is replaced by

$$-S+\beta(1+\rho)p(t-\theta)-\beta\rho p(t-2\theta). \tag{16}$$

If $\rho = 0$, we get production on the basis of current price and the simple cobweb theorem. If $\rho > 0$, the price is expected to continue moving in the same direction, whereas if $\rho < 0$, it is expected to reverse. The latter would be the more sensible since it fits with the nature of the cycle. If ρ is less than one in magnitude, it may either reflect expectations of damping down of the fluctuations, or it may mean lack of certainty and hence greater reliance on current prices.

It is in contradiction to known facts, and inherently quite unlikely that all producers would have the same expectations.[6] Upon inspection, however, it turns out that the aggregate expectations coefficient ρ can be considered as a weighted average of the various individual coefficients. For example, let us suppose that there are two groups of suppliers with different expectations:

$$\begin{aligned} &-S_1+\beta_1(1+\rho_1)p(t-\theta)-\beta_1\rho_1 p(t-2\theta), \\ &-S_2+\beta_2(1+\rho_2)p(t-\theta)-\beta_2\rho_2 p(t-2\theta). \end{aligned}$$

The two slopes, β_1 and β_2, of the dynamic supply curves will be a measure of the relative importance of each group. The aggregate supply curve will be

$$-(S_1+S_2)+\{\beta_1(1+\rho_1)+\beta_2(1+\rho_2)\}p(t-\theta) \\ -\{\beta_1\rho_1+\beta_2\rho_2\}p(t-2\theta).$$

This can be represented by an equation like (16) if

$$S = S_1 + S_2,$$
$$\beta = \beta_1 + \beta_2,$$
$$\rho = \frac{\beta_1\rho_1 + \beta_2\rho_2}{\beta_1 + \beta_2}.$$

Therefore the coefficient ρ in (16) can be taken to be an average of the particular expectation coefficients with each group weighted according to its importance. More generally, if there are k groups with sufficiently uniform expectations, we get the following:

$$S = \sum_{n=1}^{k} S_n, \tag{17}$$

$$\beta = \sum_{n=1}^{k} \beta_n, \tag{18}$$

$$\rho = \frac{\sum_{n=1}^{k} \beta_n\rho_n}{\sum_{n=1}^{k} \beta_n}. \tag{19}$$

The constant ρ will be understood to mean this average value of actual individual expectations. Thus its value represents more group difference of opinion rather than individual uncertainty. Even though individuals' actions may only correspond to $\rho = +1$, or $\rho = -1$, or $\rho = 0$, an aggregation can have fractional values of ρ. Also, it is to be expected that difference of opinion would lead to rather small values of the average ρ. In any case ± 1 seem to be realistic upper and lower boundaries for the range of likely ρ.

Equating supply and demand, we get, to replace equation (9),

$$\alpha p(t) + \beta(1+\rho)p(t-\theta) - \beta\rho p(t-2\theta) = \phi(t) + D + S. \tag{20}$$

If $\phi(t)$ and D and S be set equal to zero, we then have the homogeneous equation, which means, economically, that we study only deviations from the average value of price under the condition of no shifts in the curves. Substituting

$$p = P\lambda^t$$

and letting $\beta/\alpha = a$ and $\theta = 1$, we find that λ must satisfy the following characteristic equation:

$$\lambda^2 + a(1+\rho)\lambda - a\rho = 0. \tag{21}$$

The two roots are

$$\lambda = -\frac{a(1+\rho)}{2} \pm \sqrt{\frac{a^2(1+\rho)^2}{4} + a\rho}, \tag{22}$$

or more generally

$$\lambda = |\lambda| e^{i(2n\pi \pm \epsilon)}, \quad n = 0, \pm 1, \pm 2, \ldots . \tag{22a}$$

If λ is positive and real, ϵ is zero, and if it is negative and real, $\epsilon = \pi$. If λ is complex,

$$|\lambda| = \sqrt{-a\rho} \tag{23}$$

and

$$\tan \epsilon = \frac{\pm 2\sqrt{-\dfrac{(1+\rho)^2}{4} - \dfrac{\rho}{a}}}{-(1+\rho)}. \tag{24}$$

Each root yields a set of solutions, so that allotting each an arbitrary constant P_n, and summing over all of them to get the general solution, we have

$$p = e^{(\ln|\lambda|)t} \sum_{n=-\infty}^{\infty} \{P_n e^{i(2n\pi + \epsilon)t} + P_n' e^{i(2n\pi - \epsilon)t}\}. \tag{25}$$

With these results we may answer the question of what will be the effect on the cycle of various average expectations. If the cycle is to be destroyed both roots must be positive and real, which requires that

$$\begin{cases} \rho < -1, \\ a \geqq -\dfrac{4\rho}{(1+\rho)^2}. \end{cases} \tag{26}$$

Since any value of ρ less than -1 seems to make little sense, this possibility is ruled out easily. Also the value of a would have to be large and that would make the mechanism unstable. This region lies outside FIGURE 3.3. A negative real root yields the same period of oscillation as the simple cobweb. This result is given in regions C, D and E in FIGURE 3.3, where

$$\begin{cases} \rho > -1, \\ a \geqq -\dfrac{4\rho}{(1+\rho)^2}. \end{cases} \tag{27}$$

Combinations of a and ρ lying in the regions A and B mean complex roots and hence a lengthening of period as compared with no

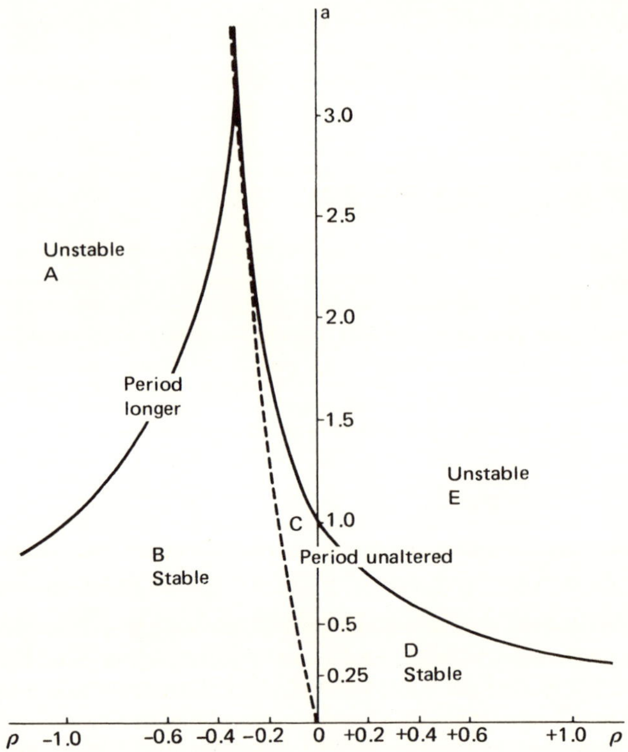

FIGURE 3.3

expectations. Beginning at the right extremity of B with a length of 2, the period increases as we move to the left gradually to twice this at $\rho = -1$, at which point the value of a plays no role in the length of period. Since this is the realistic limit of expectation, we may say that negative expectations may increase the period of oscillation up to twice what it would be without them. To the left of the line $\rho = -1$ the period[7] gradually increases without limit as it approaches the boundary (not shown in FIGURE 3.3) of the region of non-oscillatory solutions. For a given ρ, the larger a is, the shorter the period.

The cycle may equally well be destroyed by a change in the constants such as to introduce enough damping: in fact, it is in this way that an obnoxious oscillation or 'hunting' is usually eliminated in servo-mechanisms such as governors, automatic pilots, etc. Therefore the effect of expectations on stability is of great importance. In the region of real roots the condition for dynamic stability is

$$a < \frac{1}{1+2\rho}. \tag{28}$$

In the region of complex roots it is

$$a < -\frac{1}{\rho}. \tag{29}$$

This is shown in FIGURE 3.3 where regions A and E represent unstable values of the constants, while B, C and D give the stable ones. The problem may be stated as follows: given definite supply and demand conditions represented by a, what will be the effect of various expectations on stability? To the right of $\rho = 0$, the larger ρ is, the larger is the magnitude of the root. Therefore a stable market becomes less stable, or an unstable one more so. As ρ decreases from zero both terms in the root decrease in magnitude until, at the dividing line between real and complex roots (the line between B and C) the second term vanishes. Beyond this line the absolute magnitude of the roots is $\sqrt{-a\rho}$, so that it evidently increases with larger and larger negative values of ρ. Therefore the magnitude of the root is a minimum along this border line, and hence points along it represent the greatest attainable stability.

The question of whether or not simple expectations can destroy the cycle is one of degree. They can never do it entirely so long as there are any changes in the supply and demand curves. How nearly the destruction can be approximated depends on the relative strength of damping compared with the violence of shifts in the curves. The damping is sharply increased if there are mildly negative expectations. To see this quantitatively it is helpful to consider the market's *time constant*, i.e. the length of time required for a given amplitude of fluctuation to decrease to 1/2.7 of its initial value, in the absence of further disturbances. We may compare the time constant for a market with zero expectations to that of one with those expectations giving maximum stability. For various values of a, the two time constants in numbers of lag intervals are given in TABLE 3.1. It is evident that mildly perverse expectations make a great deal of difference to the damping, and therefore should much ameliorate (or in a placid world, substantially eliminate) the cycle. These are, however, optimal results only achievable by some kind of planning. If there is a widespread cycle consciousness amongst producers, this would tend to yield a higher negative value of ρ, thus lengthening the cycle and

TABLE 3.1

a	*Time constant with* $\rho=0$	ρ *giving maximum stability*	*Time constant with maximum stability*
1.0	∞	−0.17	1.1
0.9	9.5	−0.16	1.0
0.7	2.8	−0.13	0.8
0.5	1.4	−0.10	0.7
0.2	0.6	−0.05	0.4

rendering it less stable. It has been said that cycle consciousness or informed expectations would do away with cycles. Doubt is cast on this because here, in the simplest of all cycles, it is not so. It is no use to try to abolish the cycle by telling producers to understand it and allow for it: doing so would actually make it worse. If only a small part of the producers are cycle conscious they may profit heavily, and, what is remarkable, render a public service by unintentionally ameliorating the cycle.

Summarising, one may say that, there is no simple expectation that will eliminate the cycle; it may, nonetheless, be much ameliorated by slight negative expectations. These negative expectations can lengthen up to twofold the duration of the cycle, while making it less stable, even less than with no expectations. All positive expectations decrease stability; in general negative expectations lead to much greater stability than the corresponding positive ones.

All this has been demonstrated for only one type of expectations. More complicated or sophisticated ones can be analysed, but it is doubtful whether producers' reactions would ever follow such refinements. We might, for example, take acceleration as constant, i.e. assume that producers expect that the *increase* of price will increase by as much as it has just done:

$$\operatorname{ex} p(t) = p(t-\theta) + \Delta p(t-\theta) + \Delta^2 p(t-\theta).$$

Or we might take further steps in this direction, if we forget the human limitations of the producer. If they based their expectations on an exact knowledge of the cycle mechanism, then, as we might expect, the cycle would disappear in all but a trivial sense. Suppose they use an accurate estimate of the market curves to predict prices:

$$\operatorname{ex} p(t) = -\frac{\beta}{\alpha} p(t-\theta). \tag{30}$$

In this case,

$$p(t) = \left(\frac{\beta}{\alpha}\right)^2 p(t-\theta). \tag{31}$$

The solution is no longer oscillatory but rather exponential and the stability is markedly increased. We may be sure that the producers would never arrive at this result, but government advisers conceivably might help them to achieve it.

Finally, we may apply the same reasoning to these mechanisms as was applied to the simpler one in Section III. As old oscillations die out new ones are being excited by the shifting supply and demand curves. The result is that the oscillation is maintained and always changing in shape. The precise analysis is somewhat more complicated. The details for a mathematically similar case I have given elsewhere.[8]

V. Coupled Markets with Production Lags

It may easily happen that a market which is unilaterally dependent on the balance of the economy is nevertheless mutually coupled with one or more related markets. By taking account of the effect of the economy on these markets and their own interdependence, we may hope to include the primary determinants of actual behaviour. Where such conditions hold, there exists a usable halfway house between partial and general dynamics. There may be many types of interdependence, but I shall consider only the simplest one—a term in the supply or the demand curve proportional to the price in the other markets.

For the moment we may ignore the dependence on the balance of the economy. Calling the difference operator E, we may represent a system of m markets by

$$\begin{bmatrix} a_{11}(E) & \cdots & a_{1m}(E) \\ \cdots & \cdots & \cdots \\ a_{m1}(E) & \cdots & a_{mm}(E) \end{bmatrix} \begin{Bmatrix} p_1 \\ \vdots \\ p_m \end{Bmatrix} = \begin{Bmatrix} 0 \\ \vdots \\ 0 \end{Bmatrix}. \tag{32}$$

If there is coupling only on the demand side, the non-diagonal elements will contain nothing but constants. The condition for a non-trivial solution is the vanishing of the determinant of the dynamical matrix (or the characteristic equation when expressed in terms of λ). The degree of this equation will not be altered by the non-diagonal terms, so that the presence or absence of supply coupling will not affect qualitatively the types of possible behaviour. Therefore merely in order to simplify the discussion I shall omit coupling on the supply side. It is also clear that no general, algebraic solutions can be given except for the simplest cases. Thus even for two markets only, if their lags are respectively 9 and 12 months, we should have a seventh-degree characteristic equation which cannot be solved algebraically. Where the least common multiples of the lags are small, or where there are more than two markets, the characteristic equation may be solved numerically in given situations. I shall limit myself to cases simple enough to solve algebraically, but which illustrate the nature of the results for more complicated problems.

Consider two markets, coupled on the demand side, one of which has a unit production lag:

$$\beta_1 p_1(t-1) + \alpha_1 p_1(t) + \gamma_1 p_2(t) = 0, \tag{33}$$

$$\gamma_2 p_1(t) + \beta_2 p_2(t) + \alpha_2 p_2(t) = 0. \tag{34}$$

Since we are interested only in the dynamic interaction of the two markets, all constants as well as functional dependence on the rest of the economy are ignored. All constants are positive except γ_1, γ_2, which may be either positive (indicating, roughly, that the goods are complementary) or negative (competitive). These equations may be written as

$$\begin{bmatrix} \beta_1 E + \alpha_1 & \gamma_1 \\ \gamma_2 & \beta_2 + \alpha_2 \end{bmatrix} \begin{Bmatrix} p_1 \\ p_2 \end{Bmatrix} = \begin{Bmatrix} 0 \\ 0 \end{Bmatrix}. \tag{35}$$

Substituting a solution of the form $p = P\lambda^t$, we determine λ by the condition that the determinant of this matrix must be zero. Hence our characteristic equation may be written in convenient form as

$$\lambda = -\frac{\beta_1}{\alpha_1} \left[\frac{1}{1 - \dfrac{\gamma_1 \gamma_2}{\alpha_1(\alpha_2 + \beta_2)}} \right]. \tag{36}$$

So long as $\gamma_1 \gamma_2 < \alpha_1 \alpha_2 + \alpha_1 \beta_2$, which is highly likely, the root is negative and hence the other market will pick up the oscillation from the first one. The stability of the first market would be determined by the magnitude of β_1/α_1 in the absence of coupling. If the vibration remains, its stability is decreased by the coupling, since the expression in parentheses is greater than one. The amplitude of vibration in the second market is given by

$$P_2 = -\frac{\gamma_2}{\alpha_2 + \beta_2} P_1, \tag{37}$$

so that it is highly likely that the violence of oscillation will be less in the second than in the first market, as, indeed, one would expect. Furthermore, if the goods are complementary, i.e. γ_2 is positive, the two markets will swing out of phase, one price being high when the other is low. But if they are competitive they will go up and down together.

In the case of two coupled, oscillatory markets, I shall consider only identical markets, in order to simplify the algebra. More markets, non-identical ones, supply coupling, all introduce complications that are ordinarily soluble numerically; but they do not, with the exception of the effect on periods, introduce different types of result. Two markets coupled through demand may be represented by

$$p_1(t) + ap_1(t-1) + bp_2(t) = 0, \tag{38}$$

$$bp_1(t) + p_2(t) + ap_2(t-1) = 0, \tag{39}$$

where

$$a = \frac{\beta_1}{\alpha_1} = \frac{\beta_2}{\alpha_2}, \tag{40}$$

and

$$b = \frac{\gamma_1}{\alpha_1} = \frac{\gamma_2}{\alpha_2}. \tag{41}$$

Thus the markets need not be quite identical, but need only have identical ratios and lags. If we subtract (39) from (38) and make the substitution, $y_1 = p_1 - p_2$, we get

$$(1-b)y_1(t) + ay_1(t-1) = 0. \tag{42}$$

Adding and letting $y_2 = p_1 + p_2$, we have

$$(1+b)y_2(t) + ay_2(t-1) = 0. \tag{43}$$

Thus by separating variables, we reduce the problem to the solution of two uncoupled first-order difference equations, i.e. simple cobwebs. These may be solved in the manner indicated in Section II. The most evident result is that the natural periods are unaltered by the coupling (2θ and smaller in both instances). This conclusion also holds for dissimilar markets, so long as they have the same lag. By contrast, the analogous situation for dynamical markets characterised by differential equations would lead to a spreading apart of the two natural periods.

The two roots of the characteristic equations are

$$\lambda_1 = -\frac{a}{1-b}, \tag{44}$$

and

$$\lambda_2 = -\frac{a}{1+b}. \tag{45}$$

Regardless of whether b is positive or negative, one root will be larger than $-a$ (the root for an uncoupled market) and one smaller. Thus both markets will have two oscillations, one of which will be less stable, and one more stable, than their uncoupled motions. Thus stability undergoes a change in coupled difference equations analogous to alteration of periodicity in differential equations. Since the less stable solution tends always to predominate, we may conclude that coupling decreases stability. Should the product's own price be less important than the other price, b will be greater than one, which means that one, but not both, of the oscillations will go over into an exponential solution, which may be either stable or unstable depending on the size of b. If the markets are dissimilar, it is not difficult to show that the stability of the oscillation is less than that of the least stable market by itself (so long as $\gamma_1\gamma_2 < \alpha_1\alpha_2$, i.e. own prices more important than other prices).

The solutions are

$$p_1 = \tfrac{1}{2}(y_1 + y_2) \tag{46}$$

and

$$p_2 = \tfrac{1}{2}(-y_1 + y_2). \tag{47}$$

Each y represents a wave of period 2θ and arbitrary shape, and these will in general be different. In consequence of the different damping factors, they will alter relatively to one another, with the result that their sum or difference will have an ever-changing wave shape, although, damping apart, either would be simply periodic. It is worth noting that in the first constituent solution they are exactly out of phase, while in the second they are in phase. If $b > 0$ (complementary goods), the first solution tends to dominate, and hence the markets will tend to be out of step. On the other hand if $b < 0$ (competitive goods) the second solution is less stable and hence the markets will tend to go up and down together. Either constituent oscillation may be excited alone, or in any combination, so that any lead or lag of one market relative to the other is possible.

To see the effects of the coupling of dissimilar markets on their respective periods, we may take the simplest example, where one has twice the production lag of the other. Such a system is represented by

$$\begin{bmatrix} 1+a_1E & b_1 \\ b_2 & 1+a_2E^2 \end{bmatrix} \begin{Bmatrix} p_1 \\ p_2 \end{Bmatrix} = \begin{Bmatrix} 0 \\ 0 \end{Bmatrix}. \tag{48}$$

Its characteristic equation is

$$(1-b_1b_2)\lambda^3 + a_1\lambda^2 + a_2\lambda + a_1a_2 = 0. \tag{49}$$

If we restrict ourselves to the case of $b_1b_2 < 1$, i.e. $\gamma_1\gamma_2 < \alpha_1\alpha_2$, then either all the roots are real and negative, or one is real and negative and the other two are complex conjugates. It turns out, however, that, with a_1, a_2, and b_1b_2 positive and real, all the roots cannot be real. Therefore the roots must be of the form

$$\left.\begin{aligned} \lambda_1 &= re^{i(2n+1)\pi}, \\ \lambda_2 &= r'e^{i(2n\pi+\epsilon)}, \\ \lambda_3 &= r'e^{i(2n\pi-\epsilon)}, \end{aligned}\right\} \quad n = 0, \pm 1, \pm 2, \ldots, \tag{50}$$

where r, r' and ϵ are to be determined by the parameters a_1, a_2, b_1 and b_2 in (49). It follows that all the periods will be 2 or less, except one, which must be longer and has no limit on its length. The coupled periods therefore depend in a complicated way on both the uncoupled periods and on the structural parameters. Neither market, barring an exceptional case, will have the same maximum period as before. The two independent periods get scrambled into a complicated set of periods, the same set being exhibited by both markets. The longest of these may be longer than the longer of the two independent cycles, in fact there is no restriction on how long it may be. Thus there is a strong likelihood of lengthening of the duration of the cycle as a result of the coupling. Even more remarkable is the fact that it is no longer simply periodic; *it does not repeat itself, even with no outside disturbance or natural damping.* Except by accident the various periods will not dovetail, because they are not integral multiples of one another, and hence in each cycle they will join in a new way, resulting in an ever-changing wave shape. Although the two markets will contain the same set of periods, their time shape will not be the same. This is so because the amplitudes of the corresponding constituent periods will be different as between the two markets. Furthermore most of the periods in the one will be out of phase with those in the other market.

If the two markets are unilaterally coupled with the balance of the economy, we may include a disturbance function as specified in equation

(9). Instead of (38) and (39) we should write

$$\begin{bmatrix} 1+aE & b \\ b & 1+aE \end{bmatrix} \begin{Bmatrix} p_1 \\ p_2 \end{Bmatrix} = \begin{Bmatrix} \phi_1/\alpha_1 \\ \phi_2/\alpha_2 \end{Bmatrix}. \tag{51}$$

The complete solution consists of the general solutions already given for the homogeneous equations, (38) and (39), plus a particular solution to (51). If the functions $\phi_1(t)$ and $\phi_2(t)$ may be considered as a series of terms, then, by virtue of the linearity of the system, we may calculate particular solutions, term by term, and add the results. When we transform to y_1 and y_2, we merely take the sum and the difference of ϕ_1 and ϕ_2, so that it still suffices to study the system response to any one typical term in either function.

If the ϕs are perfectly arbitrary, we may proceed in the manner of Section III and calculate the responses of y_1 and y_2 to the sum and difference of ϕ_1 and ϕ_2. Or we may calculate the system response to a unit pulse and then by summation over time find its response to a stepwise approximation to the arbitrary disturbances. There may, however, be at least some part of ϕ that is systematic, e.g. definite trends or cycles. If there is a persistent exponential trend, that term in ϕ may be written as

$$\frac{\phi_k}{\alpha} = \Phi e^{\lambda_k t},$$

where λ_k gives the rate of growth. Consequently particular solutions are

$$y_{1k} = \frac{\Phi_k}{1-b+a/\lambda_k} e^{\lambda_k t} \tag{52}$$

and

$$y_{2k} = \frac{\Phi_k}{1+b+a/\lambda_k} e^{\lambda_k t}, \tag{53}$$

so that the market will have the same trend, but with altered magnitude.

If all or a part of ϕ/α can be represented by a few oscillatory terms, we may consider a typical one in complex form,

$$\frac{\phi_j}{\alpha} = \Phi_j e^{i\omega_j t}.$$

Substituting an exponential solution into (42), we find that

$$\left(1-b+\frac{a}{e^{i\omega_j}}\right) Y_{1\alpha} e^{i\omega_j t} = \Phi_\alpha e^{i\omega_j t}. \tag{54}$$

The market will have a constituent oscillation of the same period as the rest of the economy, but an amplitude and phase altered by the constant complex number, $(1-b+a/e^{i\omega_j})$, which is determined by the dynamical structure of the market. If it be rewritten in the form $r_1 e^{i\tau_1}$, $1/r$ is the ratio of the amplitude of fluctuation in y to that in ϕ, and τ gives the lag (if positive) and the lead (if negative) of y relative to ϕ:

$$r_1 = \sqrt{(1-b)^2 + 2(1-b)a\cos\omega_j + a^2}. \tag{55}$$

The minimum effect $(r_1 = 1-b+a)$ of the excitation on the market, or anti-resonance, occurs if $\cos\omega_j = 1$, i.e. a disturbance of period equal to infinity (a constant), 1 lag unit, $\frac{1}{2}$ unit, etc. Maximum effect or resonance occurs if $\cos\omega_j = -1$ and $r_1 = 1-b-a$, which requires $\omega_j = (2n+1)\pi$, but these correspond to the natural periods of the system (13). Similarly, $r_2 = 1+b-a$. For example if $\alpha = 0.5$, $\beta = 0.3$ and $\gamma = 0.15$, then $r_1 = 0.1$ and the market's vibration will be amplified tenfold. Therefore if the economy has only a small oscillation of approximately the same period as the sector, there will be nonetheless an appreciable response.

The phase of the induced oscillation relative to the excitation, is given by

$$\tau_1 = \tan^{-1}\left\{\frac{-a\sin\omega_j}{1-b+a\cos\omega_j}\right\}. \tag{56}$$

For very long cycles in the disturbance, there is a slight lead, if $b < 1$, which increases to

$$\tau_1 = \tan^{-1}\frac{-a}{1-b}$$

for a period of 4 production lags. The lead (or lag) of the market cannot be greater than a quarter cycle no matter what the structural parameters are. At resonance the two are in phase, and for a period of 4/3, the market will lag behind the disturbance. For y_2 the phase is given by

$$\tau_2 = \tan^{-1}\left\{\frac{-a\sin\omega_j}{1+b+a\cos\omega_j}\right\}, \tag{57}$$

which shows that for a negative b, the two constituent motions are reversed. They will not, in general, be in phase with one another.

VI

To sum up, we may say that the last section indicates the complications arising with general dynamical interdependence. To go from two identical markets to *n* non-identical ones will require the prolonged services of yet unborn calculating machines. If aggregation is satisfactory, we may, of course, reduce the larger problem to one involving only a few sectors, and then the methods of Section V should be feasible.

In the many cases appropriate, the methods of partial dynamics are valuable, as, I hope, the results of this paper suggest. The cobweb theorem itself, probably the most successful attempt at dynamics, is an example of the fruitfulness of the restrictive assumptions of partial analysis. By only slightly widening these assumptions to cover the impact of the rest of the economy, we have been able to make a considerable improvement on the applicability of the theorem by giving an explanation of the maintenance and irregularity of the cycles. Similarly in the question of expectations, progress can only come through rather intensive study of a narrow segment of the economy. In fact it is likely that only through such particular analyses can we even formulate and test the meaningful hypotheses out of which any more ambitious general theory (with empirically verifiable content) must be built. In any case, for a single market we have been able to state precisely what the effect of any realistically simple expectations would be in terms of the change in stability and the length of the period.

Simple as it is, the problem of interacting economic pairs is not without wider interest as in consumption and investment, building and business cycles, etc. By the semi-isolation of two sectors, we have been able to show that both will be less stable than the less stable one without the coupling. The periods of both sectors are combined in a complicated fashion, and acquired by each with the result of lengthening the period and rendering the wave shape ever-changing. Finally, with the help of the phenomenon of economic resonance, we have been able to construct a possible explanation of why the parts of an economy often have qualitatively different behaviour patterns. Each picks up markedly the constituents most sympathetic to it in the general motion of the economy.

NOTES

1. I am indebted to Mr T. Koopmans and Mr H. Rubin for suggesting this way of expressing it.

2. 'Relative Prices and Postwar Markets for Animal Food Products', *Quarterly Journal of Economics*, vol. 59, February 1945, pp. 237–79. He finds that in some cases it is necessary to take account of one other price, in some merely own price, and in one case no price, only income.
3. I shall not consider speculative holding of stocks.
4. 'The Cobweb Theorem', *Quarterly Journal of Economics*, vol. 52, February 1938, pp. 255–80.
5. 'Verzögerte Angebotsanpassung und partielles Gleichgewicht', *Zeitschrift für Nationalökonomie*, 1934. It is perhaps not too much to say that it was this article that established the usefulness of the theorem.
6. On this point as well as on numerous others I am much indebted to Dr Hans Staehle.
7. By period I mean the longest period among the solutions.
8. 'Innovations and the Irregularity of Economic Cycles', Appendix, Section 3, p. 104, *Review of Economic Statistics*, vol. 28, May 1946.

4. An Oscillatory Mechanism with a Flexible Accelerator

INCOME, EMPLOYMENT, AND PUBLIC POLICY, 1948, ED. L. A. METZLER

Almost everyone is agreed that investment constitutes the key to the problem of cycles. Some theorists go so far as to say that the investment process, by itself, contains practically the whole of the explanation. The classic exposition of this view is Professor Schumpeter's, and it is in this direction that Professor Hansen appears to incline. In opposition to this are most of the 'self-generating' theories, which maintain that the whole of the economic structure determines the periodic reversals. Neither theory alone is, in my opinion, quite satisfactory. The structural approach is condemned to the sterility of one constantly repeated wave form, which must either die out or explode in ever-increasing violence. The innovational theory handles both these difficulties well, but is not altogether convincing on what constitutes the strong point of the other theory—the unmistakable element of regularity in the recurrence of booms. The mere fact of the bunching of innovational investments cannot be taken as proof of an inherent tendency. The circumambient economic structure may alternately inhibit and encourage investment, and hence contain the explanation of the bunching. Surely, a combination of the two types of theory possesses the desired qualities.

In his treatment of capital and investment, Keynes followed traditional theory. Given a rate of interest, there is, under given conditions, a corresponding amount of capital, but should the existing amount not correspond, there is no specification of the size of investment, i.e. no determination of the rate of progression from the old to the new equilibrium quantity of capital. This lacuna can be found in many economic theories, but it is crucial in capital theory. One way of filling it is by consideration of Keynes's point that the rate of current investment controls the cost of capital goods, and hence has a negative effect on the marginal efficiency of capital. Keeping to linear relations, we may then represent the marginal efficiency of capital by

$$r = -\mu k - \nu \dot{k} + \Lambda \tag{1}$$

where r is the rate of interest and Λ a shift parameter. With a given rate of interest and a given Λ, the rate of investment, as well as the amount of capital stock, becomes completely determinate. The difficulty with this formulation is that the schedule is subject to large shifts. Indeed, the role of the shifts is probably much greater than that of r. These changes in the value of Λ are partly the result of changed expectations about future output, and partly the result of innovations. We may say that the schedule holds only for a given state of technique, and for a given level of present and expected income. Making the simplest possible assumption about the influence of income (proportionality), means inserting the acceleration principle into the marginal efficiency of capital. Stated in this context, the accelerator becomes suitable for business cycle analysis.

The rate of interest is generally held to play little role in the investment process, and, in any case, its variation cannot be explained by the reduced system under consideration here.[1] Therefore its variation, along with changes in expectations, may be absorbed into the innovational shift function, which we may call $\phi(t)$. With a convenient redefinition of constants, the marginal efficiency of capital, (1), expanded to include the acceleration principle, and with the rate of interest neglected, may be written as

$$\xi \dot{k} + k - \kappa y = \phi(t) \tag{2}$$

where ξ is a constant and κ is the acceleration coefficient.

There is an alternative and illuminating way of appraising this formulation. It implies that there is an asymptotic approach to any persisting equilibrium level of capital; it is simply a flexible form of the accelerator. When there is no net investment, i.e. when perfect adjustment exists, capital is linearly related to income (for a given state of technique etc.). If equilibrium is not attained, then the rate of investment is proportional to the difference between the equilibrium or ideal quantity of capital, and the actual quantity, as can be seen by rearranging (2) as follows:

$$\dot{k} = 1/\xi(\kappa y + \phi - k).$$

Like κ, ξ has the dimensions of time, and may be interpreted as meaning that any excess or deficiency of capital is removed at a rate which would abolish it in ξ years, if nothing else changed. The ordinary accelerator implies that capital is always perfectly adjusted to income. This is its major shortcoming, for we know that there are times of excess capacity, and other times of short capacity.

The nature of the flexible accelerator can most easily be understood by studying the reaction to a sudden increase of income to a new constant level. If, for convenience, we take the previous level of income, capital and investment as zero, we have, for an increase of income to Y at $t = 0$,

$$k = -\kappa Y e^{-t/\xi} + \kappa Y. \qquad (t \geq 0) \tag{3}$$

Thus, capital gradually approaches the value given by the customary accelerator as a limit. Investment, being the first derivative of k, decreases from a maximum value of $\kappa Y/\xi$ to zero.

$$i = \dot{k} = (\kappa/\xi) Y e^{-t/\xi}. \tag{4}$$

The flexible accelerator, acting as the generator of income, combined with the dynamic multiplier, functioning as the propagator of income, constitutes a determinate system which can explain business cycles. In order to show this, we consider the homogeneous part of the two equations.

$$-\dot{k} + \epsilon \dot{y} + (1-\alpha) y = 0. \tag{5}$$

$$\xi \dot{k} + k - \kappa y = 0. \tag{2a}$$

The characteristic equation for these simultaneous equations is

$$\xi \epsilon \lambda^2 + [\xi(1-\alpha) + \epsilon - \kappa]\lambda + 1 - \alpha = 0. \tag{6}$$

Since this equation for λ may have either real or complex roots, the coupled system may have either real exponential or oscillatory solutions. The condition for the latter type solution is

$$[\xi(1-\alpha) + \epsilon - \kappa]^2 < 4\xi\epsilon(1-\alpha). \tag{7}$$

Quite plausible values of the constants satisfy this condition, so that such a model is a possible basis for a theory of the intermittent breakdown of capitalism. If it is to be a satisfactory explanation of these cycles, it must be stable, but not too stable, and it must give a relatively long period. We may require, for example, that the period be nine years, and that the amplitude of swing decline by one-half in one cycle and by three-fourths in two, in the absence of outside disturbances. These two requirements put the following conditions on the constants (taking ϵ to be 0.25):

$$1 - \alpha = 0.124\xi; \tag{8}$$

$$\kappa = (1 - \alpha - 0.05)\xi + 0.25. \tag{9}$$

These conditions are in turn satisfied by the following reasonable set of values:[2]

$$\begin{cases} \alpha = 0.60; \\ \kappa = 1.4; \\ \xi = 3.2; \\ \epsilon = 0.25. \end{cases} \tag{10}$$

Only ξ seems to be higher than one might expect.

In view of the unfavourable empirical evidence presented in other sources, it may seem altogether unconvincing to base a cycle theory on the acceleration principle. '. . . it is a mistake, at least from the short-run point of view', says Professor Hansen, 'to place too much emphasis upon the Principle of Acceleration.'[3] It is conceivable that the accelerator is not a useful tool after all, but its attractions are nevertheless great. It is the simplest expression of the one fundamental dynamic fact in economics — that capital is a stock, investment a flow, and that both are intimately related to income.

In addition to its *a priori* plausibility, the accelerator can explain the two basic, well-established facts about the cycle, the greater relative violence of investment fluctuations, and their lead over income and consumption. The modified accelerator also explains the existence of excess capacity in certain phases of the cycle. This is easily seen to be true by considering a representation in the form of rotating vectors, a device of considerable convenience in oscillation problems. A complete rotation represents a full cycle, and hence the angle (divided by 360°) between two vectors shows the fraction of a cycle lead or lag between them. In the accompanying diagram, equation (5) is interpreted by letting investment, $\dot{k}$, be the vectorial sum of $(1-\alpha)y$ and $\epsilon\dot{y}$. Utilising the values given in (10), investment is seen to lead over income by something less than one-eighth cycle or about one year, while capital lags behind income by less than one-fourth cycle. Equation (2a) states that investment is proportional to the excess or deficiency of capital. Therefore, excess capacity appears before the middle of the downswing, and lasts through the early upswing. This behaviour agrees with Keynes's only explicit statement about a closed cycle theory, though he based his conclusions more on the life span of capital goods than upon the acceleration principle. ' . . . if the rate of investment falls below a certain minimum level', he said, 'it is merely a question of time (failing large fluctuations in other factors) before the marginal efficiency of capital rises sufficiently to bring about a recovery of investment above this minimum.'[4] The flexible accelerator is no doubt rather too rigid,

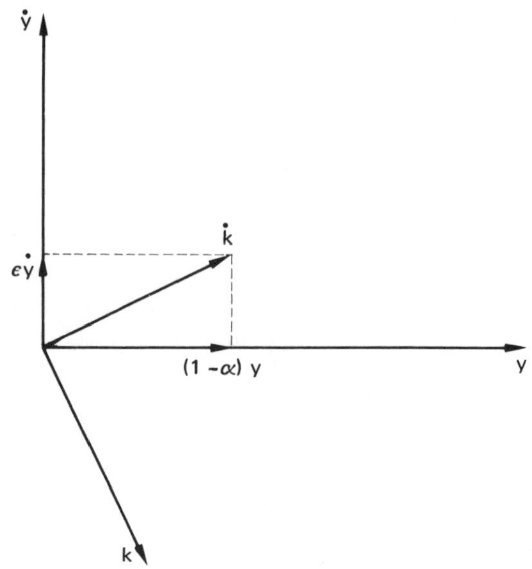

FIGURE 4.1

because it implies a gradual falling off of investment with declining income, whereas, once the horizon darkens, there is little to prevent a rapid drop. This might explain the asymmetry between upswing and downswing, although such asymmetry can also result from the tendency for autonomous investment to be concentrated in the upswing.

NOTES

1. The role of monetary policy may easily be taken into account by keeping r explicitly in (1) or (2). The rate of interest is related to idle money, which is linked to active money through the total quantity, and active money is dependent on income. All this is a subsidiary matter for our present purposes, however, since r in fact does not vary much.
2. Since (8) and (9) represent only two equations in three unknowns, an arbitrary value may be assigned to one of the three, and the equation solved for the other two. The value $\alpha = 0.60$ is close to the 'cyclical' propensity to consume, and may therefore be used as a starting point to determine ξ and κ.
3. A. H. Hansen, *Fiscal Policy and Business Cycles* (New York: 1941) p. 282.
4. J. M. Keynes, *The General Theory of Employment, Interest, and Money* (New York: Harcourt, Brace and Co., 1937) p. 253. Reprinted by permission.

5. A Non-linear Theory of the Cycle

REVIEW OF ECONOMICS AND STATISTICS, 1950

When a leading theorist has his attention diverted to business cycle analysis, the result is usually a happy one, as witness the examples provided by Schumpeter, Pigou, Frisch, J. M. Clark, Harrod and Haberler. The most recent of Professor Hicks's works continues this impressive record.[1] It is a book which no one interested in the cycle—and what economist is not?—can afford to miss reading. The following bare enumeration of its accomplishments should suffice to make this clear: (i) an elegant restatement of the *General Theory* on dynamic lines, (ii) a basic elaboration of Mr Harrod's multiplier–accelerator version of Keynes, (iii) an alteration of accelerator theory which removes its major flaw (as distinguished from numerous lesser ones), (iv) the use of this alteration to suggest a solution to a central, unsolved problem, i.e. the persistence of cycles, and (v) a reaffirmation and restatement of the role of money in the cycle in such a way as to give it an ancillary, though important, role. Such a theoretical offering, so well written, in such narrow compass (168 pp.), for so little ($2.25), is most welcome, especially if we compare it with the ponderous, uninspired, expensive texts which are continually being hurled at us. It will speak most directly to the professional economist, for it is essentially an experimental effort, a true 'model', but my guess is that it was also aimed at the better undergraduate and graduate students as well. A preliminary trial has convinced me that, while it has to be taught, the book's central thesis can be understood by honours undergraduates.

Professor Hicks launches his model with a humility rare amongst economists:

> I do believe that the argument which I am going to set out is quite likely to be the main part of the answer to the great question with which I am concerned. . . . I am not by any means positive that the

> answer which I have found is the right answer; one cannot begin to be sure of that until one has tested one's theory against the facts, and I am well aware that any testing which I have been able to do has been extremely superficial. If the theory which is here offered stands up to theoretical criticism, the next stage will be the concern of statisticians, econometrists, and (most of all) economic historians,. . . . (Preface.)

In this short note, I propose to restrict myself to the theoretical issues and to leave — with some misgivings — the empirical aspects to others better equipped for carrying out the arduous task of testing.

With an engaging frankness, the author spells out in detail his Trinitarian source— Keynes for the multiplier, Clark for the accelerator and Harrod for growth phenomena — so clearly that one might almost miss the element of originality involved in erecting a quite new building out of old and familiar building blocks. He then proceeds to lay out the nature of the dynamical multiplier in such a way as to undo the damage done by Keynes in telescoping the Kahn process. If only this lucid exposition had been available fifteen years ago, what mountains of confusion and quibbling we might have been spared. The chief new element is contained in his careful discussion of the difficult problem of distributed lags and in his demonstration that they do not alter fundamentally the conclusions derived from a simple lag hypothesis.

In Chapter IV is the second pillar of the edifice, for 'The theory of the multiplier and the theory of the accelerator are the two sides of the theory of fluctuations, just as the theory of demand and the theory of supply are the two sides of the theory of value.' (p. 38.) Here appears one of the two non-linearities which distinguish Hicks's theory from its predecessors: 'The expansion in investment, induced by a rise in output, can be as large as it likes, provided that the necessary resources are available; but the corresponding contraction is slowed up by the condition that Gross Investment in fixed capital cannot be negative.' (p. 66.) There is also a discussion of the acceleration theory of liquid and working capital where the asymmetry is not necessarily present. The simple income–expenditure lag is here (p. 52 ff.) reinterpreted in terms of stocks of goods and entrepreneurial reactions. While this step seems desirable, it does involve non-clock time, which presents treacherous problems and leaves a certain vagueness in the length of the cycle. There is in my mind some doubt as to whether Professor Hicks has really succeeded in side-stepping the difficulties of a full-dress, dynamical treatment along the lines of the Frisch carry-on function (an integral rather than a difference equation).

Mr Harrod's Regularly Progressive Economy is accepted as possible but not probable, for the reason that it is an unstable equilibrium motion, so that a small deviation does not set up a tendency to return to the steady motion. After the rejection of smooth growth, Professor Hicks quite naturally turns to cyclical theory, for which he chooses a variant of the Hansen–Samuelson formulation of the multiplier–accelerator interaction. Since he utilises income and not consumption for the acceleration effect, he loses the second difference in his equation (and hence the possibility of oscillation). This second lag he unobtrusively, and without much attempt at justification, reinserts as a single period lag in investment outlays, although subsequently he considers the more realistic and immensely more difficult case of distributed lags. From this, purely linear, model we get the familiar four behaviour types—exponential (compound interest) growth, exponential decay, explosive oscillation (complex exponential) and attenuated oscillation. Beyond this there are murky waters, with the result that the real argument is transferred to the mathematical appendix, the text being used to report a few, rather tentative, conclusions. The reason is that even this very simple model is too rich in possibilities to allow one to take explicit account of the complications of introducing the realistic assumption of distributed lags in both consumption and investment outlays. While it is not possible to be rigorous or precise, Professor Hicks does make a pretty convincing argument that these complications are indeed complications and not matters of basic importance, so that they may be substantially ignored in analysing the major cycle. This very useful result is typical of the many subsidiary pieces which adorn the book.

Finally, the central point of the book is reached: how do cycles persist? For all linear models there are three possibilities, the first of which—explosive oscillations—may be summarily rejected. Secondly, we know that an acceleration coefficient of one *exactly* will lead to a persisting, undamped cycle. Professor Frisch long ago argued quite conclusively, against the early models of Tinbergen and Kalecki, that this will not do.[2] Since that time, it has been fashionable to assume a damped system with renewal of amplitude through erratic shocks. Professor Hicks rejects this solution in an elegant, but rather too compact, passage (pp. 90–1), for the full understanding of which the conscientious reader will have to wrestle with paragraph 27 on pages 193–5 in the appendix. The gist of the argument is that since random shocks will work both with and against the cycle, the *net* effect is too small to be relied on to keep the cycle going with any appreciable amplitude.

Having disposed — correctly I think — of the existing hypotheses that will explain the persistence of the cycle, he is then free to develop a new one. Since the basic importance of the problem, and its difficulties, are not likely to be familiar to the economist (indeed, it is not clear that they are even to the author), I should like to indicate briefly something of its history and present situation. The simple linearised pendulum theory which we all learn, fails to explain most observed oscillations, i.e. the ones that neither die away nor explode as in the cases of clocks, steam engines, electric bells and buzzers, wind and string instruments, vacuum tube oscillators, the human heart and a great variety of other similar phenomena. The first reasonably successful assault on the analysis of the problem was made late in the nineteenth century in acoustic theory (a tuning fork oscillator) by Lord Rayleigh. At about the same time the great mathematician Henri Poincaré succeeded in blocking out a large part of the basic theory and applied it to certain problems in celestial mechanics. Neither effort had much effect on the general theory of cycles, however, until the advent of vacuum tube circuits made a non-linear oscillator theory imperative. About two decades ago B. van der Pol gave a satisfactory account of what he called relaxation oscillations, and this work has been extended by Philippe Le Corbeiller and others. Research is being actively pursued in many places, especially the United States and Soviet Russia, where notable results have been achieved. A superior account of the whole field is to be found in the *Theory of Oscillations*, by A. A. Andronow and C. E. Chaikin.[3] As a result of all this we have a reasonably all-embracing and much profounder theory of oscillations. It has become abundantly clear that self-maintaining cycles occur because of essential non-linearities in the structure of the system.

Since Professor Hicks proposes a theory which will explain the maintenance of oscillation, we can be sure, on formal grounds, that this implies a non-linearity. In fact, he assumes two — the lower limit of zero in gross investment and the upper limit of full employment in real income. From the point of view of systematic vibration theory, his model is probably best regarded as an over-energetic clock. The ordinary clock maintains its oscillation by delivering to its pendulum in each swing a blow which is timed by the escapement. The economy seems to have a strong tendency to instability, and hence would swing in ever greater arcs were it not for the inevitable limit of full employment, which thus provides an essential non-linearity. By analogy, we may visualise a clock placed next to a wall; it is so constructed that each swing of the pendulum is greater until it begins to hit the wall; thereafter it will oscillate perpetually with this uniquely determined amplitude. Even if it is slowed down or speeded up or nearly stopped, it will always work back to its proper limit cycle.

Actually Professor Hicks considers two quite distinct 'constraints'.[4] It is evident that full employment constitutes a barrier because in order to get there we must have a rate of expansion, and hence a level of investment, of real income which cannot be maintained when once we have attained it. Hence induced investment must fall with consequent drops in income and employment.[5] This one barrier would suffice to maintain a steady oscillation, but in fact there is a second barrier of a quite different sort from the first. There is no effective lower limit to income short of zero, but there is one to investment. Net investment cannot drop below a negative value equal to depreciation. The economy cannot, however, remain permanently at this depressed level, because replacement outlays will have eventually to be undertaken and then income increases, positive investment takes place, and the boom is on again. Between the floor and the ceiling the economy bounces back and forth. Indeed the economy need have no tendency to oscillate at all, apart from the two thresholds, but need only be explosive in both upward and downward directions.

Abstracting from trend and autonomous investment, we may state the theory as follows: today's income is greater than yesterday's income by the difference between today's investment and the saving, $s(y)$, out of yesterday's income. If to this we add the accelerator as sole determinant of investment we have a complete theory. Today's investment is determined as some multiple, say two, of the difference between yesterday's income and day-before-yesterday's income. Calling the acceleration coefficient v, we have symbolically

$$\begin{aligned} \Delta y_t &= i_t - s(y_{t-1}), \\ &= v\Delta y_{t-1} - s(y_{t-1}), \end{aligned}$$

which becomes Hicks's equation if $s(y)$ is linear. It is reasonable to assume that the system is unstable since any v, the ratio of capital to output, greater than one implies it.

The whole theory is susceptible of a quite simple graphical development which Professor Hicks neglects to present.[6] As shown in FIGURE 5.1, given any two, arbitrary, initial values such as y_{-2} and y_{-1}, we find i_0 as twice their difference. Then y_0 will be greater than y_{-1} by the difference between i_0 and $s(y_{-1})$. As is indicated, this is conveniently carried out by projecting a 45° line from the $s(y_{-1})$ until it cuts the horizontal i_0 line. The horizontal co-ordinate of this point is y_0. Next the difference between y_{-1} and y_0 determines i_1 and from this and $s(y_0)$, we

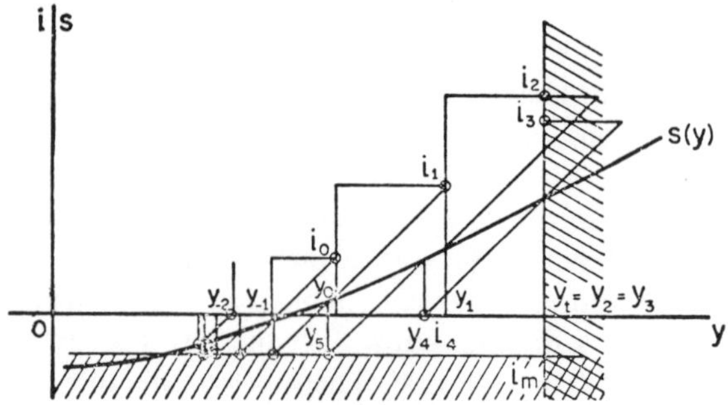

FIGURE 5.1

locate y_1, and continuing thus we finally reach the full employment threshold, y_t. If, as is almost certain to be the case, the last step carries us beyond the threshold, this means that an inflationary situation has arisen — a condition analysed with much insight in the last two chapters of the book. Neglecting these complications we may say, simply, that real income becomes constant, $y_2 = y_3$ in our example, and hence i_4 drops to zero. Therefore income must drop sharply to y_4, which in turn would entail an enormous further drop in investment. But here the second threshold (this time in investment) becomes operative and i cannot fall below a certain minimum i_m. In this way, income falls at a decreasing rate until that rate becomes less than one-half of i_m, at which point some replacement is required. If, as in FIGURE 5.1, this raises investment to the level of saving, income no longer falls. Hence investment is further increased to zero, but this means an increase in income, investment becomes positive, and the upswing commences.[7] This model possesses at once simplicity and great analytic power. It will oscillate for a wide variety of different savings functions and of acceleration coefficients. It tends to a *limit cycle* of a typical sort independently of how it commences or how it is disturbed. There is no assumption that the supply of capital is perfectly adjusted to the demand for it (as with the simple accelerator). The cycle will not die away, nor will it explode, but rather the conditions for its *maintenance* are built into it. Either the 'ceiling' or the 'floor' will suffice to check and hence perpetuate it. Thus the boom may die before hitting full employment, but then it will be checked on the downswing by the limit on disinvestment. Or again it may, indeed it ordinarily does, start up again before eliminating the excess capital as a result of autonomous outlays by business or government.

The way in which Professor Hicks introduces a trend, following Mr Harrod, seems to me highly doubtful. He assumes a *steady* growth in autonomous investment and in the full employment ceiling, quite independently of the cycle. Significantly enough Schumpeter's name is never mentioned, and yet surely some form of his innovational theory is essential to the description of the contours of capitalistic evolution, particularly in relating trend to cycle. This leads into another problem, peculiar to Keynesian theory, on which Professor Hicks is less than adequate. Even if we include secular progress in the form of the accumulation of capital and labour, whether steadily or in spurts, we are still left with an awkward question about the savings function. If $s(y)$ is as drawn in FIGURE 5.1, it is adequate for cycle analysis, but we get into trouble over the long run, for we would always return to the same trough level, e.g. a depression in 1920 would carry us down to an 1820 level and back up again but only with fantastically high levels of savings and investments. We escape this difficulty (by drawing a flatter $s(y)$ curve passing through the origin) only to fall into another (income would go to zero or lower in each cycle).

This dilemma may be resolved by a resolute application of Professor Duesenberry's 'ratchet effect', whereby savings depend not only on income but on the previous highest income.[8] As a result of secular progress the full employment limit moves to the right, and once we pass the previous highest income we proceed along the secular savings function as distinguished from the cyclical one. Yet the threshold does exist and, being encountered, reverses the boom. But now we descend along a new cyclical savings function, which is simply the old one translated to the right by the difference between the old peak and the new. In this way, without too great a strain on our geometrical intuition, we can fuse trend and cycle in a more satisfactory manner that is strongly reminiscent of, and parallel to, the Schumpeterian innovations theory. An example is given in FIGURE 5.2, with no particular attention to accuracy or realism, of such a cyclical–secular process. By joining together with a solid line the points representing successive combinations of investment and income, we get a vivid picture of how the economy may slip and slide along. Each forward lurch along the secular savings function (the straight line) generates consumption habits which produce a new cyclical curve, which we follow down and back up again. No account has been taken of autonomous investment, but it is easily inserted by simply adding it to induced investment, and, since it is likely never to be of the same magnitude, it imparts to each cycle an historical individuality.

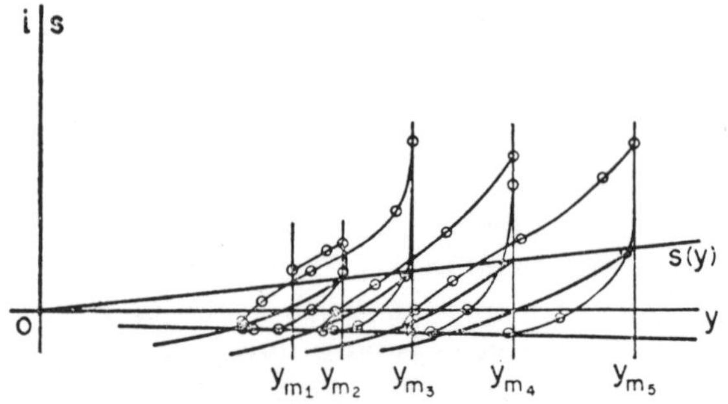

FIGURE 5.2

In this short compass I have tried only to suggest to the reader the main outlines of a most impressive performance. My purpose will have been served if I have sent him hurrying to the original, to which he must repair for a proper view of the rich embroidery of theoretical detail. There he will find illuminating discussions of inflation and the monetary theory of the cycle, of a hitherto unnoticed cobweb in the Keynesian theory (but surely not as a result of disuse!), of distributed lags, of difference equations (the mathematical appendix provides perhaps the best available introduction to that important subject), of the dynamics of the pure theory of investment and of the distinction between its fixed and liquid forms, of the theory of the secular steady state, and finally of the many problems of saving and investment in a dynamical multiplier process.

NOTES

1. J. R. Hicks, *A Contribution to the Theory of the Trade Cycle* (London: 1950).
2. It is interesting to note that radio engineers originally made essentially the same assumption and have been gradually forced to give it up as an unsatisfactory way to explain the maintenance of oscillation.
3. English translation published by the Princeton University Press, 1949.
4. His choice of word 'constraint' to describe a non-linearity seems most unfortunate. It has in dynamics a well-defined meaning which has nothing to do with non-linearities. A much better word would have been threshold, for threshold oscillators are a clearly-defined class, e.g. household heating systems with thermostatic controls.
5. This point has not, of course, by any means gone unnoticed before. For example in *Monetary Theory and Fiscal Policy*, Professor Hansen writes on p. 199, 'In the first place, when the *rate of increase* of output has begun to decline, as it must as full employment is approached, the *induced* investment

in inventories and in fixed plant and equipment will fall.' It is in this form that the Hansen–Frisch–Clark controversy (*Journal of Political Economy*, October 1931 and subsequent issues) should have been posed. Then it would have been clear that Professor Clark was really right, although formally Professor Frisch (and Mr Harrod and Professor Domar after him) was right in saying that a smooth exponential growth will always satisfy a first order differential equation. The point is that if by induced investment we rise from unemployment to full employment, there must at that point occur an impasse and the smooth development breaks down. Even if the structural parameters were such as to permit a steady 3 per cent growth rate — which seems to me quite unrealistic — once unemployment existed it would never be reduced and hence we would never reach boom and full employment.

6. Possibly the reason is that he wished to include the trend, which is not so easily done in the graph. Yet it surely is a good thing to separate trend and cycle analytically. On the other hand, in his defence, it can be said that trend makes much more difference in non-linear than in linear systems. It is even possible to cite systems which will oscillate about a trend but would remain in equilibrium if left alone (although Hicks's system would oscillate indefinitely in the absence of trend, it would do so in a peculiar and unrealistic way). Another questionable feature of the book is that in a book on a non-linear cycle we are presented with nothing but *linear* theory, even in the mathematical appendix. It is, however, much easier to cavil than to suggest what might have been done, for non-linear difference equations represent virgin territory mathematically — except for that extraordinary, but deceptively simple, performance of Professor Leontief in 'Verzögerte Angebotsanpassung und partielles Gleichgewicht', *Zeitschrift für Nationalökonomie*, 1934. Combining the difficulties of difference equations with those of non-linear theory, we get an animal of a ferocious character and it is wise not to place too much confidence in our conclusions as to behaviour.
7. It should be said that the complexity of reality escapes this form of diagram, for in the course of the slump excess capacity is accumulated, so that a cessation of decline alone is not enough to ensure replacement investment. Some autonomous investment, or failing that ultimately the mere lapse of time with continuing output, is necessary.
8. James Duesenberry, *Income, Saving, and the Theory of Consumer Behaviour* (1949), Chapter VII. Unfortunately, the important results obtained by Professors Duesenberry and Modigliani appeared too late for incorporation in the book (cf. p. vi of the Preface).

6. The Non-linear Accelerator and the Persistence of Business Cycles[1]

ECONOMETRICA, 1951

By taking account of obvious and inescapable limitations on the functioning of the accelerator, we explain some of the chief characteristics of the cycle, notably its failure to die away, along with the fact that capital stock is usually either in excess or in short supply. By a succession of increasingly complex models, the nature and methods of analysing non-linear cycle models is developed. The roles of lags and of secular evolution are illustrated. In each case the system's equilibrium position is unstable, but there exists a stable limit cycle toward which all motions tend.

Introduction

Almost without exception economists have entertained the hypothesis of linear structural relations as a basis for cycle theory. As such it is an oversimplified special case and, for this reason, is the easiest to handle, the most readily available. Yet it is not well adapted for directing attention to the basic elements in oscillations—for these we must turn to non-linear types. With them we are enabled to analyse a much wider range of phenomena, and in a manner at once more advanced and more elementary.

By dropping the highly restrictive assumptions of linearity we neatly escape the rather embarrassing special conclusions which follow. Thus, whether we are dealing with difference or differential equations, so long as they are linear, they either explode or die away with the consequent disappearance of the cycle or the society.[2] One may hope to avoid this unpleasant dilemma by choosing that case (as with the frictionless pendulum) just in between. Such a way out is helpful in the classroom, but it is nothing more than a mathematical abstraction. Therefore, economists will be led, as natural scientists have been led, to seek in non-linearities an explanation of the maintenance of oscillation. Advice to this effect, given by Professor Le Corbeiller in one of the earliest issues of this journal, has gone largely unheeded.[3]

Mention should also be made of the fact that there exists an alternative way out of the dilemma—that of an impulse-excited mechanism. There are two basically different classes of such mechanisms to be distinguished. (a) There are the synchronised systems of which the most familiar is the ordinary pendulum clock. Here the pendulum executes damped motion, but its own motion is used to time regular shocks so that it settles down to a steady routine in which the energy that is dissipated in friction during each cycle is exactly replaced. The wider system, including the feedback mechanism (the escapement) for delivering the shocks, is a particular type of non-linear oscillator since it is autonomous and maintains a uniform cycle independently of initial conditions. (b) Significantly different is a system subject to random shocks. Here the mechanism itself is damped, but an outside, unexplained source keeps it going, and in this sense it is not a complete theory, for the source of maintenance lies outside the theory. Also, since the shocks are not synchronised with the cycle, they work both with and against it so that their effects largely cancel out. That they do not entirely cancel out can be seen by the fact that, if the system were to come to rest, the next shock would excite it and the motion would be cyclical, so that there will always be a small tendency to cyclical motion. The shocks, however, would have to be large to produce much of a continuing cycle, which would make it desirable to analyse the individual causes and consequences of each shock rather than to treat them as a random element collectively. It also raises the question of whether or not the cycle would be more swamped in the random motions than is actually the case. Somewhere in between these two types lies the theory which might be called the Schumpeter clock (although it would be a chronometrically bad clock). The steady evolution of ideas leads to intermittent, irregular, but not random, bursts of expenditure. If these large and variable outlays impinge on a damped cycle, they may seriously alter its character and keep it from dying away. Professor Frisch has provided the basic analysis of this range of problems, and I shall attempt to indicate its relevance to non-linear theories below.[4] The difficult question remains as to what extent the explanation lies entirely with the innovation, giving forced oscillations, and to what extent there is mutual conditioning, leading to an erratic clockwork (and hence non-linear) theory.

Along with explaining the maintenance of oscillation, non-linear theory does away with the necessity for 'initial conditions'. No matter how the mechanism is started, it tends to a certain type of cycle. Otherwise we are involved in believing that the magnitude and turning points, for example, of a cycle now are completely determined by events which took place many years ago. The absurdity of such an assumption is obvious.

Another advantage lies in the possible treatment of the acceleration principle. Because statistical studies (e.g. Tinbergen's 'Statistical Evidence on the Acceleration Principle')[5] have shown that it does not correspond to the facts, many economists favour dropping it entirely. Yet this would surely be mistaken since it is merely the statement of a simple consequence of the one omnipresent, incontestable dynamic fact in economics — the necessity to have both stocks and flows of goods. In any case, it is worth while to try assumptions which take account of this fact but do not require any rigid proportionality. In doing this we may avoid another shortcoming of linear theory — the requirement that the upswing be essentially the same type of thing as the downswing. With non-linear theory we may make the depression as different from the boom as we wish; in fact this is one way of assessing the degree of non-linearity.

I shall proceed in order of increasing difficulty, taking up a series of models which are all variants of the simple multiplier and accelerator principles. The first is a threshold oscillator in which the economy once started up continues until it removes the capital deficiency which started it, and then it goes down until it removes the excess capacity with which it started downward. The second model introduces a simple linear trend (which is more important to non-linear systems than to linear) which makes it unnecessary to await the wearing out of all the capital from the preceding boom before beginning the coming one. A third model consists of a combination of a dynamical accelerator and a less crude form of the non-linear accelerator. This gives a more complicated evolution, but it still contains sudden shifts from declining to rising income and the reverse. This unreality is eliminated in the final model by taking account of the lag between investment decisions and the resulting outlays.

The Simplest Model

The central difficulty with the acceleration principle is that it assumes that actual, realised capital stock is maintained at the desired relation with output. We know in reality that it is seldom so, there being now too much and now too little capital stock. For this there are two good reasons. The rate of investment is limited by the capacity of the investment goods industry. Furthermore, entrepreneurial expectations are such that, even if it were possible to expand plant in the boom, there would be a great resistance to it. At the other extreme there is an even more inescapable and effective limit. Machines, once made, cannot be unmade, so that negative investment is limited to attrition from wear, from time, and from innovations. Therefore, capital stock cannot be increased fast enough in the upswing, nor decreased fast enough in the downswing, so that at one time we have shortages and rationing of orders and at the other excess capacity with idle plants and machines.

Call k capital stock, ξ the desired capital stock (proportional to income or output), c consumption, y income, and α, β and κ constants. Then, with a linear consumption function,

$$\xi = \kappa y, \tag{1}$$

$$c = \alpha y + \beta, \tag{2}$$

$$y = c + \dot{k}, \tag{3}$$

where $\dot{k}$ is dk/dt, the rate of change in capital stock and, hence, net investment. I shall assume that the economy seeks the perfect adjustment of capital to output and that it does so in either of two extreme ways, capacity output of investment goods or zero gross investment. If actual capital equals desired capital, no adjustment is necessary and capital is simply maintained with zero net investment. When the stock of capital, k, is insufficient, the rate of investment, $\dot{k}$, proceeds at capacity, $\dot{k}^*$, and when it is in excess, it is retired by scrapping at a rate, $\dot{k}^{**}$, so that

$$\dot{k} = \begin{cases} \dot{k}^*, & \xi > k, \\ 0, & \xi = k, \\ \dot{k}^{**}, & \xi < k. \end{cases} \tag{4}$$

Combining (1), (2), (3) and (4) we have

$$\xi = \frac{\kappa}{1-\alpha}\dot{k} + \frac{\kappa\beta}{1-\alpha},$$

which gives ξ^*, ξ_0, ξ^{**} upon substitution of the corresponding values for $\dot{k}$. ξ has therefore only three possible values because it is linearly related to $\dot{k}$, which has only three by hypothesis.

If we plot this system in phase space we get the picture shown in FIGURE 6.1. By contrast, a linear system would be a single straight line sloping upward to the right. The arrows indicate the direction of movement. The point ξ_0 is an equilibrium point ($k = \xi$ and consequently $\dot{k} = 0$) and satisfies the relationships defining the system. It is, however, an unstable equilibrium, since a small displacement in the phase plane leads to a large displacement from which it never returns. For example, if to ξ_0 we add $\Delta\xi$, then $\dot{k}$ changes from zero to $\dot{k}^*$ and ξ becomes ξ^*, and hence we are transferred to a point near E in the phase diagram. From there we travel continuously to C, at which point the system exhibits discontinuous change in $\dot{k}$, At C, $k = \xi$, which means $\dot{k}$ drops to zero, but that makes $\xi = \xi_0 < k$; hence $\dot{k} = 0$ is not a possible value and $\dot{k}^{**}$ is required. Thus the representative point in the phase plane jumps discontinuously from C to D and then travels continuously at a much slower pace, to A, where it jumps, for the opposite reasons, to B and thence to C, and so on indefinitely. Therefore we arrive at the limit cycle $ABCD$, and it is always the same cycle no matter where we start. The time series of k and y corresponding to the limit cycle are shown in FIGURE 6.2.

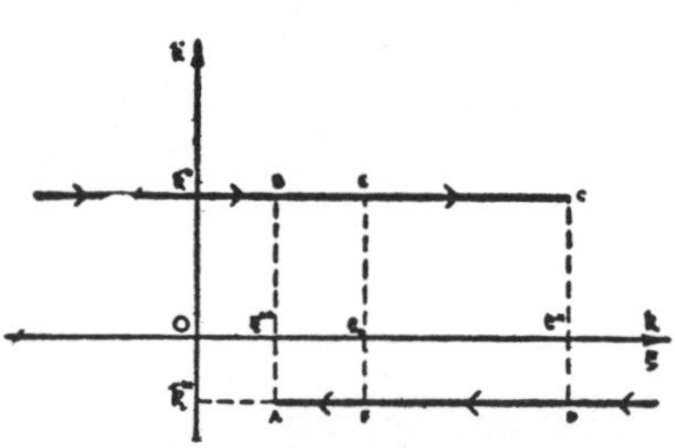

FIGURE 6.1 Simplest limit cycle in phase space

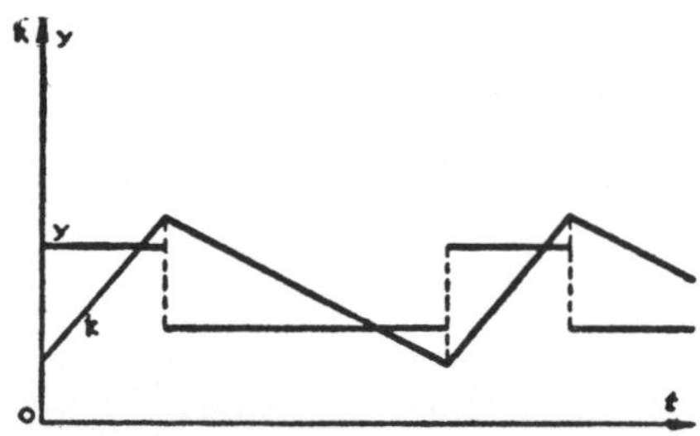

FIGURE 6.2 Time series for simplest model

For any initial stock of capital we get a determinate path for all subsequent time. To the left of B we travel on the top line, to the right of D on the bottom one. Between these two limits we have to specify not only the stock of capital but also whether it is increasing or decreasing since, as in any oscillation, the same quantity position must be traversed twice, once going up and once coming down. It is to be noted that very rapid changes are possible in investment but are quite impossible in the stock of capital. Hence, whenever the system reaches an impasse of any sort, the necessary discontinuity (which may be taken as an idealisation of a very rapid change) must occur in $\dot{k}$, not in k.

It would be difficult to imagine a cruder or more oversimplified model of the business cycle, but it does serve to illustrate clearly the general characteristics of non-linear oscillators:

(1) The final result is independent of the initial conditions.

(2) The oscillation maintains itself without the need of any outside 'factors' to help in the explanation. In this sense it is a complete, self-contained theory.

(3) The equilibrium is unstable and therefore the mechanism starts itself given even the smallest disturbance. Yet in spite of this instability it is a usable theory because the mechanism does not explode or break down but is kept within limits by the non-linearity.

(4) No questionable lags are introduced. The mechanism operates by its own structure.

While such a crude model cannot claim to be a representation of actual cycles, it does have many of the basic characteristics (as opposed to the refinements) of the picture of cycles that economists have agreed on. In particular, its nature is such that when there is heavy investment, businessmen desire more capital than they have and when there is no investment, they have too much capital. Yet neither of these apparently circular and hence self-sustaining conditions can persist indefinitely because of an *inherent* dynamical contradiction. The boom generates its own ruin by fulfilling its purpose, and the depression brings about its own cure by removing the source of its being. One striking short-coming of the mechanism is its tendency to spend much more of its time in depression than in boom, since capital can be built much more rapidly than it is worn out. Our mechanism gets rid, during depression, of all the capital created during the boom. Clearly, any account of growth will change this and remove the shortcoming.

Technological Progress

To make a crude allowance for technological progress, we may assume a steady growth in the desired amount of capital. Altering (1) accordingly, we get

$$\xi = at + \kappa y; \qquad \dot{\xi} = a, \tag{1a}$$

where t is time and a the constant growth rate in the capital requirements. Keeping the other relations (2), (3), (4), we find that, as might be expected, no equilibrium exists, since $\dot{k} = 0$ means that k is constant and hence that ξ would become greater than k and hence that $\dot{k}$ would cease to be zero.

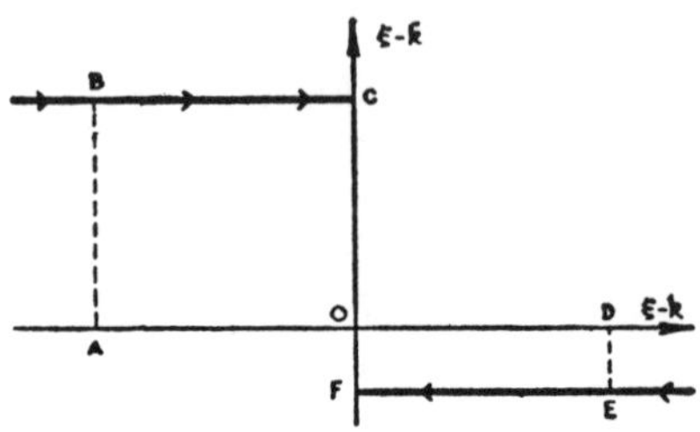

FIGURE 6.3 Phase diagram with steady growth

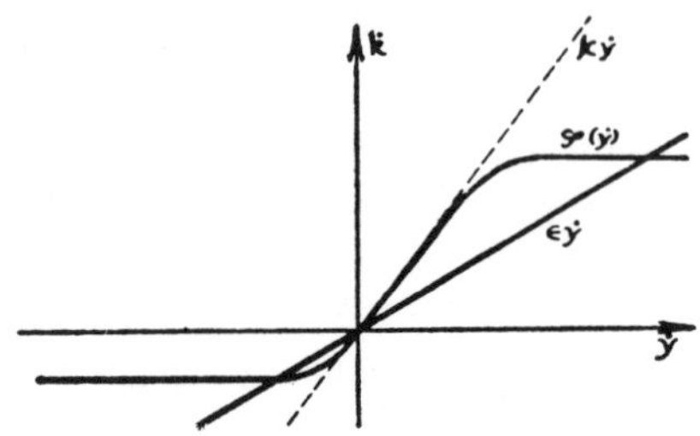

FIGURE 6.4 The non-linear accelerator–multiplier

Desired capital, ξ, depends on time and on the level of income, and hence

$$\xi = \begin{cases} at + \xi^* , & \xi - k > 0; \\ \dot{a}t + \xi^{**}, & \xi - k < 0. \end{cases}$$

It is more convenient to plot $\dot{\xi} - \dot{k}$ against $\xi - k$, as is done in FIGURE 6.3. $\dot{\xi}$ is always equal to a except at the points of discontinuity, whereas $\dot{k}$ has two values, $\dot{k}^*$ and $\dot{k}^{**}$. If a is greater than $\dot{k}^*$, the economy can never catch up with its capital needs. Excluding this unrealistic case, we find that in boom the economy proceeds slowly along the path EF, gradually catching up with its requirements (desired capital, ξ, is greater than actual capital stock, k). When enough capital has been accumulated ($\xi = k$), investment ceases, but this means a great fall in income and hence capital requirements, so that decumulation begins. Hence we *add* to $\dot{\xi} = a$ the *negative* net investment $\dot{k}^{**}$, and hence (with $k > \xi$) we proceed rapidly along the line BC—rapidly because excess capacity is being eliminated both through failure to replace and the steady occurrence of capital-using innovations. The distance AO is equal to OD since in each case the distance from the origin represents the jump in the value of ξ consequent upon a shift from $\dot{k}^*$ to $\dot{k}^{**}$ or vice versa. But while ξ shifts by the difference between ξ^* and ξ^{**}, k does not alter at the time of shift. Given any initial value of $\xi - k$, the path of the system is uniquely determined. If the mechanism was not already oscillating, it will, in the course of one motion, commence to vibrate on the closed cycle *BCEFBC*, and so on indefinitely in the absence of a change from 'outside'.

In addition to the characteristics of the first example, this one has certain other important aspects:

(1) So long as there is technological progress, it has no equilibrium point; it can never settle down, even for a moment. It strains to get to its equilibrium point, but once there it relaxes, and that relaxation means that so much capital is no longer needed. Then it strains to slough off the excess capital, which, once eliminated, changes the situation again.

(2) The depression is almost certain to be shorter than the boom and in any case is not symmetrical with it. The relative length of the two phases depends entirely on the rate of secular progress.

(3) There is secular progress with capital accumulation.

(4) The mode of action of this progress has considerable affinity with the Schumpeterian theory of innovations. New ideas requiring investment occur regularly, but nonetheless investment goes by spurts. Thus one of the most fundamental aspects of non-linear oscillators is demonstrated: they are frequency converters. A steady change (zero frequency) is converted into a fluctuating motion with a positive frequency, or period.

(5) In the simplest possible way, autonomous and induced investments are combined.

By virtue of its simplicity, this model has great flexibility. We may consider any variable rate of progress that we wish by taking short periods of constant rates of progress but allowing the rate to be different in each short space of time. In this manner we may easily introduce an historical element, prolonging or shortening the boom or depression according to the actually realised rate of progress.

The Dynamical Multiplier and the Non-linear Accelerator

There are two directions in which we may soften the crudities of the theory. The first is by considering the dynamical operation of the multiplier and the second by doing the same for investment decisions and outlays (to be taken up only in the next section). The use of the instantaneous multiplier introduces a quite unreal and unnecessary awkwardness, while clarifying and simplifying the problem. It is certain that the process of multiplication takes time, and in any dynamical situation it is important to take this into account. I propose to do this by replacing equations (2) and (3) by

$$y = \alpha y + \beta + \dot{k} - \epsilon \dot{y}. \tag{5}$$

This is a multiplier, with a lag introduced by $\epsilon\dot{y}$, where ϵ is analogous to the lag in the usual time period analysis.[6] If we rewrite (5) in the form,

$$y = \frac{1}{1-\alpha}(\beta + \dot{k} - \epsilon\dot{y}),$$

we see that it states that income is the multiplier value of investment plus consumer injections less a kind of saving or disinvestment (it can be interpreted as either) resulting from a changing level of income.

The investment, $\dot{k}$, consists of an autonomous part, $l(t)$, and an induced part, φ. About induced investment we may make the less crude (than the previous one) assumption that the acceleration principle ($\xi = \kappa y$) holds over some middle range but passes to complete inflexibility at either extreme, as is shown in FIGURE 6.4. The upper limit is the $\dot{k}^*$ of the previous models and the lower limit the $\dot{k}^{**}$. $d\varphi(\dot{y})/d\dot{y}$ is equal to the acceleration coefficient, κ, in its middle range and zero (or some quite small value) at either extremity. If we let

$$\psi(\dot{y}) = \varphi(\dot{y}) - \epsilon\dot{y}, \tag{6}$$

it will have the shape shown in FIGURE 6.5 when it is merely 'multiplied' by $1/(1-\alpha)$. It is assumed that $d\varphi(0)/d\dot{y}$ is greater than ϵ. If, for the moment, we measure y in deviations from its (dis)equilibrium value, we may ignore β and l. Thus we get the result shown in FIGURE 6.5 which represents the equation

$$y = \frac{1}{1-\alpha}\psi(\dot{y}). \tag{5a}$$

Thus for every value of y we can find whether it is increasing or decreasing and by how much. Therefore, once we specify an initial income, its whole subsequent evolution is determined.

We find that there is an equilibrium point, E, at the origin, but that it is unstable, as indicated by the arrows. Therefore, a small change in outside conditions leads, for example, to explosive growth to A, where the development becomes untenable with a discontinuous change in $\dot{y}$ to point B. And thence to C to D to A, and so forth, so that we have a closed path constituting a self-sustaining cycle.

The points A and C are critical points and there one of the variables suffers a discontinuous jump. Which variable can only be decided in terms of knowledge about the variables involved. In our case it is clearly $\dot{y}$ and not y, which is analogous to the jump from $\dot{k}^*$ to $\dot{k}^{**}$. The discontinuity should be considered as an approximation to a rapid change. That there must be a jump can be deduced from the two facts that (i) the point, representative of the economy, must be on the curve, and (ii) it must follow the direction of the arrows.

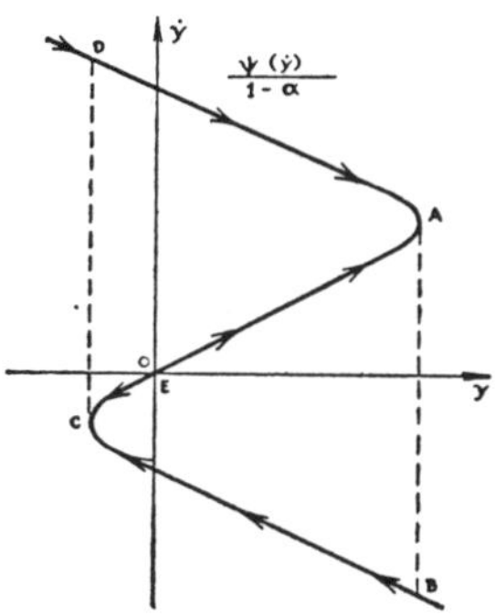

FIGURE 6.5 Phase diagram for accelerator–multiplier

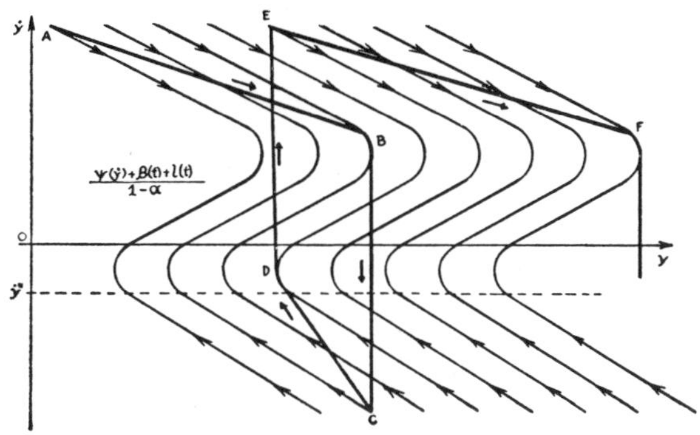

FIGURE 6.6 Path in phase space with steady growth

The model abstracts from secular progress, and by taking account of it we escape the peculiarity that the model spends more of its time in depression than in boom. As our system stands, income always returns to its previous low, but if we introduce a shifting of the curve to the right, then it is intuitively evident that the upswing will be lengthened and the downswing shortened. In order to include autonomous as well as induced investment we must rewrite (5a) as

$$y = \frac{\psi(\dot{y})}{1-\alpha} + \frac{\beta(t)}{1-\alpha} + \frac{l(t)}{1-\alpha}, \tag{5b}$$

where $l(t)$ is the historically given investment outlay, which does not depend on output and which may be roughly associated with innovations and governmental injections of purchasing power. As an interesting, though not essential, refinement, we may say that $l(t)$ is identically zero whenever $\dot{y}$ is below some negative threshold value, indicated as $\dot{y}^*$ in FIGURE 6.6. $\beta(t)$ is the historically given upward drift of the consumption function. This may be associated with rising population (because a given level of output means ever greater numbers of unemployed, all of whom consume without income) and with the accumulation of capital leading to greater *fixed*, short-run outlays of business. It is also possible to regard the long-run consumption function (with β as zero) as basic and the short-run one as a deviation from it depending on the previous high income.[7] The graphical technique is somewhat more complicated (the ψ curve is elongated in the upper phases of the boom) but the results are otherwise much the same. For simplicity of exposition only, I shall take the simple case of a steady increase in $\beta(t)$ and an $l(t)$ irregularly positive in boom and zero in deep depression. The effect of any increase in β and l is to translate the $\psi(\dot{y})$ curve to the right by the multiplier value of the current rates of outlay which they represent.

The resulting trajectory is no longer a closed curve, which merely expresses the fact that it is an evolutionary and not a stationary economy. It goes from A to B to C to D to E to F, and so on. The most important formal result is that the boom is lengthened and the depression shortened, thus avoiding the unrealistic behaviour that the depression would otherwise have to last long enough to wear out all the capital constructed in the boom. It is possible to construct a good approximation to the trajectory in this phase space for any arbitrary $l(t)$. Thus every cycle may be (and certainly will be) different in shape and duration. Large innovational outlays lengthen the boom and carry it further. On the other hand, if there is only induced investment the upswing will not last so long. If innovational outlays commence early in the depression they will shorten it but not (unless very large) stop it. But, coming late in the depression, they may well reverse the downward motion of income; it is this case which is shown in FIGURE 6.6. Should no innovational outlays occur, the depression may drag out for a long time.

By graphical integration from FIGURE 6.6, we may determine the behaviour of national income over time. The rate of growth of income is greatest at the beginning of the boom and then declines somewhat but not to zero. It changes at the peak to a decline, first great and then ever milder. The kind of behaviour implied is shown roughly in FIGURE 6.7.

Expanded Model with Investment Lag

The second lag that must be considered in order to come closer to reality is the lag between decisions to invest and the corresponding outlays. We may say that outlays will tend to lag behind decisions by approximately one half the length of time required for fabrication, which is longer than the time required for consumption goods. Therefore we may say

$$O_I(t+\theta) \approx O_D(t) = \varphi[\dot{y}(t)],$$

where O_I equals investment outlays, O_D investment decisions, and θ is one half the construction time of new equipment. Hence equation (5) is more correctly written as

$$\epsilon\dot{y}(t+\theta)+(1-\alpha)y(t+\theta) = O_A(t+\theta)+\varphi[\dot{y}(t)], \tag{5c}$$

where O_A stands for the sum of the autonomous outlays β and l. Expanding the two leading terms in a Taylor series and dropping all but the first two terms in each, we get

$$\epsilon\dot{y}+\epsilon\theta\ddot{y}+(1-\alpha)y+(1-\alpha)\theta\dot{y}-\varphi(\dot{y}) = O_A(t+\theta), \tag{5d}$$

where $\dot{y} = dy/dt$ and $\ddot{y} = d^2y/dt^2$. Or, shifting our autonomous injections by θ time units and calling it O^*, we get

$$\epsilon\theta\ddot{y}+[\epsilon+(1-\alpha)\theta]\dot{y}-\varphi(\dot{y})+(1-\alpha)y = O^*(t). \tag{5e}$$

For the moment we may take $O^*(t)$ to be a constant, O^*. Then we may study deviations from the equilibrium income $O^*/(1-\alpha)$ by substituting

$$z = y - O^*/(1-\alpha),$$

which gives us

$$\epsilon\theta\ddot{z}+[\epsilon+(1-\alpha)\theta]\dot{z}-\varphi(\dot{z})+(1-\alpha)z = 0. \tag{5f}$$

If $d\varphi(0)/d\dot{z} < \epsilon+(1-\alpha)\theta$, we get damped oscillations, and if it is considerably less, we get non-oscillatory stable motion. In these cases we may write a linear approximation by taking $d\varphi(0)/d\dot{z}$ as a constant, and thus we will get a valid representation for small motions around the equilibrium point. But if $d\varphi(0)/d\dot{z} > \epsilon+(1-\alpha)\theta$, which there is good reason to suppose to be the case, the system explodes beyond the limited region of valid linear approximation. Then we must resort to the Poincaré–Liénard method of graphical integration.[8] First, however, (5f) must be reduced to a dimensionless form. Let

$$\psi(\dot{z}) = [\epsilon+(1-\alpha)\theta]\dot{z}-\varphi(\dot{z}),$$

$$x = \sqrt{(1-\alpha)/\epsilon\theta}\, z/\dot{z}_0,$$

$$\dot{x} = dx/dt_1 = \dot{z}/\dot{z}_0,$$

$$\ddot{x} = d^2x/dt_1^2,$$

$$t_1 = \sqrt{(1-\alpha)/\epsilon\theta}\, t.$$

$\dot{z}_0$ is any convenient unit in which to measure velocity. Noting that

$$\ddot{z} = \dot{z}_0 \frac{d^2x}{dt_1 dt} = \dot{z}_0 \sqrt{\frac{1-\alpha}{\epsilon\theta}} \frac{d^2x}{dt_1^2},$$

we may substitute these new variables in (5f), which becomes, after simplification,

$$\ddot{x} + \frac{\psi(\dot{z}_0\dot{x})}{\dot{z}_0\sqrt{\epsilon\theta(1-\alpha)}} + x = 0. \tag{7}$$

Letting

$$X(\dot{x}) = \frac{\psi(\dot{z}_0\dot{x})}{\dot{z}_0\sqrt{\epsilon\theta(1-\alpha)}}, \tag{7a}$$

we get

$$\ddot{x} + X(\dot{x}) + x = 0. \tag{7b}$$

An illuminating way to regard this is to write it as

$$\ddot{x} + [X(\dot{x})/\dot{x}]\dot{x} + x = 0, \tag{7c}$$

where the expression in square brackets may be regarded as a variable damping coefficient. As is well known, a positive coefficient leads to an attenuating cycle and a negative one to an exploding cycle. $X(\dot{x})$ differs only in scale from $\psi(\dot{y})$, and therefore $X(\dot{x})/\dot{x}$ has the general form shown in FIGURE 6.8. Consequently the system oscillates with increasing violence in the central region, but as it expands into the outer regions, it enters more and more into an area of positive damping with a growing tendency to attenuation. It is intuitively clear that it will settle down to such a motion as will just balance the two tendencies, although proof requires the rigorous methods developed by Poincaré. It is interesting to note that this is how the problem of the maintenance of oscillation was originally conceived by Lord Rayleigh and that our equation is of the Rayleigh, rather than the van der Pol, type. The result is that we get, instead of a stable equilibrium, a stable motion. This concept is the more general one, for a stable equilibrium point may be considered as a stable motion so small that it degenerates into a point. Perfectly general conditions for the stability of motion are complicated and difficult to formulate, but what we can say is that any curve of the general shape of $X(\dot{x})$ [or $\psi(\dot{y})$] will give rise to a *single*, *stable* limit cycle. Of another equation mathematically equivalent to ours, Andronow and Chaikin say: 'Thus while there is no convenient method for solving van der Pol's

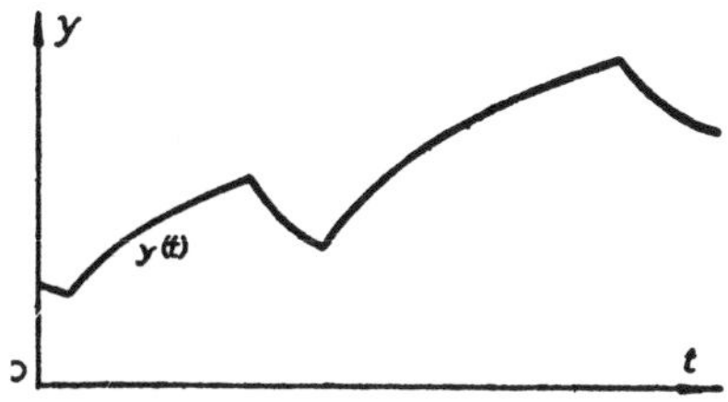

FIGURE 6.7 Time series with steady growth

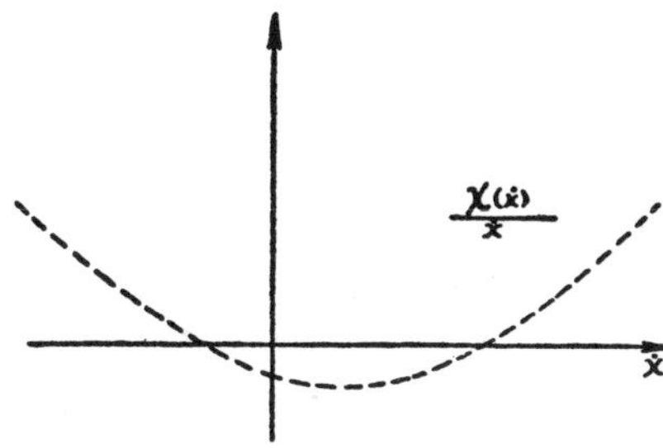

FIGURE 6.8 The variable damping coefficient

equation, it is known that: (a) there is a unique periodic solution and it is stable; (b) every solution tends asymptotically to the periodic solution. These two properties manifestly provide most valuable practical information.'[9] Therefore, making only assumptions acceptable to most business cycle theorists, along with two simple approximations, we have been able to arrive at a stable, cyclical motion which is self-generating and self-perpetuating.

For performing the graphical integration it is convenient, letting $v = \dot{x}$, to rewrite (7b) as

$$v\frac{dv}{dx} + X(v) + x = 0. \tag{7d}$$

Thus we have an extremely simple, non-linear, first order, differential equation, which may easily (the Liénard method makes it truly easy) be integrated graphically, provided we have an empirically given $X(v)$ curve. $X(v)$ need not be expressible in any simple mathematical form, although some approximation, say by a cubic expression, does facilitate qualitative discussion of the type of system. In our case we have only a very rough idea of the X function, which we may derive from the structural parameters, ϵ, θ, α, and the acceleration coefficient operative when there is no excess capacity. Regarding these parameters we have but a crude idea of their order of magnitude, nothing more. In estimating the fabrication period (twice the time lag) of consumption goods we must remember that it includes not only the time required to make any one article but also the raw materials that go to make it, and those that go to make the raw materials, and so on. If we replace all this by a single hypothetical firm producing consumption goods, we must make the assumption of a fairly long fabrication time, say one-half to one and one-half years. Taking the mean of this range, we might put the time at one and hence ϵ at 0.5. Professor Frisch estimated the fabrication time for capital goods on the average at three years, and I shall take it to be two, which makes θ equal to 1.0. There is good evidence that in the course of the cycle α is around 0.6.[10] The acceleration coefficient is the ratio of national capital to national income, which was around 4.0 for Britain in the 1930s and was undoubtedly of this order of magnitude for the United States, although accurate statistics are still lacking. There is no doubt, however, that the marginal coefficient operative in a boom is much smaller. I shall assume that the slope of $\varphi(\dot{y})$ (the acceleration coefficient, κ) is 2.0 in the middle range and zero at either end. There remains only to determine the possible limits of net annual investment. From Kuznets's data for the great boom and depression, these might be placed at -3.0 and $+9.0$ billions of dollars per year.

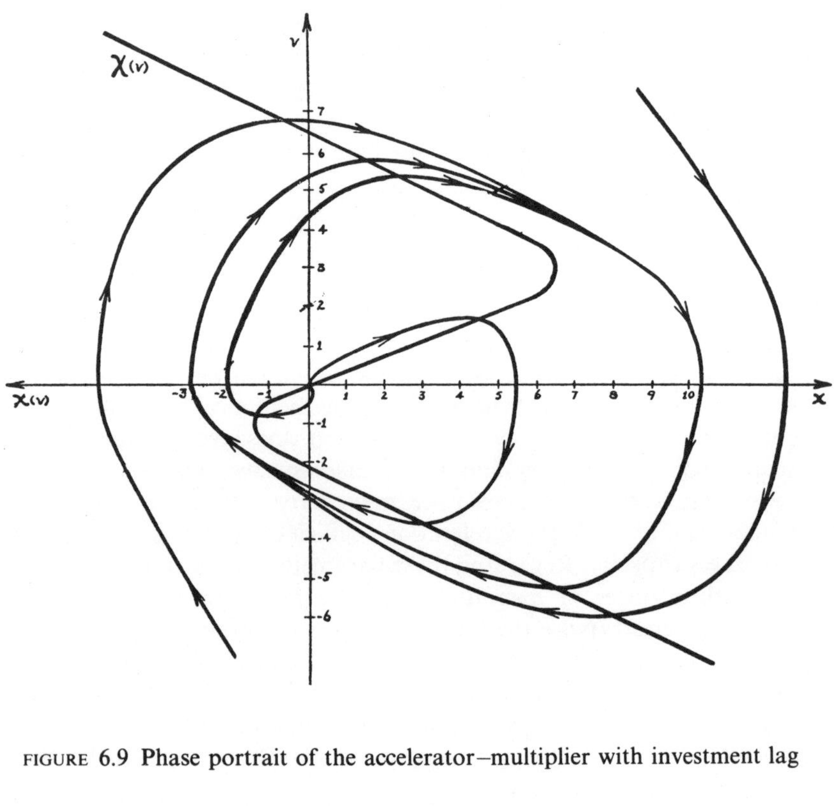

FIGURE 6.9 Phase portrait of the accelerator–multiplier with investment lag

In FIGURE 6.9 is given the Poincaré limit cycle for the foregoing values of parameters. Also represented are four possible phase trajectories, starting from arbitrary initial conditions and approaching asymptotically the unique limit cycle. All points in the phase plane represent pairs of initial conditions, the vertical axis giving the initial velocities and the horizontal axis the initial levels of income (in deviations from some steady level). Through every point in the phase plane passes a single trajectory, which leads ultimately to the one limiting motion. In FIGURE 6.9 we have velocity as a function of income, and hence, by a second graphical integration, we can get income as a function of time for the undisturbed or limiting cyclical form. The range of fluctuation is from − 5.0 in the trough to + 19.0 billions of dollars per year at the peak, and the period is slightly over nine years. The ease with which such models explain long cycles is a notable feature, and it does not depend in any great degree on the lags but rather on the amount of time it takes to produce the desired amount of capital goods.[11] FIGURE 6.9 also gives an idea of the extent of departure from simple harmonic motion as represented by a sine curve. The closed phase diagram for a sine curve is a circle, whereas this phase diagram is very uncircular. The upswing gets under way more quickly and the high level of activity is held longer than with a sine curve. The upper turning point is followed by a rapid decline and a tendency to remain longer at a depressed level. In spite of the obvious asymmetry of X (v), the two phases have approximately the same duration, a little more than four years being spent in the region of increasing income and a little more than four and one-half years with decreasing income. Our model is, however, of an unprogressive economy in which income and capital always return to their previous lows. In a

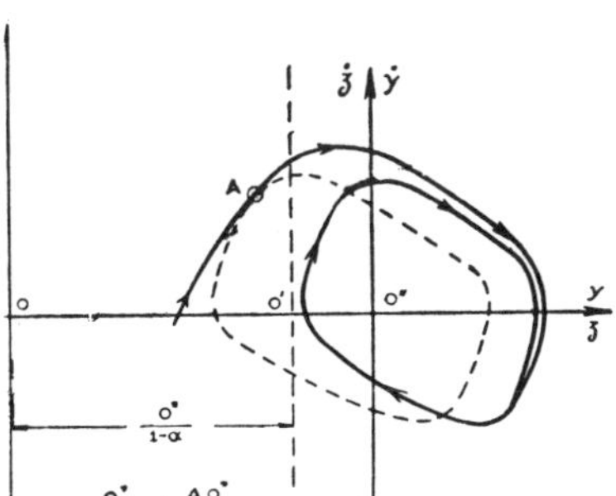

FIGURE 6.10 Effect of a single shift on phase path

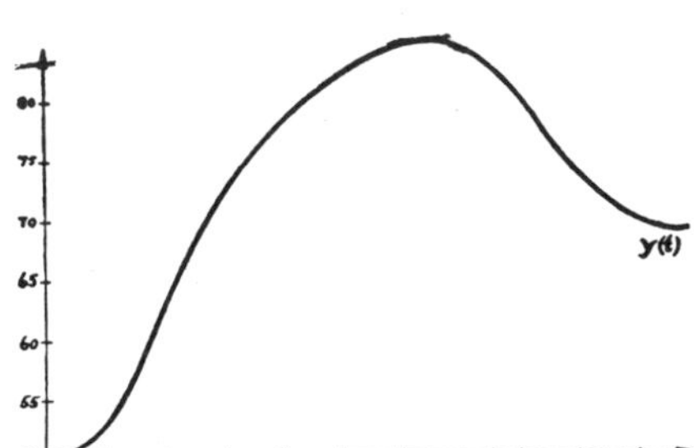

FIGURE 6.11 Time series of a non-sinusoidal cycle with growth

progressive society the limit cycle would shift irregularly to the right and the representative point would pursue it in a complicated spiral to the right. We can see this by considering a single shift to the right brought about by an increase in O^* to $O^* + \Delta O^*$, as shown in FIGURE 6.10. The origin for y is O and the origin for z is O'; the previous steady regime is given by the broken contour and the new one by the solid one. The representative point will be at some point, say A, on the broken contour at the moment of the shift. This then specifies the initial conditions (level and rate of change) for a transient motion towards the new regime. We may consider a continual, regular or irregular, shifting to the right so long as it is not too rapid as compared with the undisturbed motion (i.e. adiabatic change).

Plotted roughly in FIGURE 6.11 is the resulting time series of income from a steady shifting (about 3 per cent per year) to the right of the limit cycle. We see that the upswing is prolonged to 6.5 years and the downswing shortened to 4.2 years. The whole cycle is moderately lengthened to 10.7 years. Income rises from 50 to 85 billions of dollars and falls back to 69. The introduction of historically given innovational outlays would make each cycle different.

Finally, it should be noted that, while I have assumed a particular shape for $\varphi(\dot{y})$, the power of the Liénard construction is shown by the fact that an equation containing any given curve may be easily integrated. Therefore, whatever sort of investment function is found actually to hold, that type may be completely analysed in its cyclical functioning. If we look closely into this problem, we find that what is really necessary is to take individual account of many different industries because while one industry may still have excess capacity, another may be short of fixed capital. Therefore, the combined operation may depend as much on the points at which different industries fire into investment activity as on the actual shape of the X function for each industry or any conceivable aggregation of all of them. Thus we will have a kind of propagation of an impulse through an industry space with the (possibly quite slow) staggered responses of the various industries, with a resultant sluggishly cumulative boom.

NOTES

1. This paper, with the exception of a few modifications in the last section, was presented at the 1948 meeting of the Econometric Society in Cleveland, and it was summarised in *Econometrica*, April 1949 (vol. 17, pp. 184–5). In its various metamorphoses it was followed with great interest and many helpful

comments by the late J. A. Schumpeter. His influence on the whole of it is so pervasive, and I hope so evident, that particular acknowledgement would be inadequate.

2. Cf. any good book on mechanics, e.g. A. A. Andronow and C. E. Chaikin, *Theory of Oscillations* (English translation by S. Lefschetz) (Princeton: Princeton University Press, 1949) Chapter I.
3. Philippe Le Corbeiller, 'Les systèmes autoentretenus et les oscillations de relaxation', *Econometrica*, vol. 1, July 1933, pp. 328–32. 'If statistical data lead us to believe that a given magnitude varies periodically, and if we look for the cause of these oscillations, we may suppose that that magnitude executes either (a) forced oscillations, or (b) maintained oscillations, which may be either (bα) sine-like, or (bβ) relaxation type.' My debt to Professor Le Corbeiller is very great, not only for the original stimulation to search for the essential non-linearities, but also for his patient insistence, in the face of the many difficulties which turned up, that this type of analysis *must* somehow be worked out.

   Since the statement in the text was written, I have discovered that there has been an increasing amount of work on non-linear theories, culminating in Professor Hicks's admirable book, *A Contribution to the Theory of the Trade Cycle* (Oxford: Clarendon Press, 1950, 199 pp.), which appeared while I was making final revisions on this paper. Professor Tinbergen has also attacked the subject in his article, 'Ligevægtstyper Og Konjunkturbevægelse' (*Nordisk Tidsskrift for Teknisk Økonomie*, vol. 32, nos. 2–4, 1943, pp. 45–63). This development corroborates the position of Professor Le Corbeiller and promises much good for economics. In Hicks's book the reader will find reference to other investigations as well as a much more complete statement of why non-linear cycle theory is necessary. I find most impressive the extent to which he and I have hit on the same problems and, substantially, the same answers, although his techniques appear, on the surface, to be quite different since he deals with difference equations and since he does not approach the subject in terms of formal, non-linear theory. The similarities are not purely accidental, partly because we have both started from the unsatisfactory, but profoundly stimulating, dynamical closure of the Keynesian system put forth by Mr Harrod in his book, *The Trade Cycle* (Oxford: Clarendon Press, 1936, 234 pp.).
4. Cf. Frisch, 'Propagation Problems and Impulse Problems in Dynamic Economics' in *Economic Essays in Honour of Gustav Cassel* (London: George Allen and Unwin Ltd., 1933) pp. 171–205, and also my own 'Innovations and the Irregularity of Economic Cycles', *Review of Economic Statistics*, vol. 28, May 1946, pp. 95–104.
5. *Economica*, vol. 5 (New Series), May 1938, pp. 164–76.
6. Cf. my paper 'Secular and Cyclical Aspects of the Multiplier and the Accelerator', in *Employment, Income, and Public Policy*, Essays in Honor of Alvin H. Hansen (New York: W. W. Norton and Co., 1948) pp. 108–32.
7. Cf. James S. Duesenberry, *Income, Saving, and the Theory of Consumer Behavior* (Cambridge, Mass.: Harvard University Press, 1949) 128 pp. and Franco Modigliani, 'Fluctuations in the Savings–Income Ratio: A Problem in Economic Forecasting' in *Studies of Income and Wealth*, vol. XI (New York: National Bureau of Economic Research, 1949) pp. 371–438.

8. A particularly lucid and illuminating account of the entire subject, as well as of the Liénard construction, may be found in Philippe Le Corbeiller, 'The Non-Linear Theory of the Maintenance of Oscillations', *Journal of the Institution of Electrical Engineers*, London, vol. 79, September 1936, pp. 361–78. A good account of the general methods employed in this, as well as of a much wider range of topics, will be found in the English translation, already referred to, of the important work of the two Russian scientists, Andronow and Chaikin.

   [$d\phi(0)/d\dot{z} = \epsilon + (1-d)\theta$ is a bifurcation point, a concept that has become important in the qualitative dynamics of state space. A system whose parameters yield exactly or approximately this value is *structurally* unstable: a small variation in a parameter will alter the *type* of motion and thus be an example of what would now be called Catastrophe Theory. See also chapter 14. R.M.G. 1980.]
9. Andronow and Chaikin, op. cit., pp. 4 and 302 ff.
10. For simplicity I choose to ignore the thesis of Professors Duesenberry and Modigliani that the marginal propensity to consume has different values according to the recent past levels of income. But it is interesting to note that such hereditary effects (level dependent on path) have few terrors here since analytic solutions are impossible and graphical or arithmetical methods are used in any case.
11. This can be seen perhaps more clearly in the model without time lags which I have presented in Chapter XXI of *Business Cycles and National Income* (New York: W. W. Norton and Co., 1950) by Alvin H. Hansen. There I have also indicated how we may take general full employment rather than full employment in the investment goods trades as our upward limiting factor.

7. Iteration, Automatic Computers, and Economic Dynamics

METROECONOMICA, 1951

In the continuing effort to erect a useful dynamics, we need all possible helpful sources of hypotheses. One such is the traditional mathematical device of solving equations by trial and error and its vigorous modern stepchild, the automatic computing machine or zeroing servo, i.e. a mechanism which keeps trying solutions until the resulting error is reduced to zero.

It always takes time to solve an equation by approximative methods, and if our methods for determining the successive approximations are made analogous to the structure of economic decisions, then we may regard the sequence of steps as entirely parallel to an actual process of economic dynamics in time. The convergence of the approximations to the correct answer is the same as the dynamical stability of the economy. We have found the answer when our trial input is correct with zero error. Thus we keep putting in a trial answer and when we get the same answer back we have a solution. Hence a solution corresponds to an equilibrium value. Similarly we may regard economic dynamics as such a series of iterated trial solutions which actually succeed one another at realistically great, regular intervals of time. The existing economic relations determine the method by which the economy makes its repeated tries and a solution is a stationary value of a variable which satisfies these relations in the sense that the same value will be repeated and no further adaptation is necessary. If the relations are such as to yield a stable system, then an undisturbed mechanism will find its stationary solution; otherwise it will depart from it or forever oscillate about it.

Correspondingly in an iterative process we will approximate closer and closer to a solution or depart from it, or endlessly over and underestimate it, depending on (i) the nature of the equations, and (ii) the kind of approximating process we use. All these things are fairly easy to grasp in the case of difference equations, since we always proceed iteratively, by finite steps, which can be exhibited in the form of differences. What is not so clear is that continuous processes (with differential equations) may also be regarded as trial and error methods of solution to static equations. The reason why it is not so easy to see is that no human being can make continuous trials infinite in number. This gap in our grasp of the problem has been closed by the perfection of electronic and electro-mechanical computers — sometimes called zeroing servos — which continuously feed back their errors as the basis for new trials until the error has disappeared. Such a machine is an exact analogue of a continuous dynamic process. Therefore it seems entirely permissible to regard the motion of an economy as a process of computing the answers to the problems posed to it. One might reasonably ask why it is that the computing is never finished, why it is not possible to settle down to a correct answer and keep it, thus providing a stationary process to which we could apply static theory with justification. To provide an answer to this question is precisely one of the key problems of dynamics.

There are two possible explanations, only one of which has been utilised in economics. It would be difficult to improve on Walras's statement of it.

> *Tel est le marché permanent, tendant toujours à l'équilibre sans y arriver jamais par la raison qu'il ne s'y achemine que par tâtonnements et qu'avant même que ces tâtonnements soient achevés, ils sont à recommencer sur nouveaux frais, toutes les données... ayant changé... comme d'un lac agité par le vent et où l'eau cherche toujours son équilibre sans jamais l'atteindre.*[1]

Quite distinct from this is the possibility that the methods of seeking for a solution, as implied by the structure of the economy are such that we do not converge to a solution. In general this will lead to perpetual, self-maintained oscillations. Probably both types of phenomena are present in economic reality.

To facilitate the understanding of the matter, it is desirable to take the simplest possible example, the Kahn–Keynes multiplier. We begin with the well-known equation, in which c is consumption, y income, i investment,

$$y = c(y) + i,$$

and we wish to find a root (solution). A standard procedure in such cases is to guess at a value, y_0, for the root and simply substitute it in the right-hand side. Then we calculate y and see if we have guessed correctly, in which case we would get back the same value that we put in. Barring rare good luck this will not happen, but now we have a new value, y_1, to use as a basis for a second trial. We therefore proceed by iteration thus

$$
\begin{aligned}
y_1 &= c(y_0) + i; \\
y_2 &= c(y_1) + i; \\
&\ldots\ldots\ldots\ldots \\
&\ldots\ldots\ldots\ldots \\
y_t &= c(y_{t-1}) + i.
\end{aligned}
$$

Evidently this is the dynamical multiplier if we regard the succeeding trials as the various values of income at regular intervals of time. It is easily shown that the process will converge (or that the economy will be stable) if $dc/dy < 1$. dc/dy is assumed positive.

A better view of what is happening is attained if we subtract y_{t-1} from both sides,

$$
\begin{aligned}
\Delta y = y_t - y_{t-1} &= c(y_{t-1}) - y_{t-1} + i \\
&= i - [y_{t-1} - c(y_{t-1})].
\end{aligned}
$$

The term in square brackets is saving, so that income increases if investment is greater than saving and income decreases if saving is greater than investment.

Modern automatic control devices (servomechanisms) work by error control, e.g. guided missiles, homing missiles, automatic pilots, anti-aircraft fire control, thermostatic heat controls, etc. A desired value is given and the actual value of the device is subtracted from it and this error is fed back to the device in such a way as to diminish the error. In the dynamical multiplier we have a special form of error control. The desired value is not known, but rather the difference between successive trials is taken as the error and this is successively reduced to zero — hence the name zeroing servo. At this point we have found the answer, our process repeats itself until disturbed. Thus the economy may be regarded as slowly computing the answer to an ever-changing problem.

The foregoing example is altogether trivial. But we may make a restatement of it which is by no means trivial. Suppose that we divide the economy into n sectors and that each sector behaves as we have assumed that the whole economy behaves: each sector always spends some fraction (smaller than one) of the receipts of the previous period. Further assume that everything may be approximated by linear relations. Then we have

$$0 + a_{12}y_2(t-1) + \dots\dots\dots\dots\dots + a_{1_n}y_n(t-1) + i_1(t-1) = y_1(t).$$
$$a_{21}y_1(t-1) + 0 + a_{23}y_3(t-1) + \dots + a_{2_n}y_n(t-1) + i_n(t-1) = y_2(t).$$
$$\dots\dots\dots\dots\dots\dots\dots\dots\dots\dots\dots\dots\dots\dots\dots\dots$$
$$\dots\dots\dots\dots\dots\dots\dots\dots\dots\dots\dots\dots\dots\dots\dots\dots$$
$$a_{n^1}y_1(t-1) + a_{n^2}y_2(t-1) + \dots + a_{n,n-1}y_{n-1}(t-1) + 0 + i_n(t-1) = y_n(t).$$

We may rewrite this suggestively as

$$[a]\{y_{t-1}\} + \{i(t-1)\} = \{y(t)\},$$

where $[a]$ and $\{y\}$ and $\{i\}$ are complex quantities. We get a single *matric* equation which is identical with the aggregative equation and we may repeat the whole of the argument almost exactly. Here, however, there is very real point to the iterative aspect, for if we wish to find a solution to the system of equations

$$[a]\{y\} + \{i\} = \{y\},$$

this is often the best way to do it. Also we have effectively inverted the matrix $[I-a]$ for we have found a y such that

$$\{y\} = [I-a]^{-1}\{i\}$$

That we are really calculating an inverse by our trial and error method we see from the following restatement, taking i as a constant:

$$\begin{aligned} y_t &= i + ay_{t-1}; \\ &= i + a(i + ay_{t-2}); \\ &= i + ai + a^2(i + ay_{t-3}); \\ &= i + ai + a^2i + a^3(i + ay_{t-4}); \\ &\dots\dots\dots\dots\dots \\ &\dots\dots\dots\dots\dots \\ y_t &= [I + a + a^2 + a^3 + a^4 + \dots]i. \\ &= [I-a]^{-1}i. \end{aligned}$$

Therefore we may calculate an inverse without making the trial solutions but rather simply by raising the matrix to a high power. Naturally it must be convergent, but ours always is by virtue of marginal propensities to spend of less than unity. Further refinements along these lines (more rapid convergence, calculation of remaining error, etc.) will be found in a brilliant succession of recent papers by Frazer, Duncan, Collar, Hotelling, Morris, Bingham, and others.

A servomechanism regulates its behaviour by its own behaviour in the light of its stated object and therein lies the secret of its extraordinary finesse in performance. Thus a guided missile sets its rudders according to its deviation from the desired course. Similarly a human being in picking up an object succeeds in this complicated operation by moving the hand so as always to diminish the distance between hand and object.[2] It is a matter of considerable interest that Walras's conception of and term for dynamical adjustment — *tâtonner*, to grope, to feel one's way — is literally the same as that of modern servo theory. Unfortunately he confused the matter by not being altogether clear as to whether he was talking about an iterative solution or about an actual temporal process. In this paper I am trying to turn this confusion to good account, but it should not be forgotten that the distinction between a method of solution and economic reality is as vast as it is vital.

As a second example consider an isolated, simple market with a demand curve (the inverse of the Marshallian), $q_d = q_d(p)$ and a supply curve, $q_s = q_s(p)$. A solution (in the sense that all traders are unwilling to make further bargains at a single price) requires supply to equal demand. Therefore a solution is any real positive root of

$$q_d(p) - q_s(p) = 0.$$

To find this root by iterative methods we may proceed as follows: let

$$p = q_d(p) - q_s(p) + p.$$

Substitute any trial solution in the right hand side (*prix crié au hasard*) and obtain a second approximation from the other side; thus

$$\begin{aligned}
p_1 &= q_d(p_0) - q_s(p_0) + p_0;\\
p_2 &= q_d(p_1) - q_s(p_1) + p_1;\\
&\dots\dots\dots\dots\\
&\dots\dots\dots\dots\\
p_t &= q_d(p_{t-1}) - q_s(p_{t-1}) + p_{t-1}.
\end{aligned}$$

The series will converge to a solution if, in the neighbourhood,

$$q_d'(p) > q_s'(p),$$

which is the Walrasian stability condition. If we rewrite this as

$$\Delta p = p_t - p_{t-1} = q_d(p) - q_s(p),$$

we see that this is a true representation of Walrasian tâtonnement;

> Two goods being given, in order to have market equilibrium so far as they are concerned, or stationary price of the one in terms of the other, it is necessary and sufficient that the effective demand of each of these two goods be equal to its effective offer. When that equality does not exist, it is necessary, in order to get to the equilibrium price to increase the price of the good whose effective demand is greater than its effective supply, and to lower the price of one whose effective supply is greater than its effective demand.[3]

Walras disavowed in advance the use of this kind of market adjustment as a practical device in the manner of Professor Lange's exposition of socialist market theory. He explicitly states that it is only a mathematical method of solution and not the practical one exemplified in the behaviour of real markets. At other points, however, he seems to assert the contrary, as, for example, in the following passage: 'This feeling the way, then, takes place naturally . . . under the regime of free competition, because, under this regime, one raises the price of services when the demand is greater than the supply, and lowers it when the supply is greater than the demand.'[4] Unfortunately for the theory no one raises or lowers any price under perfect competition.

If we look for an empirically verifiable or falsifiable hypothesis upon which to rest the Walrasian theory, we may consider stocks of finished goods, s, as dependent on price, thus

$$s = f(p);$$
$$\frac{ds}{dt} = f'(p)\frac{dp}{dt} = q_s(p) - q_d(p);$$

or

$$\frac{dp}{dt} = \left(\frac{1}{-f'(p)}\right)[q_d(p) - q_s(p)],$$

which is equivalent to the previous formulation, if we change Δp into dp and simply introduce a possibly variable, factor of proportionality.

By contrast we may consider the equality of price (demand price) and cost (supply price) as our required equilibrium condition. We seek then an output such that

$$p_d(q) - p_s(q) = 0,$$

and proceed exactly as before.

$$q_1 = p_d(q_0) - p_s(q_0) + q_0;$$
$$q_2 = p_d(q_1) - p_s(q_1) + q_1;$$
$$\cdots\cdots\cdots\cdots$$
$$\cdots\cdots\cdots\cdots$$
$$q_t = p_d(q_{t-1}) - p_s(q_{t-1}) + q_{t-1}.$$

The subtle and rich investigations of the various aspects of this kind of behaviour constitute Marshallian Time Analysis. 'When therefore the amount produced . . . is such that the demand price is greater than the supply price [long-run normal cost], then sellers receive more than is sufficient to make it worth their while to bring goods to market to that amount, and there is at work an active force tending to increase the amount brought forward for sale.'[5] Although he did not investigate it so profoundly, Walras also considered the same type of adaptation mechanism. 'This feeling the way, then, is precisely what takes place of itself, in product markets with free competition, when entrepreneurs flow toward enterprises or leave according as profits or losses are being made.'[6]

It should be noted both in this and in the previous case, in passing from a trial and error solution (which does not necessarily actually take place) to a dynamical process which does happen, one must re-interpret the symbols. In searching for a solution, q_s need not equal q_d and p_s need not equal p_d. But in reality on a single competitive market there can be only one quantity and one price. In the first case the quantity actually traded is equalised through variations in stocks of finished goods. In this second example p_s must not be strictly interpreted as a price, since that must be the same for buyer and seller, but rather as an average or long-run cost.

There exists another possibility which apparently was overlooked both by Walras and by Marshall. Instead of having pure price or pure quantity adjustment, we may have a mixed price quantity process. Thus we may use the following iterative method, which assumes the simultaneous existence of only one price and one quantity:

$$p_d(q_0) = p_0; \quad q_s(p_0) = q_1;$$
$$p_d(q_1) = p_1; \quad q_s(p_1) = q_2;$$
$$\cdots\cdots\cdots\cdots$$
$$\cdots\cdots\cdots\cdots$$
$$p_d(q_{t-1}) = p_{t-1}; \quad q_s(p_{t-1}) = q_t.$$

If we rewrite this in the form

$$q_t = q_s[p_d(q_{t-1})].$$

we recognise the famous hog cycle (cobweb theorem) which is perhaps the most securely founded empirically of all dynamical hypotheses. In fact it is the theory of all product markets in which there is a significant fabrication period.

It is interesting to construct a diagram of the two types of market adaptation as if they were servomechanisms.

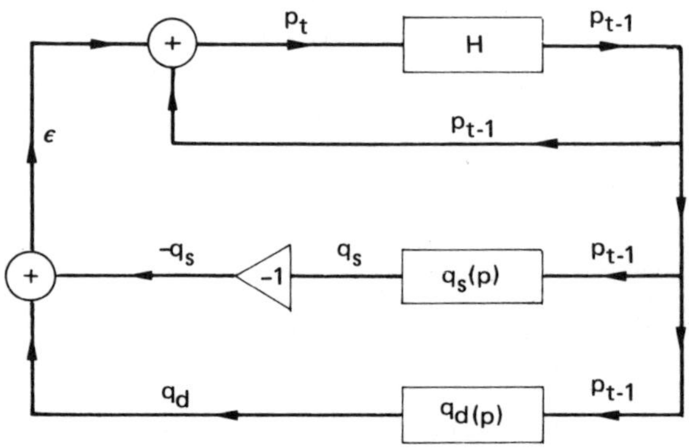

FIGURE 7.1 The Walrasian market

In this diagram ϵ stands for the error with

$$\epsilon = q_d - q_s = p_t - p_{t-1},$$

so that

$$p_t = \epsilon + p_{t-1}.$$

H stands for the lag operator $1-\Delta$ such that

$$Hp_t = p_{t-1}.$$

The Marshallian market is exactly the same as the Walrasian market except that p and q are interchanged. In this way we see the extraordinary symmetry between the two processes.

NOTES

1. L. Walras, *Éléments d'Économie Politique Pure*, édition définitive, 1926, pp. 369–70.
2. Norbert Wiener, *Cybernetics*, p. 14 *passim.*
3. Walras, op. cit., p. 64.
4. Ibid., p. 226, my translation.
5. A. Marshall, *Principles of Economics*, Book 5, Chapter III, paragraph 6.
6. Walras, op. cit., p. 221, my translation.

8. The Nature and Problems of Cycle Policy

BUSINESS CYCLES AND NATIONAL INCOME, 1951,
ALVIN H. HANSEN

We should give some consideration to the nature and problems of cycle policy in the light of econometric models.[1] As the matter stands now, we cannot place enough confidence in any one model as a representation of complex reality to base a positive, quantitative policy on it. Yet it is stimulating and useful to consider how we would go about such problems if, as ultimately we must hope will be the case, our model were adequate to the task.

In constructing a theory one's ultimate aim is to lay the foundations of an intelligent course of action. The Marxian theory, although seriously incomplete, leads — or perhaps jumps — to the conclusion that nothing can be done, and this must be accounted as a policy. The Keynesian analysis prescribes a positive range of possible courses of action to bring the cycle to an end, or at least to ameliorate it.

The Keynesian programme has one great strength; it does not rest on any detailed cycle theory. Rather it simply prescribes more spending and/or less taxing whenever full employment is not attained. It is significant that no one has proposed a simple policy for bringing the economy to full employment and holding it there. This problem is more intractable than is generally realised. On the simplest level, if a government has economic advisers, they may study the state of the economy and recommend appropriate increases in the government deficit or surplus. But if the government refuses to delegate to this body the power to tax and spend — and this has always been held to be the core of state authority and to be in its essence *political, not technical* — then a considerable lag will ensue between the observing of the deviation from full employment and the taking hold of the corrective measures.[2]

Without working out a detailed mathematical analysis, our intuition based on servomechanism analogies is helpful. The relationship of the Council of Advisers to the President, and of the President to the Congress, constitutes a clear example of a feedback mechanism, and one that can easily function badly. The Council of Advisers is an 'error-detecting device' and reports on the deviation between desired course and actual course. The Congress amplifies this signal into some large-scale input of the creation or destruction of purchasing power. Such a 'servo' system will overshoot, as we have seen, and, depending on its structure, may take to 'hunting' its course without ever finding it. In the case of the steering of ships we have some of the oldest 'servo' systems, sometimes with and sometimes without a human link. A rudder is set according to the deviation of the actual course from the changing desired course. If the course is not altered too frequently or too violently and if the mechanism is properly designed, the feedback will produce a good result. 'On the other hand, under certain conditions of delay, etc., a feed-back that is too brusque will make the rudder overshoot, and will be followed by a feed-back in the other direction which makes the rudder overshoot still more, until the steering-mechanism goes into a wild oscillation or *hunting*, and breaks down completely.'[3] The discovery of hunting almost a hundred years ago has led to extensive study of how to avoid it; and the great progress made in the last twenty-five years may be the source of helpful hints, though scarcely more than that, to the economist and statesman.

> It is important to note that this instability is closely related to the time lags in the system. The probability of getting into an unstable situation becomes materially reduced as the reaction time of the rudder to small errors in heading becomes extremely short. The stability can also be increased and errors reduced if the rudder displacement is made proportional to the heading error (proportional control). The behaviour of the system can be improved even further by anticipation control. Anticipation in this application implies that in the setting of the rudder, use is made of the fact that the gyro-compass error is decreasing or increasing; it may go as far as to take into account the actual rate at which the error is increasing or decreasing.[4]

It might be maintained that the problem may easily be solved by a government counter-cyclical policy which was equal but opposite in timing to private investment. Then, it seems, total spending would be constant and the economy would be kept at full employment. In general this is a difficult question to answer, but *if* we have a linear system like the last one, mathematical cycle theory enables us to answer immediately that it is not so. Rigid adherence to a simple cyclically varying government deficit would lead not to the erasure of the cycle but rather to its intensification. In this case we have a driven cycle, analogous to the sunspot hypothesis, and the cycle would follow the spending instead of opposing it, and we would get an exaggerated cycle — indeed, in the case of some cycle models, a cycle of perpetually increasing violence. No doubt the advocates of this policy have in mind a flexible spending adjusted to the actual course of events, but then we are back to the problem of a control theory and it must be analysed as such.

The engineer, observing a machine which functions badly, will set about redesigning its structure in such a way as to alter its behaviour for the better. In the case of unwanted oscillations, this means changing the constants, or even the nature, of the system so that the stability is increased. In our model the stability depends on constants describing the behaviour of consumers and producers — e.g. the slope of supply and demand curves for capital, the marginal propensity to consume, and the acceleration coefficient. If we could alter these behaviour constants in the right way, we could ameliorate the cycle, and if we could alter them at will we could make the economy respond so quickly and smoothly to changes that the cycle would cease to be of any interest. There seems, however, little hope that we can have much effect on the behaviour of people in a free, capitalistic economy, the essence of which is the freedom of people to do whatever they think best for themselves. In socialist or mixed-type economies the situation becomes quite different. The public servant managers may be told to follow some other rules of action. For this policy to be successful in doing away with the cycle, we must have a reasonably complete, quantitative model of the economy; otherwise we shall not be able to calculate the effect of a given change of decision structure. Here again control theory is suggestive. For almost the first time, scientists have been faced with the problem of designing a complicated mechanism which will yield a given desirable performance. This process of *synthesis* is to be contrasted with the classical one of the *analysis* of a given mechanism. Instead of proceeding by trial and error until some acceptable result is achieved, a real start has been made in the problem of saying what the mechanism *must* be, *given* the aims. Econometrics has been concerned mostly with analysis, but in fiscal policy and other methods an approach is being made which really requires the methods of synthesis.

NOTES

1. The basic treatment of this question is to be found in Tinbergen's *Les Fondements mathématiques de la stabilisation du mouvement des affaires* (Paris: Hermann & Cie., 1938).
2. On this point, consult the illuminating discussion by Arthur Smithies, 'Federal Budgeting and Fiscal Policy' in H. S. Ellis (ed.), *A Survey of Contemporary Economics* (Philadelphia, 1949).
3. Reprinted from Norbert Wiener, *Cybernetics*, published by The Technology Press of the Massachusetts Institute of Technology, John Wiley & Sons, Inc., and Hermann & Cie., 1948, p. 14. A more quantitative discussion of the general nature of the problem is given in Chapter IV.
4. I. A. Getting, 'Servo Systems', in H. M. James, N. B. Nichols and R. S. Phillips (eds.), *Theory of Servomechanisms*, M.I.T. Radiation Laboratory Series, p. 3. Courtesy of McGraw-Hill Book Co., New York, 1947.

9. The Problem of Trend and Cycle[1]

YORKSHIRE BULLETIN OF ECONOMIC AND SOCIAL RESEARCH, 1953

No problem in economics is more difficult than the one posed by the almost universal evidence that while capitalist economies grow, they do not expand steadily. On the contrary they sometimes advance rapidly but at other times they stagnate or decline. How are we to handle this delicate and unsolved problem of the mutual conditioning of these two types of behaviour?

The usual answer is simple enough: we have long-run changes in technique, population, etc. which give rise to a trend and we have a short-run dynamic structure which leads to alternating expansions and contractions. These two separate behaviours may be superimposed by simple addition to give the kind of behaviour we actually observe. Yet we are entitled to ask: can we reliably discuss the cycle in ignorance of the fact whether the average level, from one boom to the next, is rising or falling? Or again, would the rate of growth be the same in a planned society, with cycles eliminated, as it would be in an unplanned one with regular periods of depression and unused resources? My impression is that we would have to answer both questions in the negative, and in so doing we would be implicitly condemning the current theories. I shall try to discuss the problem and to indicate briefly a possible way of fusing the two analyses more closely. There is no obvious solution to this question, and I know of only one economist, Schumpeter, who has ever really constructed a unified theory of growth and cycle.

We are all familiar with the nature and problems of the decomposition of economic time series into trend, cycle, seasonal and residuals. This was an important contribution to our understanding of economic reality. While there may be some doubt about the 'removal' of seasonal variation, on balance the concept is clear and fairly acceptable. But as to the 'removal' of trend, the situation is by no means as satisfactory. There are not two clearly separate and identifiable causes, the one producing trend and the other generating a cycle. On the contrary, if we accept Schumpeter's theory, they are one and the same phenomenon. Technological progress, in producing a trend, first generates a boom, and then, as an inevitable consequence, a dislocation which is the depression. He, in fact, gave an emphatically negative answer to the question: would cycles exist in the absence of growth? Yet, if we 'remove' trend, we are implying precisely this.

There is another way of looking at the matter. It is a well-known fact that we may take *any* time series and analyse it into a sum of cycles. To these cycles we cannot, in general, assign any particular causal significance or consider them as evidence of the structure of the mechanism. There is, however, a special case of great importance, that of a *linear* dynamical system, and if we feed into it a time series consisting of, say, two cycles and a trend, then we may analyse its response to each of these separately. Then to get the total response we simply add these separate and independent responses. Each of the motions evolves completely independently of the others. This fact is known as the superposition principle and is a direct consequence of the linearity of the system. Conversely, we may 'decompose', by suitable means, the observed behaviour of such a system into components, and these components may be identified with distinct parts of the input plus the free functioning of the system in the absence of any input. If, by contrast, we have a non-linear system, the superposition principle ceases to hold and neither of these statements follows. In recent years a number of non-linear cycle models have been proposed, for example, by Kalecki, Kaldor, Hicks and myself. If we decompose the behaviour of such a model into trend and cycle, the result must be regarded as purely descriptive and with no identifiable counterpart in the model.

The problem of trend has been relegated to the economic historians for fairly obvious reasons. I am not prepared to deal with the historical aspects, but rather with the question of a theory or possible theories of trend. In classical economics there was a thorough-going, dynamical theory of trend. Essentially it consisted of working out the implications of Malthusianism for wages, profits and rent. As we all know this theory proved inadequate and was superseded by the neoclassical theories of Marshall and others. In this change to a more subtle and complex analytical construction it was generally overlooked that the theory of long-run trend got lost. Granted that any long-run theory is bound to be a pretty weak and shaky affair, still it is most regrettable that modern economists essentially gave up the effort to construct one.

The credit for bringing us back face to face with this problem belongs very largely to Mr Harrod. Beginning with his famous article in the *Economic Journal* for 1939 and continuing with his book on dynamic economics, he has laid out a theory that has at the same time great simplicity and a grand sweep. The Keynesian theory had much to say about what were the consequences of some given level of investment, but it had very little to say about what determined investment. Mr Harrod filled this empty box neatly and elegantly by recalling the acceleration principle, i.e. the assumption that capital stock is proportional to the rate of output. Keynes's vision was directed primarily at short-period analysis, and he certainly did not aim to provide a theory of long-period growth. Mr Harrod thought that he was merely completing the work of his master in this respect, for his original statement of the theory was made in 1937 in a book called *The Trade Cycle*. But, as Professor Tinbergen pointed out in his review, this theory gives rise to a compound interest rate of growth, not to depression, stagnation or cycle. Mr Harrod appears to have accepted this view, for subsequently he restated his theory in terms of long-run growth. Thus almost unintentionally, a startlingly new type of economic theory swam into view — one that was quite different from that elaborated by the 'dismal science' of 150 years ago. The theory received an apparently striking verification in the publication of Kuznets's secular data for the U.S. economy which showed a 10 per cent steady savings ratio for nearly 100 years. This, combined with the evidence for a capital to output ratio of about three to one, and applied to the Harrod formula by Professor Domar, gave a predicted growth rate of slightly above 3 per cent a year, which fits roughly Kuznets's data as well as the educated guesses made by various other economists.

There is, however, a fatal flaw in all this. As Mr Harrod himself has always emphasised, this theory describes not what *does* happen but what *could* happen. Since it takes time — sometimes a very considerable time — to produce capital goods, the future would have to be foreseen perfectly in order to have the capital accumulated in a quantity exactly to match output. But this is not the worst of it: once an error is made, any attempt to get back into adjustment will only lead to further displacement from the proper adjustment. The so called equilibrium path is an unstable one, and thus it corresponds to a pendulum in a vertical position with the weight directly above the suspension point. This position will almost never be realised, and even less will it be held. Thus Mr Harrod's growth curve is most unlikely to be attained, and if attained, will not be maintained.

In spite of its apparent similarity to actual historical trends, we must reject the Harrod growth theory as an explanation of fact. Professor Hicks then stepped in (with his book on the trade cycle) with a very slight modification which meets this objection. Entrepreneurs order capital goods in accordance with already realised sales, so that no perfect foreknowledge is assumed. This trivial change in the timing of events produces a revolutionary alteration in the behaviour; the theory ceases to be one of trend and becomes one of a cycle, and, it should be emphasised, a cycle about a constant level; all growth elements disappear. This rather startling fact is obscured by the Hicksian device of imagining the economy as bouncing back and forth between a rising ceiling and a rising floor. Yet if we look closely we discover that he provides essentially no theory of why these two limits should be growing. The rising average level is generated by long-range, autonomous investment, which is really an unexplained trend. Worse still, the capital goods issuing from this autonomous investment have no function, since induced not autonomous investment provides all the capital needed for the rising levels of output. Thus the rising level of effective demand resulting from the trend in autonomous investment apparently cures a depression by removing excess capacity, but actually this need not happen, since the autonomous spending must be adding to capacity as well as to demand, and the addition to capacity is cumulative to capacity but not to demand. Professor Hicks's work provides a convincing demonstration of the fact that in adapting Mr Harrod's theory to explain fluctuations we lose any explanation of trend.

In practice it is extremely difficult to provide a single theory of both trend and cycle in their interaction. Yet I have always felt that Schumpeter was right that these two fundamental features of historic capitalism are inseparable. Specifically, it is the vigorous boom which does generate the trend, and it is this leap forward into new levels of output which governs the subsequent slump.

I want to sketch briefly a theory which will unite the two aspects. Its central feature consists of the fact that to increase output, we *first* make increased outlays (which inevitably lead to increased demand) and *then* get increased output or supply. It is this essential time structure of capitalism as pointed out long ago by M. Aftalion, which makes smooth progress so difficult, and which explains why we get buoyant markets followed by dislocation and transitional stagnation.

For the propagation of impulses through the economy I propose to go back to an old and well established theory (Lundberg and Metzler), that of stocks of goods, including raw materials, goods in progress and finished goods. The central importance of inventories is easily demonstrated, for example, by the fact that in the American data for 1919–38 in constant prices, in the five expansions of gross national product, an average of 23 per cent went into additions to stocks of goods and in the five contractions 47 per cent came out of such reductions (see M. Abramovitz, *Inventories and Business Cycles*, N.Y., 1950). I shall make the following assumptions: first, plans are made for periods of, say, six months and not altered during the period; second, that production for the next period is set equal to sales this period plus production for stock; third, production for stock is equal to the difference between the desired level of stocks and the actual level; fourth, the desired level of stocks is proportional to sales, i.e. the acceleration principle; fifth, income generation proceeds according to a dynamical multiplier mechanism.

While it is not at all obvious, these assumptions define a mechanism which will almost certainly lead to a cycle. Thus if we have too small stocks, entrepreneurs step up production in the following period enough to fill out their stocks, but as a necessary consequence of their higher rate of production, sales the next period will be higher so that they will fail to achieve sufficient additions to stocks. But, barring extreme cases, they will have partly done so, and hence in subsequent periods they will gradually reduce their deficiency of stocks. When they have finally got enough they will cut production to equal sales, but this will cut sales, which will mean they have too large stocks, and so it goes.

At first the stocks of finished goods will rise, only to fall later as production and sales are cut heavily. The reduction of stocks implies production lower than sales, so that when stocks are finally reduced to the desired level, production must be raised to equal sales. This, however, brings higher sales and necessitates further increases in output and hence the expansion is re-commenced. If this revival carries the economy back up to near the previous high levels of output, then we must bring in the derived demand for fixed capital goods. The orders placed for fixed capital goods may be taken to be equal to the difference between desired stock (proportional to actual sales) and actual stock. The rate of production and hence generation of derived sales will be equal to the orders placed in the previous period, subject to the capacity of the capital goods industry. The net result is to make the system explosive so that the economy advances well beyond the previous peak. The reason for this is that the attempt to remove the discrepancy between actual and desired capital only leads to an accentuation of it, because the first effect is to expand sales and hence to expand desired capital by a multiple. The economy becomes explosive but not wildly so because of the limitations on the achievable rate of production of capital goods, which in turn is due to the existing capacity of the capital goods industry and the limited flow of investible funds. The consequence of this is a large backlog of unfilled orders for capital goods, which in turn means that the boom will last for a considerable time.

At this point it is vital to invoke the fundamental Marshallian distinction between fixed and variable costs. In the later stages of the boom we expand the scale of output, and hence 'fixed' costs cease to be fixed and expand along with variable costs. The most obvious example is fixed-interest debentures, but also we have stable dividend policies, managerial, sales, research and maintenance staffs. All these categories tend to vary with the capacity of firms, not with the short-run level of output. Professor Duesenberry has pointed out that a similar phenomenon occurs with consumers, who expand their hitherto more or less fixed contractual payments for housing, automobiles, education, clubs, etc., payments which cannot be easily contracted in the event of a fall in incomes. In substance, there exists a body of 'fixed' outlays corresponding to the accumulation of 'fixed' capital. Both the capital and the outlays are 'fixed' for a very much longer period in the downward than in the upward direction. This is but a simple application of Marshall's famous principle that the short period is very much shorter for expansions than for contractions.

When, therefore, the economy has finally accumulated enough capital, investment is reduced, sales fall, investment is further reduced and sales fall further. But, whereas investment will be reduced to the same level as in the last depression, sales will not because of the great additions during the boom to the body of the 'fixed' outlays (and hence sales). This then is one half of the picture; a high level of sales once attained will not be entirely lost. The other half of the picture is the explosive effect of the induced investment in fixed capital which invariably occurs in the later stages of the boom. Thus in each swing the economy goes higher than it did previously, but it does not swing back lower than previously, because of the nature of the cost structure.

In this model we thus fuse indissolubly the cycle and the trend. This theory is parallel to but not the same as Schumpeter's, in that it is the boom which generates the trend, and one cannot discuss the one without the other. When output is falling it is falling, and that is all there is to say. There is no such thing as a trend factor which continues to rise right through the depression. Conversely, the cycle would be quite different were it not for these special relations which give rise to the trend.

Therefore we cannot separate out trend and cycle and discuss each independently.

In my analysis I have started with a cycle and shown that this model will tend to drift in the upward direction. This gives the appearance of according to the cycle a logical priority over the trend. In part this is so, and it comes out in the fact that the cycle could exist without the trend, but not vice versa. We can, however, begin the other way round and emphasise the close interdependance of the two types of behaviour.

Consider a Harrod type growth process; because of physical limitations (output per man hour and number of man hours), it is impossible for output to grow at greater than some given rate. What is possible is growth at some lesser rate. This means that sooner or later the output gets below its maximum value. This permits subsequently a growth rate greater than can be maintained in the long run. For example, accumulation may proceed at a 10 per cent rate for a while until full employment is reached, after which it can only grow at, say, 3 per cent. But, as Mr Harrod long ago pointed out, this situation cannot continue, so that we get a reduction in investment, a fall instead of a rise in output and a rapid extinction of all fixed capital investment. Then the inventory process takes over, and we get first excessive stocks and then their gradual elimination. When this is completed output rises and we are off again with a new boom.

As the fixed capital accelerator takes hold we are again in a Harrod growth process at a greater rate than can be maintained. We ride upward beyond the previous peak because of increases in output per man hour and in man hours. Upon reaching full employment we again turn down, but this time the same low level of gross investment corresponds to a higher level of effective demand, so that just as the peak is higher than last time, so also will be the trough. Thus we have shown that following a trend will lead to difficulties, and these difficulties entail downturn and reversal with renewed pursuit of the general upward drift. Thus we may say that the trend will generate a cycle just as easily as that the cycle will create a trend.

From this model we can gather some insight into the anomalous behaviour of the aggregative savings function as revealed by the researches of Professor Kuznets. In his data for 1919–38 he found a marginal propensity to save in the neighbourhood of one-half along with a negative intercept. By contrast in his long-run data, 1869–1938, he found a marginal and average propensity to save of around one-tenth. The key to this apparent contradiction lies in the fact that the secular data refer to decades and hence cover approximately one full cycle each. In a cycle we have both investment and disinvestment, which tend to cancel when summed. Thus if we had a cycle without growth, we would find zero marginal and average propensity to save over a whole decade, even though from year to year any variation in incomes would be half saved. It is precisely in the drift upward from one cycle level to the next that we get net accumulation (saving) over a cycle. Here the Harrod considerations hold, i.e. how far upward has the economy risen in ten years, how great an accumulation of capital is required for this, and what proportion of total output has gone into capital formation? All this does not give us any indication about the short-run savings function, nor does it, by itself, explain why what did happen did in fact happen.

I do not propose to say much about the vital factor of technological progress. For one thing there is probably very little that economists have to say about it. Its incidence serves to strengthen and enrich the foregoing analysis. To have innovational (Schumpeterian) investment it is not necessary to have less than the desired amount of capital. Therefore under the favourable conditions of rising sales, we will tend to get investment in fixed capital at an earlier stage than would be the case with induced investment only. This makes the expansion more vigorous, and carries it both further and faster. If the outlays incidental to innovations are small we will get a weak expansion, if large, a strong one. The magnitude of innovational outlays undoubtedly varies from cycle to cycle, and in this way we may explain the great differences between the behaviour of individual cycles. By this fact we also explain the variations in the realised rates of secular expansion.

Appendix

The essential suggestion embodied in the rather composite model I have proposed here is that we take a simple cyclical structure, one which would by itself be slightly damped, and give it a favourable, strong shock about mid-way in each boom. This will render the model explosive but will not by itself introduce any trend. Then we add the Marshall effect, which means that the downswing will be each time of approximately the same size measured from the peak. This, combined with the explosiveness, which implies each peak higher than the last, means that each cycle unfolds itself at a higher average level than the last one.

Specifically, our cycle model consists of a sales equation,

$$w_t = \alpha u_t + z_t, \tag{1}$$

where w is sales, α the marginal propensity to consume, u the output (and income), and z all sales not determined by the level of output (including sales resulting from induced investment, to be discussed below). Second, there is a production equation, consisting of production for sales and production for stocks,

$$u_{t+1} = w_t + (\mu w_t - s_t), \tag{2}$$

where s is stocks and μ is the desired ratio of stocks to output. From (2) we get

$$\Delta u_{t+1} = (1+\mu)\,\Delta w_t - \Delta s_t, \tag{2a}$$

and, by definition,

$$\Delta s_t = u_t - w_t, \tag{3}$$

so that

$$\Delta u_{t+1} = (1+\mu)\,\Delta w_t - u_t + w_t.$$

We may eliminate w by substituting from (1), giving

$$\Delta u_{t+1} = (1+\mu)\,\alpha\Delta u_t - (1-\alpha)u_t + z_t + (1+\mu)\,\Delta z_t. \tag{4}$$

For a constant z we may plot Δu against u and draw a straight line equal to $(1-\alpha)\,u + z$. Given any initial u and its increase from the previous period, Δu_t, we multiply the latter by $(1+\mu)\,\alpha$ and plot this height above u_t. The difference between the point and the line will be Δu_{t+1}, so that by a simple 45° line we get u_{t+1}. Now we repeat the process and thus generate the evolution of the economy.

This simple behaviour is then complicated in two ways. First somewhere in the course of the upswing we cease to have excess capacity

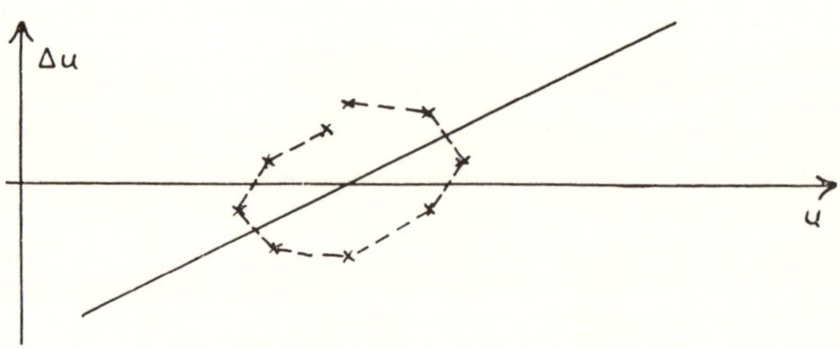

FIGURE 9.1

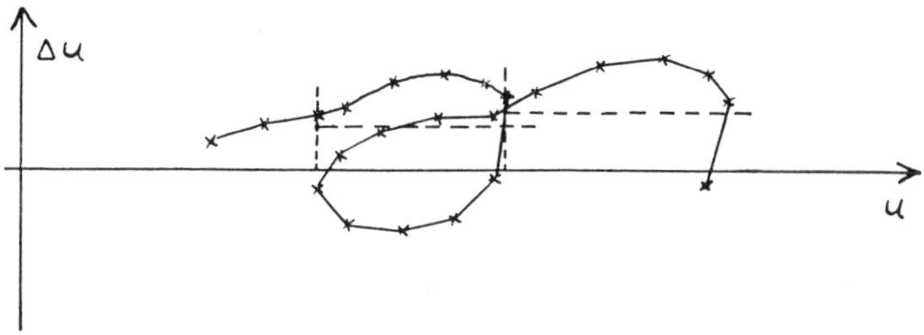

FIGURE 9.2

and thus we must add the amount of induced investment in fixed capital. This will ordinarily be subject to a maximum rate of output of fixed capital and this maximum will quickly be reached. Therefore we may make a reasonable approximation to the behaviour by adding a constant, represented by the upper dotted line in the figure, to the induced investment in stocks. Similarly we may subtract a smaller constant in the downswing. The second complication is that our straight line will shift to the right in the latter part of the boom (fixed outlays accumulating as does the fixed capital), but will not shift back appreciably in the depression. The downswing and early upturn are like those of a linear cycle, but after that we have the impressed investment outlays which determine the vigour and duration of the boom on quite different principles from those of a simple harmonic model. Depending on the assumptions, the boom may be prolonged to any extent, and it is this prolongation which generates the trend. Although there is an identifiable cyclical structure, we cannot say that we have a cycle added to a trend. There would be no growth without a cycle, although the converse is not necessarily true. Indeed for a weak cycle there exists a 'dead region' in which the motion would slowly die out, in the absence of disturbances. In this case it would require something like a war or Schumpeterian innovations to re-excite the self-sustaining oscillations of the system.

NOTES

1. This paper was presented to the University of Leeds Economics Seminar at Grantley Hall on 15 March 1953, and in French at the Institut de Science Economique Appliquée on 14 April and was printed in French in *Economie Appliquée*.

10. A Model of Cyclical Growth

THE BUSINESS CYCLE IN THE POST-WAR WORLD, 1955, ED. E. LUNDBERG

I. Interrelations of Growth and Cycle

My primary concern in this paper is with the simultaneous existence and mutual conditioning of economic growth and economic cycles. It is clearly desirable to have one theory that encompasses both or, at least, to have a more intimate union of the two analyses than is ordinarily effected. It may be argued that this is too ambitious an aim and, in the light of the difficulties that I have encountered, I am inclined to agree. It is better to isolate problems and attack them one by one. Yet, in this particular case, I feel that there are strong reasons to doubt the soundness of analysing on the one hand steady development and on the other stationary cycles. It may well be that many of the serious difficulties of each, considered separately, will yield to a combined attack. But to achieve an advance in this direction we must pay a price, and the price is the abandonment of all but the crudest elements of economic theory.

We all know of the nature and problems of the decomposition of time series into trend, cycles and residuals. The great pioneer work in this field has improved our understanding and has been crucial in establishing the existence of a 'cycle' problem. At the same time, however, there is a danger that the 'removal' of trend will give us a false picture of reality. Worse still, in terms of some of the models developed by Kalecki, Kaldor, Tinbergen, Hicks and myself, it is definitely not permissible. In the case of a linear system, by virtue of what is known as the superposition theorem, we may analyse all sorts of motions, e.g. trends, cycles, impulses, steady levels, etc., one at a time, and simply add the results to get the correct total behaviour. Or conversely we may 'decompose', by spectrum analysis or any other method, the observed behaviour into its independent parts. For a non-linear system the theorem does not hold, and decomposition is invalid, how invalid depending, of course, on the structure of the system. It remains to be established empirically that there are important non-linearities in the economy, but, for the time being, we must, I think, regard with grave misgiving the removal of trend, since this might remove much of the real problem.

The issue has been stated clearly by Mr Harrod in his two articles in the *Economic Journal*[1] and in his *Dynamic Economics*.[2] He holds that the same theory must explain both growth and cycle, but it is, I think, fair to say that few have been convinced that he has provided such a theory. As Professor Tinbergen remarked in his review of Harrod's *Trade Cycle*[3] the multiplier–accelerator combination, considered simply, gives rise to an exponential trend, not a cycle. In effect, Mr Harrod seems to have felt this too, for he has not, since then, attempted an explicit cycle theory. In Professor Hicks's *Trade Cycle*,[4] we see how difficult is the problem, for in elaborating the Harrod theory into a cycle model he loses the theory of the trend in all but a trivial sense. Professor Hicks gets a trend by putting in an exponential autonomous investment, but this trend is unrelated to required capital or indeed to anything except the necessity to get a trend. It is true that this meets Mr Harrod's strictures against the models of the type of Kalecki or Hansen–Samuelson, but these can always be transformed into oscillations about a trend, by inserting a trend as a function of time. And this separation of trend and cycle is justified *if* reality is approximately linear. One should add, however, that the trend is not really explained if we merely apply a rising trend factor to our model. Evidently it is more difficult than Mr Harrod concedes to construct a single theory which will explain both.

II. Schumpeter's Theory of Growth and Cycle

In order to fuse growth and cycle unalterably we may make the following two assumptions: (*a*) economic progress is not steady but comes in spurts, these spurts occurring primarily in the booms; (*b*) the cycle is not a case of over- and under-shooting of a stationary level, but rather it is dominated by—and possibly would not exist without—economic growth. The source of these two assumptions is Schumpeter and, in my opinion, it is in his work that we shall find the most fruitful ideas for the analysis of the problem of trend and cycle. He was surely correct in saying that *the* essential element in the theory must be the occurrence of revolutionary advances in technique. It is not that Schumpeter is the only one to hold these views — one has only to think of Wicksell or Professor Robertson amongst others — but he has the most fully developed and integrated theory, and it is with his way of thinking that I am most familiar. Also basic, but not quite so fundamental, is growth in the labour force. By itself, population increase will not suffice, as is amply illustrated, e.g. in Ireland or China, but in conjunction with (and in some very complex way caused by) technical improvement it is a powerful driving force.

Schumpeter's theory, as he often complained, is difficult to formulate in simple mathematical terms. Therefore such use as I shall make of it may seem rather a caricature, and definitely requires supplementing by reference to his own exposition and rich illustration of it. Beyond this I cannot follow him in his rejection of the Keynesian effective demand analysis. There seems no obvious reason why this important tool should not be used to strengthen his system, though he always rejected its assistance in forcible terms. By incorporating effective demand it is possible to lessen the excessive strain that is put on his special theory of the innovational process. Essentially he places *the* explanation of the cycle on the internal dynamics of successful innovation, subsequent imitation and consequent exhaustion of the new combinations. It may sometimes be so, but that it has always been so over more than 150 years is difficult to accept. If, on the contrary, we emphasise the mutual conditioning of innovating and the state of trade, it becomes relatively plausible, indeed almost inevitable, that innovations will be carried out in swarms.

Schumpeter's original, pure theory can be put simply: 'The recurring periods of prosperity of the cyclical movement are the form progress takes in capitalist society.'[5] Throughout his many vagaries in elaborating this schema in historical, statistical and theoretical directions he never abandoned this central part of his 'vision' of capitalist reality. He thus fused into an organic whole the concepts of growth and cycle, and implied that the one could not exist without the other. The vital necessity of this view has been obscured in recent years because of the widespread preoccupation with the Keynesian system, but second thoughts, prompted both by Mr Harrod's speculations and by the discovery of awkward statistical material, have brought us again face to face with a longer run reality in which Schumpeterian concepts are bound to play a central rôle. This is not to say, however, that we are back where we were before *The General Theory*. It has always seemed to me that the theories of effective demand and liquidity preference could be used to bring greatly enhanced usefulness to Schumpeter's theory, but it is plain that he would have none of it.

III. The Essential Features of a Model

To make quite sharp the essential point of the Schumpeterian theory, we may construct a simple model which, it should be emphasised, is not designed to do justice either to his schema or to economic reality. We assume a curve $p(k)$ of present value of all known capital projects as a function of the quantity of capital, k. Correspondingly, there is a curve, $s(\dot{k})$, giving the supply price of new capital as a function of the rate of net output of new capital, $\dot{k}$. Given competitive entrepreneurs, these two will be brought into equality, and the dynamic evolution of the system determined. The special feature of Schumpeter's thought can be represented by putting a hook in the curve $s(\dot{k})$, as shown in FIGURE 10.1. There is a range of neutral equilibria between A and B, but the system is stable, for if the price and quantity were above or below this range they would tend to return to it. There is no oscillation. If we now introduce steady progress in the simplest form by assuming a regular rate of shift to the right $p(k)$ we get a very different result. The profitable opportunities increase, but for all the reasons which Schumpeter has so vividly described nothing is done until they are potentially so high $(B-A)$ that an innovator successfully carries out a new combination. The path being opened, he is followed by many with a burst of investment at a rate F slowly declining to E. Then net investment ceases, and we again slowly accumulate investment possibilities as the present value rises slowly to B, at which point the barrier is again broken and we jump to C and so forth. If the steady advance is such as to require a rate of accumulation between O and E this process will continue indefinitely. In this case the

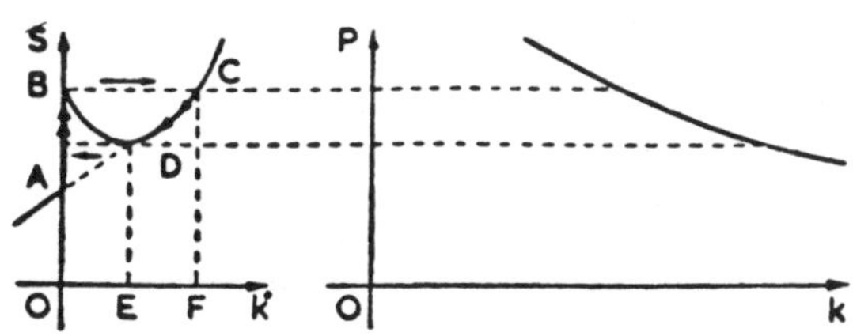

FIGURE 10.1

growth is the explanation of the cycle, and the latter would not exist without the former. Here we see quite clearly that it would be totally inadmissible to draw a trend line through the resulting time series and 'remove' it. The resulting cyclical appearance would correspond to no structural reality, and if we attempted to set up a model to explain it we would be talking nonsense.

In the physical sciences, whenever a steady source to an apparatus results in a fluctuating output, it has always been found that there is a non-linearity somewhere. This gives us a clue as to a technical requirement of the Schumpeterian theory, for we have a steady growth in ideas giving rise to bursts of investment and increases in output. In the preceding example the non-linearity is the hook in $s(\dot{k})$, and a somewhat different one will figure prominently in the model to be described below. It is not always necessary that there be growth to generate the oscillation. Thus a piece of chalk will only screech if moved across the blackboard, but an electric bell will ring about a stationary position; but both are non-linear oscillators and their difference is not fundamental.

The model to be presented below will be readily seen to be unsuitable for statistical testing. Rather is it analogous to the economy, and is meant to suggest the kind of development that goes on without, however, being able to take account of the rich complexities of what actually happens. There is general agreement that we need further investigation of hypotheses to be tested, and further testing of these, and that both activities are essential. I have endeavoured, in so far as possible, to keep to quantities that are potentially measurable.

IV. The Historical Validity of the Model

Once progress is admitted on the ground floor of a theory the awkward question arises about the historical validity of the system. The relevance and usefulness of economic theory to economic history has been small. If anything, business cycle theory has done better than some other branches. The situation becomes more serious the moment we restrict ourselves to a theory simple enough to be written down in a few equations. To imagine any connection between such a model and economic history seems grotesque, and yet, if there is no relation, there seems little use in constructing it.

To my mind there is no doubt that the special circumstances of each cycle and of each country seriously alter the character of the fluctuations. By seriously I mean gross distortion, so that a true cycle cannot really be said to exist, and can scarcely, if at all, be detected by screening the statistics. Some sort of alternation there is, but clearly there is no strict periodicity, and there may not be enough of a tendency to regular recurrence to allow us to speak of a cycle.

The fact that this tendency to alternation in levels of economic activity has appeared more or less uniformly in all advanced capitalist countries argues that there is some typical set of relations which would tend, in the absence of disturbance, to produce a regular cycle. The degree of uniformity, in the midst of all the tremendous changes of the past century, is as striking a fact as the lack of uniformity. There must be basic features of capitalism which will explain why these fluctuations have appeared in so many different countries over such long periods. It is these features which we must seek to isolate by ingenuity and perspicacity, even though they are hidden by the stormy history of capitalism. These elements must be capable by themselves of producing a cycle, and they will explain what uniformity there is in cycle after cycle. But any such theory must have many 'open ends' through which we may insert the impact of historically given events, which will explain the enormous variability and irregularity of the cycle. Thus it is not that we can expect any simple, mathematical model to explain the wave-like character of economic history, but rather merely to explain the remarkable fact that there is some degree of uniformity in the otherwise unique course of development.

V. The Structure and Functioning of the Model

First, we may go over in outline the structure and functioning of the model. The indispensable growth elements are improvements in techniques and the increase in the labour force, both of which are taken as given and more or less continuously growing. Innovational investment characteristically does not require increased output but, on the other hand, both greater employment and greater productivity mean larger output which will, with given techniques, call for more capital. The possibility of greater output is not the same as its realisation, and for the answer to this we appeal to the Kahn–Keynes multiplier. The existence of a cycle means that aggregate demand is not always adequate to realise the full productive capacities of capitalism, and at first sight we might be tempted to wonder that they are ever realised. In general, new techniques require heavy investment outlays which swell demand, so that both the increased output per labourer and the increased number of labourers are absorbed. When the economy has achieved its new higher levels of output and capital it cannot hold them, because the great burst of investment (both innovational and accelerational) is necessary to create the effective demand, and, when it ceases, demand and output drop, thus creating unemployed capital and unemployed labour. Therefore we have a dynamic, but not a static, breakdown theory. Just as output rises each time to new heights, it also does not fall to its previous low, because the expansion generates fixed outlays which break the fall at higher levels on each swing. The revival awaits the accumulation of sufficient pressure for innovational investment. In the first approximation no lags are introduced, with the result that we have a two-phase cycle, full employment and deep depression. It is assumed throughout that the structural coefficients are such as to give explosive behaviour. Therefore investment, once begun, carries the economy to full employment, and this upper limit rises rapidly with the accumulation of capital, which allows the realisation of the technological advance.

In simple terms the economy is strongly expansionist in both output and demand. It is always straining to get to the full employment limit, but, by the mere fact of being there for a time, it is projected downward again. To think of a mechanical analogy, we may picture a gas-filled balloon underneath a stairway. A slight draught carries it steadily forward and it rises until it hits the ceiling, but then it bumps downward. After a time it begins to rise again, yet, having moved forward, it now passes the old level and rises until it hits the bottom of the next step. Thus it is essentially non-oscillatory, but is converted, by successive steps, into an intermittent upward drift. The central feature of the analogy is the parallelism between stair steps and full employment ceilings: it is these limits which control the character of the growth. It seems to me that full employment must, in some fairly intimate manner, guide the long-range behaviour of the model, otherwise it is difficult to see why we would not find that the model would predict, after a time, a cycle around a level of 50 or 150 per cent of full employment, which is unrealistic. The concept of full employment I employ uncritically, and I do not think the many reservations required make any serious difficulties.

Throughout the argument capital stock will be taken as the central explanatory variable. Since the behaviour of capital is taken to be the main feature of the cycle this seems logical. The reason why I have not followed Professor Hicks and Mr Harrod in taking income as the dependent variable, is that once we break the simple proportionality between capital and income, the behaviour of income no longer tells us anything conclusive about the behaviour of investment. To see this we must juxtapose actual stock to the desired stock of capital, and in view of this it seems preferable to work throughout with capital stock. Upon doing this we quickly realise how utterly hopeless it is to explain the lower turning point in terms of the necessity for replacement of a wasting capital stock.

There are more serious objections against the use of the quantity of capital than against the use of the quantity of output. Capital has never been satisfactorily defined quantitatively, and it is doubtful whether we can attach any useful meaning to the concept of variations in the stock of capital. However, at the cruder level of approach used here there is perhaps no very serious objection. Capital is taken to mean the stock of equipment, in the broadest sense, that is used in production, so that an increase in output calls for more capital, and a decrease for less. It is useful to pretend that capital stock is the sum of all past net investments, but since it is output and not capital that really matters, we need not worry if the resulting quantity of capital is partly fictitious. This problem arises sharply in the case of innovational investment which, in our system, means an unequivocal addition to capital stock. But our crude aggregative model ignores the fact that innovational investment also destroys capital, so that in fact we cannot be sure whether there has been an increase or a decrease.

Throughout I shall use the 'flexible accelerator' as the explanatory principle for investment. I have described it in my contribution to *Income, Employment and Public Policy: Essays in Honor of Alvin H. Hansen*,[6] and more recently it has been discussed, with supporting evidence, by Dr Chenery.[7] According to this principle, net investment will be undertaken as long as desired capital is greater than existing capital, and disinvestment in the contrary case. Desired capital, ξ, I shall assume to be determined by

$$\xi = vy + \beta(t), \tag{1}$$

where v is the acceleration coefficient, y is output, and $\beta(t)$ is a parameter to be associated primarily with changes in technique. Thus innovation means that more capital is desired with a given output, and the accelerator means more capital is desired only with increased output.

It is to be noted that, even if we ignore $\beta(t)$, this is not the acceleration principle, which assumes a perfect adjustment of capital to output at all times. On the contrary, it is assumed here that with a given stock of capital we can produce more (by overtime etc.) than it was designed to produce, and, obviously, also less. Furthermore, in designed capacity, there is usually some stand-by or peak-load capacity which can be used. The point is that this high-level operation involves higher variable costs, strain on staff and equipment, delays, etc., all of which create pressure to expand capital and capacity. Therefore the short run is characterised by a failure to exemplify the acceleration principle, but it is also dominated by efforts to attain the accelerational quantity of capital. The assumption here is that entrepreneurs behave on homeostatic principles as exemplified by automatic control mechanisms. We sidestep the question of expectations, although the rate at which investment proceeds in response to a given excess or deficiency of capital is a kind of measure of confidence in the continuation of current rates of output.

For the sake of simplicity, we assume that the pressure to expand is proportional to the difference between ξ and k, subject to two crucial non-linearities. The lower one is set by the rate of wastage of capital at zero gross investment, and the upper one by the maximum output of new capital goods obtainable with given capital and labour supply. The picture is as drawn in FIGURE 10.2, and we may write it for convenience as,

$$g(\dot{k}) = \xi - k. \tag{2}$$

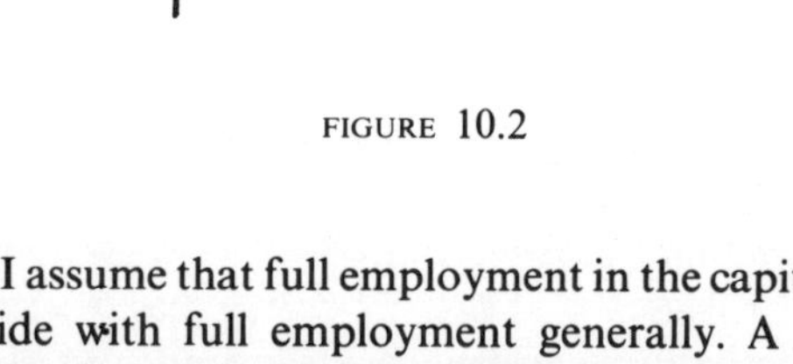

FIGURE 10.2

Beyond this, I assume that full employment in the capital goods trades tends to coincide with full employment generally. A little reflection shows that it must be so, else we should either never attain full employment, or else have violent inflation in all booms. In general this result may come about in the following way: as the boom proceeds we may tend to hit capacity limits in the instrumental trades before general full employment; these trades, facing a backlog in any case, will divert some of their output to enlarging their own capacity; this process will continue so long as there is unemployed labour available. Thus we arrive, if not initially, finally, at simultaneous full capacity output in both producers' and consumers' goods industries. Beyond this point it is dangerous for the former to go, since it would mean sharply rising costs along with falling output in consumption goods. There is a tendency to moderate inflation in most booms, and it could be assumed that the maximum output in durable goods lies slightly above the general limit so that the investment trades often try to bid resources away from the others.

If this relation between capital goods output and general output is to be maintained it follows that, with full employment, further growth in output must be split between the two in the proportion given by the secular multiplier. Thus, if the multiplier is 5, a rise of 10 in total output will include a rise of 2 in the output of new capital. The assumption is clearly necessary to the proper functioning of the model, but it is bound to appear somewhat arbitrary unless we assume some equilibrating mechanism behind the scenes.

There remains the stimulating question whether or not innovations, which continually increase the amount of desired capital, raise the acceleration coefficient. My own inclination has always been to assume that the coefficient is increased, and I owe to the persuasive analysis of Mr Harrod[8] and Mrs Robinson[9] my present strong doubts on this score. The point is that new methods of production almost always require additions to capital stock, but they also destroy capital, sometimes by making it obsolete, sometimes by reducing the cost of replacing it. Therefore we may be continually adding to our capital autonomously but find that, after many years, a routine addition to output requires the same addition to capital stock as before.

In the absence of any information, or grounds for believing one effect or the other to predominate, it is simplest to assume that the acceleration coefficient v remains unchanged, and this I shall do. It seems much better not to lump this problem with the much more identifiable one of whether or not innovations are capital using or capital saving. Whereas Mr Harrod defines capital using in terms of v,[10] I prefer to define it in terms of the increase or decrease of $\beta(t)$. The important point is 'that major innovations and also many minor ones entail construction of new plant (and equipment). . . .'[11] The fact that net investment with constant output need not make industry 'more capitalistic' is only paradoxical, because we are dealing with aggregates which suppress all structural interdependence.

To incorporate a theory of effective demand and the generation of income, we may follow well-established Keynesian lines and write

$$y = f(\dot{k} + \gamma(t)), \tag{3}$$

where $\gamma(t)$ is 'public spending' suitably defined, and everything is in constant prices. I shall not discuss government anti-cyclical policy, and hence I shall suppress $\gamma(t)$, but the reader will find no difficulty in introducing it.

The slope of this function is the multiplier, and its inverse is the aggregate savings function (all lags are ignored and the equality of savings and investment is assumed). The uniqueness of this function has been one of the first central Keynesian doctrines to waver. Following Professor Duesenberry[12] we may represent the shape of this function as in FIGURE 10.3. When going down we follow the steeper slope, and only when we venture again into new, higher ranges of income does saving again grow only slowly. The necessity for some such contrast between short- and long-run phenomena is clear, but the explanation of this anomalous savings function is not quite so well established.

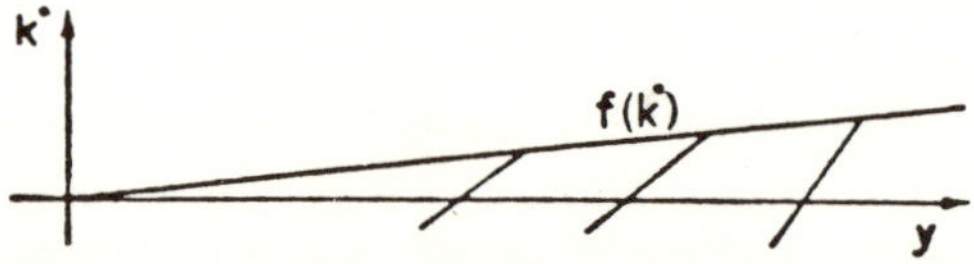

FIGURE 10.3

Professor Duesenberry has advanced an ingenious explanation, and I should like to suggest some further considerations which also may help. Fundamentally, it may be an expression of the familiar Marshallian distinction between the long and the short period. The long period is much longer in the downward than in the upward direction. Thus, as the scale of output is expanded, all outlays go up easily, but a part of them 'freeze' and become 'fixed' and cease to be quickly reducible in the event of a fall in output. We can think not only of 'fixed' interest but stable dividend policies, irreducible managerial, maintenance, sales and research staffs. Many workers also are not discharged, but many are and cease to be a cost to the firm. But to society they remain a fixed charge, and they continue to consume, though at a lower rate, whether through savings, charity, credit or public relief. Similarly, as Professor Duesenberry has shown, the consumer finds that his outlay is fairly easily variable in the upward direction, but is awkwardly rigid downward. In the long run, this would cease to be so. Finally, it is almost a law of political science, as well as a political slogan, that government outlays expand easily but resist contraction to an extraordinary degree. A related though distinct phenomenon is the fact, stressed by Mrs Robinson,[13] that in the early stages of the boom there is a large increase in output before there is much increase in capacity, leading to large profits which are mostly saved. As the prosperity continues the accumulation of capital may lead to a fall in profits and hence in savings. This could generate the kind of savings function shown in FIGURE 10.3, for in depression there is no significant decumulation, and hence the savings function will not be reversible. Here again aggregates conceal the real problem, for we must appeal to a classical competitive behaviour to explain why entrepreneurs undertake investment which *lowers* profits.

VI. The Complete Model

We are now in a position to assemble the various parts into a working model. Combining equations (1), (2) and (3) we get

$$\xi - k = vf(\dot{k}) + \beta(t) - k = g(\dot{k}),$$

or, rearranging,

$$k = vf(\dot{k}) - g(\dot{k}) + \beta(t). \tag{4}$$

The function $vf(\dot{k})$ is the same as $f(\dot{k})$ only much flatter, and therefore the situation at any point of time is as shown in FIGURE 10.4.

If we subtract $g(\dot{k})$ from $vf(\dot{k})$, call it $\phi(\dot{k})$, and add $\beta(t)$ to it, we get the result shown in FIGURE 10.5. It is evident that an increase in $\beta(t)$ simply

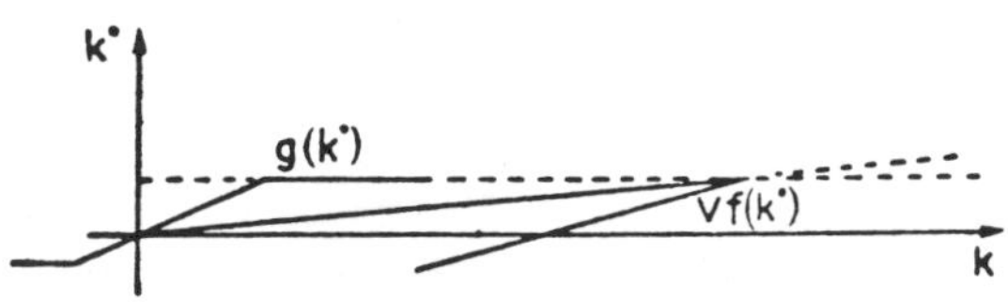

FIGURE 10.4

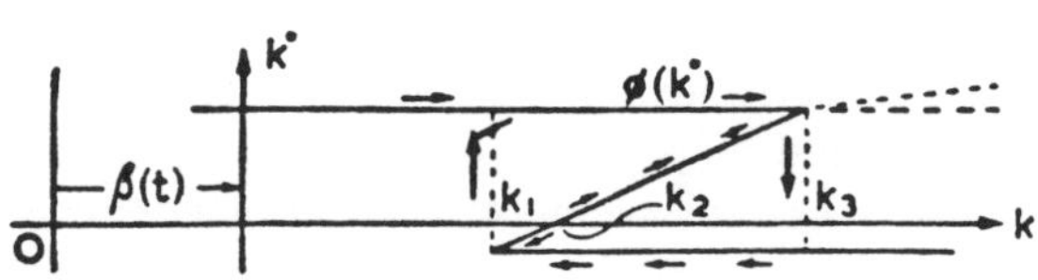

FIGURE 10.5

shifts the $\phi(\dot{k})$ curve to the right. All our relations are satisfied if we remain on the curve. All lags have been abstracted from in the interest of simplicity, and with the conviction that these are of secondary rather than of primary importance for the cycle.

To begin with, let us consider the case of a completely unprogressive economy with $\beta(t)$ constant, no increases in productivity and no growth in the labour force. If we begin at the upturn, we have capital k_1, and start accumulating at the peak rate. This means peak output, and a much larger amount of capital is desired than the existing stock. The capital goods fill this backlog at the maximum attainable rate until we reach the amount k_3. At this point entrepreneurs would begin to slacken in their rate of new investment, but this proves impossible because the more they slacken the investment the lower is income and output, and hence the lower is desired capital by a multiple. There is no feasible position short of zero gross investment, below which point they cannot go and to which they instantaneously jump. This instantaneous jump from full boom to deep depression is a direct consequence of abstracting from lags, and we shall at a later point drop this assumption.

In consequence of zero gross investment output is now low, and the existing stock of capital, k_3, is greatly in excess of desired capital. Capital is now decumulated at the maximum possible rate until k_1 is reached, and then the process is begun all over again. If, as a result of a war or some such large disturbance, capital is slightly in excess of the equilibrium amount, k_2, and combined with a low rate of net investment, we get an accelerated rise to k_3. This behaviour corresponds rather closely to the familiar 'multiplier–accelerator process', but it is executed by this model only under exceptional circumstances.

The model is completely unrealistic in its depression behaviour. Even under favourable circumstances it would remain depressed much longer than in boom. The curve of FIGURE 10.5 probably much over-estimates any actually achieved rate of physical wastage of capital assets. Our model identifies two things which are in fact not the same. Zero gross investment means the non-spending of depreciation allowances, and hence determines the lower level of income as represented. But unfortunately this does not represent actual disappearance of capital goods, especially since, following a boom, their age composition will be abnormal and actual disappearance quite small. Some reduction there will be, and also a general ageing which will be conducive to investment, but these effects will be weak. It should be admitted that this is a shortcoming both in this model and in that of Professor Hicks.

VII. The Sources of Growth

There are two sources of growth and these may be conveniently considered in turn. In the first place there is the rise in the full employment level, both because the size of the labour force increases and because the productivity of labour rises through innovation. The organic connection between cycle and trend will be most sharply emphasised if we assume that all growth in the full employment ceiling occurs only during booms. Thus, at the end of a depression there will have been some attrition in capital stock, but this may be roughly counterbalanced by the growth in the labour stock, so that we may plausibly assume that the full employment level is about the same at the end of the depression as it was at the beginning. In the ensuing boom full employment output may rise rapidly, because the capital is being accumulated to equip with newest techniques the expanded labour force. But this output rises above the previous peak and carries us into the range of the large secular multiplier. This time the acceleration coefficient gives us the large additions to desired capital which the rising output entails. The achieved rate of rise in full employment output, say of 4 or 5 per cent per year, fixes the rate of growth of desired capital, and this, in combination with the slowly accelerating capital stock, determines the length of the boom.

If we continue along the top horizontal curve we eventually reach the termination of the boom. With secular progress the full employment limit rises, and the peak output of capital goods rises in a fixed proportion to it. This means that the flat top to $\phi(\dot{k})$ slowly rises which raises the required capital and prolongs the boom. Therefore we move along a horizontal curve which is steadily rising, so that in fact we follow a slowly rising curve as is shown in FIGURE 10.6. This postpones, but does not avoid, the final accumulation of sufficient capital to induce a slackening of investment and the consequent end to the boom. Whereas the boom is prolonged, the slump is shortened, because the 'fixed' outlays

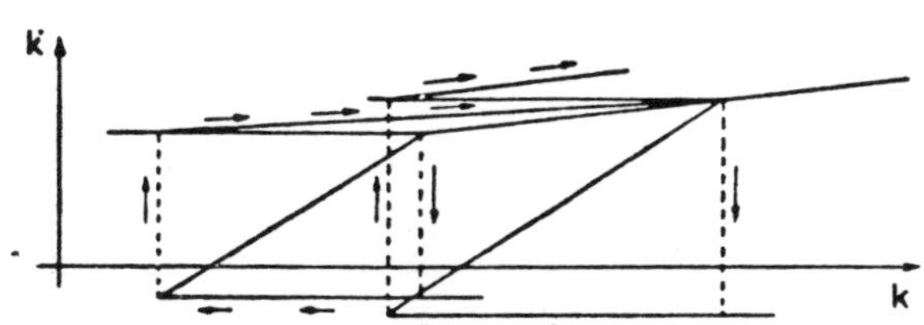

FIGURE 10.6

which have become swollen during the boom now place a higher 'floor' to output, and hence to desired capital. Therefore it is not necessary to carry out the absurdly unrealistic task of decumulating, by wear and tear, all of the capital accumulated during the preceding boom. It remains true, however, that realistic figures still give a depression that lasts longer than the boom.

The economy surges forward and plunges down, but it does not go back to its old low. There is no 'progress' during depression: it all occurs during the boom, or at least it is all 'realised' during the boom. Therefore there would be no meaning to drawing any smooth trend line through the time series of national income. Finally, it should be noted that secular growth takes place without any autonomous or innovational outlays.

We have already taken account of the results of innovation in increasing productivity; it remains only to include the fact that they ordinarily mean additional investment outlay. We therefore allow $\beta(t)$ to rise, more or less smoothly, which implies that there has been in capitalism a continuous stream of ideas for new methods of production which have required additional capital outlays. These may occur slowly at some times and rapidly at others, but $\beta(t)$, being the resultant of many small events cumulated, is likely to be fairly continuous.

Making no more definite assumptions than this we get the Schumpeterian result that the steady accumulation of potential 'new combinations' is converted into bursts of development which eventually exhaust themselves and relax into depressions. They may sometimes come as a result of his isolated, pioneer entrepreneur, but they need not. In this way we make a closer mutual conditioning between the state of trade and innovating activity.

The effect of a steadily rising $\beta(t)$ is a steady shifting of the $\phi(\dot{k})$ curve to the right. Thus it is not necessary to await the slow wasting of capital, for desired capital rises to overtake the existing stock. Therefore, depending on the given historical rapidity of growth of new methods of production, the depression may be so short as to amount only to a 'crisis', or it may drag on for many years awaiting significant technological advance. Contrariwise, the advance of $\beta(t)$ postpones the end of the boom by increasing capital requirements, so that under favourable conditions the boom may be much lengthened. Since the model, like capitalism itself, is dominated by vigorous growth, we may use variations in $\beta(t)$ to account for, in part at least, the enormous variation from cycle to cycle and country to country. Thus we can account for snap depressions such as that of 1907, or prolonged stagnation as in the 1870s or 1930s. Again, a long boom such as that of the 1920s can be fitted in. The current post-war boom can be explained by the steady accumulation of possibilities during the great depression and the war, and by the length of time needed to accumulate the capital to exploit these as well as to equip the considerably increased labour force.

A questionable feature of this model lies in the fact that it lumps together the accelerational and the innovational demands for new capital. Yet this has much to recommend it, for new methods and forms of capital will be most readily installed when rising demand requires additional capital in any case. Probably most new types of capital are installed during booms, and so innovational investment is hopelessly mixed with accelerational investment. Also, while not necessary, a high and rising demand is favourable to innovational outlays.

VIII. The Lower Turning Point

Even allowing for the vigorously expansionist nature of capitalism, the lower turning point remains a difficulty for a model built solely on capital requirements. There are numerous factors which alleviate the problem and I shall allude to three. Throughout we have taken no account of the distinction between working and fixed capital. As is well known there is no serious technical limit to the rate of disinvestment in the former, and hence the excessive stock of working capital may be quickly dissipated. As has been shown by Professors Lundberg[14] and Metzler[15] this leads to a rise in investment and output. The resultant increase in desired capital may well ignite a general boom much earlier than we would expect from the 'fixed' capital model. Second, as has been pointed out by Mr Harrod,[16] the aggregative model completely misses the vital fact of the heterogeneity of capital goods. Thus some capital wears out quickly and requires gross investment to maintain output. As the depression persists, there will be rising gross investment even though a vast amount of capital is still redundant. This means rising output and capital requirements, which rise to meet the declining stock. In fact, this dispersion in the durability of different capital goods must be a large part of the explanation of the failure of gross investment to fall to zero in deep depression. Finally, we should mention the possibility that government outlays for relief, war or public works may lift the economy enough to set off the boom. This point has been so completely discussed that it seems unnecessary to go into it.

IX. The Effects of Lags

The model has been presented in an extremely crude form, the better to bring out its essential features. One over-simplification must be softened, and this is the assumption of no lags. There are a bewildering variety of lags of which the most important is the time between the decision to produce and actual installation of new capital goods. In our model it is implicitly assumed that ordering a new capital good leads to immediate installation, and that the full effect of this on income also results immediately. The average lag, θ, due to fabrication time, is long, perhaps as long as a year or more. Taking account of the lags creates serious difficulties in our non-linear equations. One difficulty may be disposed of roughly, but perhaps fairly satisfactorily, as follows: There is a kind of average lag between the decision to invest and the outlays incident to the investment, and there is a further lag between the spending of money and its full multiplier effect; if we then take these two lags to add up to θ, we have the useful fact that a piece of capital goods and its income effect appear at the same time. The remaining difficulty may be evaded, for practical purposes, as follows: the function, $g(\dot{k})$, which regulates investment decisions, is linear except for its upper and lower limits; but these limitations determine completely the behaviour in their ranges; it is only in the rise from the lower limit to the upper limit and conversely that we are interested, and here we may without serious error assume simple linear relations. Therefore instead of $g(\dot{k}_{t+\theta})$, we write $1/a[\dot{k}_{t+\theta}]$, and instead of $f(\dot{k}_t)$, we write $m\dot{k}_t$, where m is the multiplier and a is a constant which tells the rate at which any deficiency of capital is being made up. To replace (4) we have

$$\dot{k}_{t+\theta} - avm\dot{k}_t + ak_t = a\beta(t),$$

or, if we expand $\dot{k}_{t+\theta}$ in a Taylor series and keep only the first two terms,

$$\theta\ddot{k} + (1 - avm)\dot{k} + ak = a\beta(t). \tag{5}$$

This is a linear, second order differential equation, and it will ordinarily give rise to oscillations, which will be explosive if $avm > 1$. That this can ordinarily be expected to be so we see by considering the fact that v and m are both greater than unity and that though a may well be less than unity it is unlikely to be sufficiently less. Thus if $v = 2$ and $m = 2$, then a would have to be less than $\frac{1}{4}$, which would mean that the *annual* net output of capital goods would have to be less than $\frac{1}{4}$ of the deficiency in capital goods, which is not realistic. An explosive linear oscillation in the $\dot{k}k$ plane will be a somewhat distorted, unwinding, logarithmic spiral.

Therefore, apart from the delicate point of transition, we have a cycle made up of two simple routines, the flat top and bottom, and the outward spiralling ends. The initial conditions for the two ends are specified by the horizontal slope of the phase line at the end of the depression and of the boom. Consequently, we get the kind of picture shown in FIGURE 10.7. The harshness of transition from boom to depression and back again is entirely softened. As gross investment begins after a slump, some time elapses before the multiplier–accelerator desire for more capital is fed-back into the investment decisions. Therefore, in a process spread over time, investment rises, and the more entrepreneurs invest the more they want to invest, but they are eventually restrained by the amount that they are able to invest.

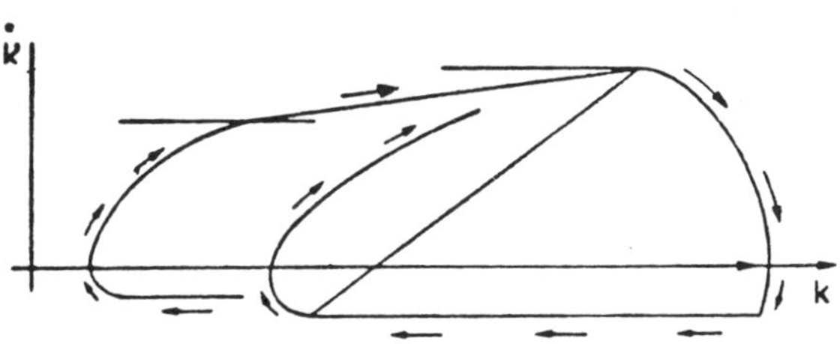

FIGURE 10.7

The model has a much shorter downswing than upswing, and in this it fits one of the most firmly established generalisations about business cycles. The actual downswing (as distinguished from depression low levels) is shorter, because it is soon stopped by the limit on gross investment. It is shorter also because the shallower savings function holds for the whole of the downswing, whereas it holds only for a part of the upswing. Finally, it is shorter because of the shifting to the right of $\phi(\dot{k})$, although this is not shown in FIGURE 10.7.

The curved portions of the diagram in FIGURE 10.7 may be constructed to any desired degree of accuracy by the method of isoclines. We first measure in deviations from the equilibrium level as determined by $\beta(t)$. Writing b instead of $\dot{k}$ we have, from (5),

$$\dot{k} = \frac{dk}{dt} = b;$$

$$\frac{db}{dt} = \ddot{k} = \left(\frac{avm-1}{\theta}\right)b - \frac{a}{\theta}k.$$

Eliminating dt, we get

$$\frac{db}{dk} = \left(\frac{avm-1}{\theta}\right) - \left(\frac{a}{\theta}\right)\frac{k}{b}. \tag{6}$$

This gives us the slope in the bk plane of the required curve for any pair of values of b and k. Hence, starting from the 'floor', we can proceed by small steps, in the direction calculated from (6), to the 'ceiling', and conversely.

NOTES

1. R. F. Harrod, 'An Essay in Dynamic Theory,' *Economic Journal*, 1939, and 'Notes on Trade Cycle Theory,' ibid., 1951.
2. *Towards a Dynamic Economics* (London: 1948).
3. *Weltwirtschaftliches Archiv*, 1937.
4. J. R. Hicks, *A Contribution to the Theory of the Trade Cycle* (Oxford: 1950).
5. *Economica*, 1927, p. 295.
6. 'Secular and Cyclical Aspects of the Multiplier and the Accelerator', *Income, Employment and Public Policy: Essays in Honor of Alvin H. Hansen* (New York: 1948).
7. H. B. Chenery, 'Overcapacity and the Acceleration Principle', *Econometrica*, January 1952.
8. *Dynamic Economics*, op. cit., *passim*.
9. J. Robinson, *The Rate of Interest* (London: 1952) p. 42.
10. *Dynamic Economics*, op. cit., pp. 23 *et seq.*
11. J. A. Schumpeter, *Business Cycles* (New York: 1939) vol. I, p. 93.
12. J. S. Duesenberry, *Income, Saving, and the Theory of Consumer Behavior* (Cambridge, Mass.: 1949).
13. *The Rate of Interest*, op. cit., p. 101.
14. E. Lundberg, *Studies in the Theory of Economic Expansion* (London: 1937).
15. L. A. Metzler, 'The Nature and Stability of Inventory Cycles', *Review of Economic Statistics*, 1941.
16. 'Notes on Trade Cycle Theory', *Economic Journal*, 1951.

11. The Optimal Growth Path for an Underdeveloped Economy[1]

ECONOMIC JOURNAL, 1961

In the course of practical planning in underdeveloped countries there arises at some point the question of what the rate of saving should be. This may be, and probably usually is, solved by pushing it as high as is politically feasible. As an answer this indicates a serious theoretical lacuna, apart from other more concrete shortcomings. The rate is ordinarily much too low and can only be raised gradually. But how rapidly should it be raised and how high? Should the savings rate continue to rise, level off or even ultimately be reduced? As time passes the policies become easier to carry out, but the prescriptions become more disputable. A related question is 'In what proportion should net capital formation be divided between capital goods industries and consumer goods industries', and it was discussed in this form in the early days of planning in the U.S.S.R. Increasing capital-goods capacity has great attractions, since machines to make machines involve growth in a way that machines to make, say, textiles do not. In fact, it is not difficult to show that by putting more capital into capital goods, consumption will ultimately benefit, even though at first it will be reduced; i.e. by shifting resources from the one to the other we will at first have less, and then later more consumption, in perpetuity, than if we did not. Yet this proves too much, because then we can *always* use promised future consumption as a reason for not consuming now, which does not provide a satisfactory basis for policy.

Ignoring all non-economic factors, we may proceed directly to the question: amongst those paths of economic growth which are possible, which is the best? The answer is not as simple as the question, nor is it likely to be attainable in practice, even if we can define it. Yet it does seem helpful to have a clear picture of the optimal time shape as a guide to the directions in which policies may be modified.

I

To discuss this problem in all its generality, we must proceed at a drastically unreal level of abstraction. I shall assume the economy is completely planned, the planners taking the long view in the sense that they give equal weight to all events from now to a specified future date. Consumption is held to be the sole aim of economic activity. All consumption is equally desirable regardless of when it occurs (i.e. any subjective time preference is explicitly rejected). The planners consider only consumption per head, thus ignoring any inequalities as well as, by implication, holding growth in numbers to be, by itself, no gain. Optimal growth is defined as the maximum of welfare over a finite period, welfare being taken as *per capita* consumption valued in some manner.

The labour force is growing at a given and constant rate. For realism it seems best to start with a considerable excess of labour, though this is not essential, since initially unemployment increases in realistic conditions. Capital goods are consequently the only scarce factor.

The problem is to transform an economy characterised by the old, low-productivity techniques into one consisting entirely of the new, high-productivity techniques. Therefore we have two distinct economies, though they contribute jointly to the common pool of real national product and they share the common inputs. Purely for simplicity the old sector is assumed, to begin with, to remain constant in output, employment and capital. Hence in the early years the economic surplus comes from the output of the old sector, and is ploughed back solely into the new. The resulting increases in output gradually make possible increasing accumulation, which will be coming in ever-greater proportion from the new sector. The old sector is held constant until general unemployment ceases, and then the labour and (more doubtfully) the capital are rapidly transferred to the new. In reality both labour force and capital would be gradually run down by non-replacement during the whole process.

Throughout the whole period each technique remains unchanged in the sense of maintaining constant average capital–output and labour–output ratios. Again solely for simplicity the capital–output ratio is taken to be the same for the two sectors. There is no question of diminishing returns, in spite of an awe-inspiring accumulation of aggregate capital relative to total labour, since capital, output and employment all expand in strict proportion in the new sector. We have thus a model with no technical change but rather a rise in the relative importance of the high-productivity as compared with the low-productivity sector. This corresponds to the fact that there is already available to underdeveloped economies a range of techniques which, when fully used, will vastly increase their average productivity. Should unforeseen new techniques become available during the change-over, the remainder of the process can be replanned, taking account of these new techniques. We are thus explicitly ignoring the question of whether or not the kind of techniques chosen should conform to the stage of development, a question which is of a higher order of sophistication and difficulty. This gives us an upper limit to the period over which we can, with this model, do our maximising. When sufficient capital goods of the new variety have been accumulated to provide employment for all the unemployed, all the accretions to the labour force, and finally, all those now employed at the old techniques, then the change-over model ceases to be applicable. Since such a gigantic task is as much as, and indeed more than, any underdeveloped economy is likely to take explicit account of, it seems reasonable to take this period as the duration of time over which welfare is to be maximised. The maximising period may be taken as shorter than this or longer, but in the latter case a second model must be used for the period after full employment under the new techniques.

In the interest of simplicity, foreign trade, loans and gifts are all ignored, although much of the surplus extracted from the old industry must be exported to acquire the capital equipment that it cannot produce. The government is entirely ignored, though some account of its activities is allowed for by taking an unusually high capital–output ratio. Intentionally I have not considered the possibilities of putting the unemployed to work with the old techniques. The extent to which this can be done will vary so much from country to country that it seems little can be said about it in general. Also it poses no issue in the sense that the more it is done, in such a way as not to decrease the surplus available, the better, since it will increase growth and raise living standards now and/or in the future.

Leaving on one side any possibilities of increasing output through absorption of unemployment, the problem becomes one involving in an essential way interpersonal and intertemporal comparisons of welfare, and as such involves an inescapable value judgement. Each act of investment involves an asymmetrical exchange of consumption now for output and possible consumption in the future. The simple comparison of pairs of dates will not do, because less consumption now means more output later, which is not simply comparable with consumption now. We have in turn to take the future added output and compare consumption then with consumption at other still more future dates. The problem must be solved in one act; it cannot be dealt with bit by bit. The planners therefore require an unequivocal and quantitative set of valuations for various levels of consumption at different times. By our assumptions the scale of evaluation must be the same for all different times. The term utility is used to describe the unique scale of valuation and carries no other meaning. Given the technical possibilities, the planners can, by varying the time pattern of investments, vary the time pattern of consumption per head. If the planners have a quantitative and unambiguous set of valuations of consumption, then by comparing the sum of valuations for any two situations possible, they can always decide which is better. All possible variations must be tried until a time shape of consumption per head is found from which no possible variation will produce a positive net change in valuation. Some consolation for such heroic assumptions may be found in the fact that any industrialisation programme inescapably involves such valuations. It is surely better to make the basic valuation explicit, and hence consistent, than to leave it unstated and arbitrary.

II

Accordingly, we write for the labour force

$$l = l_0 e^{\alpha t},$$

where l_0 is the initial labour force and α its given rate of growth. The labour force is taken to stand for the whole population, with an average number of dependants for each labourer. Also let

$$z = c/l,$$

where c is aggregate consumption and z that of the average or typical individual. Where no confusion can arise, z is referred to simply as consumption. To this consumption some sort of evaluation must be applied, because the transformation of the economy will make further increases in consumption progressively less urgent and hence less valuable. Therefore we define utility, u, as the valuation or weight put on consumption by decision of the state or the planners, and

$$u = \phi(z).$$

The planners must find amongst all possible $z(t)$s, the one which will maximise the sum of these *u*s. z is constrained by the limits of realisable output (capacity as determined by capital), by the inevitable growth of labour and, finally, by the basic contradiction that only by restraining z can it later, by capital accumulation, be increased.

There is an essential time lag between investment decisions, the actual outlay on investment and the added output available from the resulting capacity. To simplify a complex matter, I shall assume that on the average the money is all spent at a point midway between the beginning and fruition of a project. All other lags are taken as negligible by comparison. As a unit period, therefore, I take half the average time between the initial decision and the effective operation of the capacity. A two-year period giving an average time of four years construction would seem to be a realistically long lag.

By virtue of the assumption that we are making, i.e. a scale expansion of an unchanged new set of techniques, we may assume a constant capital–output ratio σ. The economy being planned, we may assume that output, y, is always at full capacity, and thus equal to k/σ, where k is the quantity of capital. Our fundamental constraints are then given by

$$y_t = k_t/\sigma,$$
$$y_t = c_t + k_{t+1} - k_t,$$
$$u = \phi(c_t/l_t),$$
$$l = l_0 e^{\alpha t}.$$

Substituting the first equation into the second, and that in turn (together with the fourth equation) into the third, we get utility as a function of capital and time,

$$u = \phi\left(\frac{(1 + 1/\sigma)k_t - k_{t+1}}{l_0 e^{\alpha t}}\right).$$

The planners' problem is to find that $k(t)$ which will render stationary, from the initial period to the final one, f, the finite sum

$$\sum_{t=0}^{f} u_t(k, t).$$

For this

$$\sum_{0} \phi'_t(z_t) dz_t = 0$$

is a necessary condition. Now

$$dz_t = \frac{(1+1/\sigma)dk_t}{l_t} - \frac{dk_{t+1}}{l_t} - \frac{c_t dl_t}{l_t^2}.$$

But $dl_t = 0$, since no change in c or y will change l. Hence our necessary condition becomes

$$\sum_0 \phi' \left[\frac{(1+1/\sigma)dk_t}{l_t} - \frac{dk_{t+1}}{l_t}\right] = 0.$$

The typical term in this series is

$$\left[-\frac{\phi'_{t-1}}{l_{t-1}} + \frac{\phi'_t}{l_t}(1+1/\sigma)\right]dk_t.$$

Because we are free to choose our dk_ts we can only ensure a zero sum for all possible variations in the dks by requiring all of the coefficients to be zero. If we can find a time series for k which will nullify all these coefficients, then no small alteration of that time series will increase or decrease the sum. This, then, will be the stationary solution we seek. Whether it is a maximum, a minimum or a saddle point must be ascertained by further inspection. Hence,

$$\phi'_t/l_t - \phi'_{t-1}/l_{t-1} = -\frac{1}{\sigma}\phi'_t/l_t, \text{ or}$$

$$\Delta(\phi'_t/l_t) = -\frac{1}{\sigma}\phi'_t/l_t$$

This is the fundamental relationship which the planners must follow. I shall call it Ramsey's Rule after its discoverer[2] (though here it appears slightly disguised due to l_t and the staggering of its lagged effects). Given the fact that the labour force grows at a constant rate, we may write the result as

$$\phi'_t = \left(\frac{1+\alpha}{1+1/\sigma}\right)\phi'_{t-1}.$$

Thus we get a simple first-order homogeneous difference equation with a constant coefficient, the solution to which is

$$\phi'_t = \phi'_0\left(\frac{1+\alpha}{1+1/\sigma}\right)^t,$$

so that even without knowing anything about our valuation function we know how its marginal value must behave throughout the whole process. From this it follows that, to obtain a solution, we do not need an explicit mathematical utility function. We may use any marginal utility function whatsoever, including simply a table of associated values of standard of living and valuation, derived from any empirical source or posited as a set of value judgements. It must, of course, be possible to interpolate between any readings, so that for any ϕ' we can always find the corresponding z. After plotting $\phi'(z)$, erect a straight line, A, with the slope $\dfrac{1+1/\alpha}{1+\alpha}$ and a 45° line as in FIGURE 11.1. Given any initial value z_0, we get, by descending steps between the two straight lines, the successive values of ϕ' for all future periods. This determines z_t from the ϕ'. z_0 is not, of course, given, but must be found from the solution to the whole problem. We have

$$\frac{k_{t+1}}{l_t} = (1+1/\sigma)\frac{k_t}{l_t} - \frac{c_t}{l_t}.$$

If we write κ_t for k_t/l_t and remember that $l_{t+1} = (1+\alpha)l_t$, we get

$$\kappa_{t+1} = \frac{1+1/\sigma}{1+\alpha}\kappa_t - \frac{1}{1+\alpha}z_t.$$

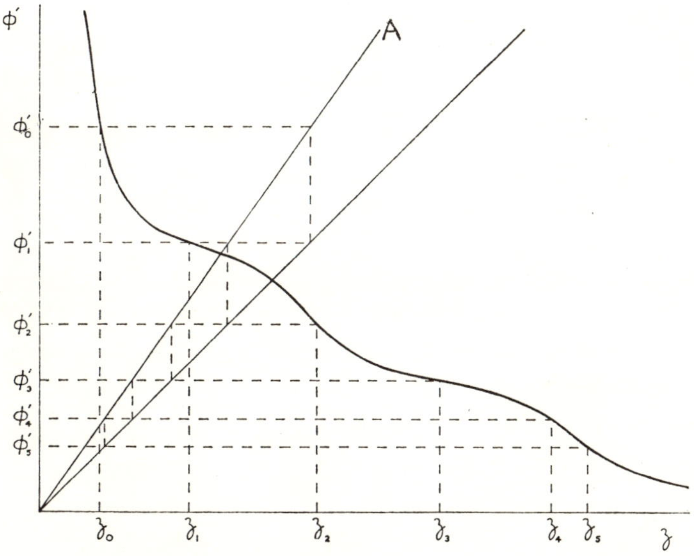

FIGURE 11.1

In order to make the problem determinate we must specify two given boundary conditions (in addition to l_0 and f). Obviously one of these is k_0 (and hence y_0). The second cannot be Δk_0, because that is one of the variables we wish to solve for, nor can it be y_f, because we can get high values of z by disinvestment at the end, but this makes no economic sense. Hence the best choice seems to be a given final rate of investment, which will safeguard the future of the economy. Therefore the planners must choose some satisfactory final growth rate, $1+v$. The boundary conditions are then given by k_0 and

$$k_{f+1} = (1+v)k_f, \quad \text{or}$$

$$\kappa_{f+1} = \frac{1+v}{1+\alpha}\kappa_f.$$

The f must be chosen so that it is less than or equal to the time at which industrialisation has been completed by the equipping of the whole labour force with the new techniques. Writing θ for $(1+1/\sigma) \div (1+\alpha)$, the solution is

$$\kappa_{f+1} = -\frac{1}{1+\alpha}\sum_{\tau=1}^{f} \theta^{\tau} z_{f-\tau} + \theta^{f+1}\kappa_0,$$

i.e. the faltung sum, or convolution, of θ and z. In this form we may incorporate our second boundary condition. We shall have found a solution when, by trial-and-error methods, we have hit upon a time series of z_t which satisfies the following equation:

$$\frac{(1+\sigma)}{1-v\sigma}z_f + \sum_{\tau=1}^{f} \theta^{\tau} z_{f-\tau} = (1+1/\sigma)\theta^f \kappa_0.$$

We can be assured that there will be a solution in practice, if $\phi'(z)$ tends to infinity at the lower end and falls monotonically to zero as z increases without limit—assumptions which are ordinarily made about the 'marginal utility of money'.

By requiring our time horizon to coincide with the completion of industrialisation, we have in effect added another boundary condition (though one not inherent in the problem). This f may then be simultaneously determined, along with our solution, from the relation

$$\kappa_f = \epsilon_N \sigma,$$

where ϵ_N is the labour productivity of the new techniques. To determine z_0 and f by these relations is laborious but practicable. The severity and perversity of our conditions completely determine the nature of the solution. Poor generations are being asked to impoverish themselves in order to enrich later, richer generations. It is only within narrow limits that the productivity is sufficiently great to justify what is, after all, intertemporal exchange the wrong way round. The later generations should subsidise the earlier, but because of the reality of the irreversibility of time, this cannot happen (if we exclude borrowing from abroad). We have so to choose our initial standard of life that the fall in the worth of goods will be balanced against the increasing abundance. For a poor community, we must begin high enough up on the marginal worth curve, so that z needs scarcely to increase at all whilst bringing down the worth of goods rapidly. This then allows the massive accumulation of capital which will permit of the required rapid growth of z in the flat tail of the curve later on. Exactly how this works out depends on the surplus above subsistence available at the start, the capital–output ratio, the population growth and the length of our time horizon, f. To simplify matters we may reverse the logic and try various likely z_0s, in each case working out the implied optimal process until the rate of growth of output is cut back to our required terminal growth rate. Proceeding this way, we can always find a z_0 which will result in our required terminal growth rate at that point in time when we have completed industrialisation.

The planners may determine the marginal utility curve in any way or may accept any sort of directive about it. Purely for illustrative purposes I propose to determine an 'empirical' curve by committing a quite illegitimate reversal of Irving Fisher's well-known proposal for determining a just income tax. It will be remembered that he proposed to use his measurements of the marginal utility of money for determining that tax structure which would impose equal psychic sacrifices. *Per contra*, if we assume we have such a just income tax, we may infer from it what the marginal utility of money is. Fisher's formula[3] needs altering so that it goes to zero for infinite income taxed at a marginal rate of unity. This will be so if we assume

$$\phi'(z) = \frac{1 - T(z)}{T(z)}$$

where $T(z)$ is the marginal tax rate by income class, z. For $T(z)$ I shall take a freely adapted version of the United Kingdom marginal income-tax schedule, 1953/4, for a married couple with two children. I assume that some rather abrupt changes, made for administrative convenience, may be smoothed, i.e. at the abrupt beginning and at the transition from standard to surtax rates. Also I have freely interpolated graphically. A zero rate, and hence an infinite marginal utility, is assumed at £375 with a smooth transition to the actual rate of 0.20 for £725.

The best way to see the problem and its solution is to take a specific example. All rates are given in annual terms, but last in each instance for two years (and are most easily calculated in biennial rates). The hypothetical community has a labour force of 10, of which only $6.5 = v$ are really essential and $3.5 = u$ are in some sense unemployed. Initial output is 100, so that crude productivity is 10. True productivity, ϵ_A, is 15.4. The labour force is rising at 2 per cent per year. The initial standard of living, z_0, will be near the crude productivity, but it must not be greater than 9.3, or else there is no possibility of industrialisation, since capital per man will be falling. Assuming that there is little 'free' surplus, we may take the minimum of subsistence to be $\bar{z} = 9.15$. This minimum may be physical, or moral, or political, but it is a very real thing in that it is that level below which the standard of living may not, under any circumstances, be pushed by a rational planner. To translate our hypothetical psychic income evaluation for the United Kingdom into one appropriate to our impoverished community, we simply equate £375 to 9.15. The capital–output ratio is taken to be $\sigma = 3.5$ years, which is rather higher than usual but may be held to allow for the fact that, since we are omitting any government accounts, some development expenditure not usually classified as investment will be included. The old and the new capital–output ratios are taken to be equal. Being in a planned economy, output is throughout taken as using full capacity. Therefore $k_0 = 350$. The new labour productivity is $\epsilon_N = 125$, about eight times the old, which is broadly realistic. When the change-over is completed, capital per labourer will be $\kappa_f = \epsilon_N \sigma = 438$. The terminal growth rate required is 5 per cent per year, but it must not be expected that we can achieve exactly this over a period as long as the last two years. It is in fact brought to 6.5 per cent, but would have become negative in the next biennial period. For the final period I have simply inserted the amount of consumption which would give a 5 per cent growth in the succeeding period. None of these data are empirical nor do they apply to any country. But they are, I think, of the right order of magnitude, and thus constituted, we have a 'real' as opposed to an imaginary problem.

Given these structural conditions and boundary values, we seek that initial level of consumption, z_0, which will lead to complete industrialisation with the required terminal growth. If we set $z_0 = 9.17$ the progress will be carried out optimally in approximately thirty-eight years. The detailed behaviour over the whole change-over is given in TABLE 11.1, and the most important control factors in FIGURE 11.2.

TABLE 11.1

t	k (1)	y (2)	c (3)	s (4)	l (5)	v (6)	u (7)	c/l (8)	c/v (9)	s/y (10)	$\Delta s/\Delta y$ (11)	$\Delta y/y$ (12)
0	350	100	19.7	8	10.00	6.50	3.50	9.17	14.1	0.080	—	—
2	368	105	95.5	9	10.40	6.54	3.86	9.18	14.6	0.086	0.20	0.025
4	388	111	99.5	11	10.82	6.59	4.23	9.19	15.1	0.099	0.33	0.029
6	412	118	103.5	14	11.24	6.64	4.60	9.21	15.6	0.119	0.43	0.032
8	441	126	108	18	11.70	6.71	4.99	9.24	16.1	0.143	0.50	0.034
10	476	136	113	23	12.16	6.79	5.27	9.28	16.7	0.169	0.50	0.040
12	527	151	119	32	12.71	6.91	5.80	9.33	17.2	0.212	0.60	0.054
14	590	169	124	45	13.15	7.05	6.10	9.41	17.6	0.266	0.72	0.060
16	680	194	131	63	13.65	7.25	6.40	9.58	18.1	0.325	0.72	0.074
18	812	232	140	92	14.22	7.56	6.66	9.82	18.5	0.397	0.76	0.098
20	998	285	151	134	14.79	7.98	6.81	10.18	18.9	0.470	0.79	0.114
22	1268	362	170	192	15.38	8.60	6.78	11.08	19.8	0.530	0.75	0.135
24	1653	473	199	174	16.00	9.48	6.52	12.4	21.0	0.579	0.74	0.154
26	2205	630	243	387	16.63	10.74	5.89	14.6	22.6	0.613	0.71	0.166
28	2980	850	327	523	17.30	12.50	4.80	18.9	26.1	0.615	0.62	0.175
30	4050	1158	549	609	17.99	14.95	3.04	30.5	36.7	0.527	0.28	0.181
32	5280	1510	852	658	18.71	17.80	0.91	45.5	47.9	0.436	0.14	0.153
34	6600	1885	1205	686	19.45	19.45	0	62.0	62.0	0.364	0.07	0.124
36	7960	2275	1770	505	20.20	20.20	0	87.5	87.8	0.222	0.05	0.104
38	9000	2570	2120	450	21.01	21.01	0	101.0	101.0	0.175	−0.37	0.065

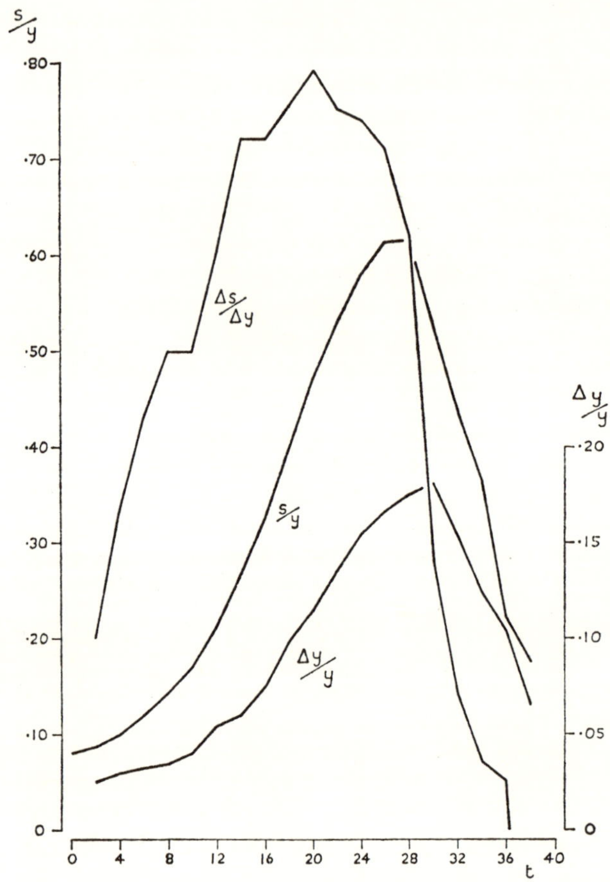

FIGURE 11.2

The general nature of the policy prescription is clear — severe restraint on consumption for the larger part of the period and full relaxation towards the end. Such a policy is a rational consequence of the advantages of exploiting the technological possibilities. The harshness towards the present generation results in spite of giving exactly the same weight to its desires as to those of future generations. So great are the gains that we are fully justified in robbing the poor to give to the rich! The considerable rise in aggregate consumption [col. (3)], is to begin with largely required for the rising population, but some modest rise in the average consumption [col. (8)] does occur right from the start. Consumption per employed worker [col. (9)], which might be taken as a measure of the real wage rate, is allowed to rise somewhat more rapidly, but these gains are in part dissipated in the earlier periods by the continuing growth in the parasitic population, u. In spite of the violence of the capital accumulation effort, unemployment proves to be highly intractable because of the low labour requirements of the high-productivity techniques being introduced. It should be added that the problem of variation of techniques according to the level of development has been excluded by hypothesis. In a broad sort of way the model is in agreement with the experiences both of the Soviet Union and of the capitalist countries. Standards of living remain low for a long time after the commencement of industrialisation. Furthermore, there is a persistent tendency to surplus labour, which is always observed.

This model, like many others, is an exercise in compounding, but it is strikingly different from the 'balanced growth' models which have been widely used in analysing economic development. Such models imply a constant growth rate, whereas here we have the rate, $\Delta y/y$, beginning at 2.5 per cent and rising steadily to 18 per cent per year and then falling back close to the required terminal growth rate of 5 per cent (TABLE 11.1 and FIGURE 11.2). Similarly, it is to be contrasted with the practice, both in model building and in the conduct of high policy, of posing the problem as one of pushing up the savings ratio to some 'satisfactory' or 'best' level. The savings ratio, starting at 8 per cent, undergoes a rapid acceleration to a maximum of 61.5 per cent of net national income. Thereafter it decelerates rapidly to 17.5 per cent. Perhaps the most crucial indicator is the implied marginal propensity to save, $\Delta s/\Delta y$, it is 'implied', because saving is determined by planning decision rather than any voluntary behaviour patterns of income receivers. As in any poor community, the *average* saving ratio is unduly low, but the *marginal* ratio may be put as high as population growth and Ramsey's Rule will permit. It begins at 20 per cent and rises steeply to 79 per cent, after which it falls to a negative value (i.e. income is rising whilst savings, though positive, are falling). The marginal savings ratio contains also the vital information of what proportion of new capital goods must be ploughed back to the capital-goods industries. If we call the additional capital required in capital-goods industries Δk_k, then its ratio to the total capital required is $\Delta k_k/\Delta k$, which will be equal to $\sigma\Delta(\Delta k)/\sigma\Delta y$. We see that this ratio is equal to $\Delta s/\Delta y$ because $s = \Delta k$. The same ratio will also tell us to what extent we are doing pure compounding at a constant rate. Thus, if aggregate consumption were kept constant we could take the initial amount of saving and turn it into added income, all of which in turn would be saved, and so forth. The result would be growth in net income at over 50 per cent compounded every two years, or about 25 per cent compounded every year. As has been recognised since the eighteenth century, long-term compounding produces spectacular results, and at such ultra high rates it does so even in short periods. And yet this 25 per cent rate is, if anything, on the conservative side, since a capital–output ratio (on which it is based) of 3.5 is rather high, and hence inhibits growth. However, we only compound at the 25 per cent rate to the extent that we plough back capital goods to capital-goods capacity, i.e. we make machines to make machines to make more machines and so on. The ratio $\Delta s/\Delta y$ tells us the best proportion in which to do pure compounding, assuming that our aim is the psychic worth of consumption and not mere size of total output. The degree to which, in practice, one can hold down the standard of living in the early stages is of crucial importance, but also highly intractable. What is required is that, as the unemployed are equipped, set to work and paid wages the incomes of the families or communities in which the unemployed were previously parasitic must be reduced so that they do not gain by being relieved of their non-earning members. This represents a degree of control which no actual state could achieve; it is also the norm to be aimed at. Evidently authoritarian governments have a much greater ability to approximate to the norm.

It is interesting to note that though subjective time preference, if it exists, has been explicitly rejected as a guide to policy, future goods become less desirable per unit, as a direct consequence of the known and foreseen rise in living standards. Therefore no rational individual would lend money for future repayment and consumption except at a positive rate of interest. If free to do so, a consumer would be willing to lend at any rate of interest greater than

$$\frac{1 + 1/\sigma}{1 + \alpha}$$

and this remains constant throughout the process. In this example it is about 23 per cent per annum. This supply price of funds exists in spite of perfect foresight and no subjective undervaluation of the future. In accord with Schumpeter's analysis, the supply price would be zero in a stationary state. This should help in explaining the long-run constancy of interest rates in capitalism. The remarkable fact is that the constancy of the subjective interest rate is consistent with massive accelerations and decelerations in the growth rate of output, showing that interest rate and growth rate need not be closely related.

III

To get beyond the elegant generality of Ramsey's Rule, it is necessary to specify some sort of valuation function. In the previous section I have shown how this may be done for an arbitrary weighting function by a numerical analysis which is somewhat laborious and cumbersome. On the other hand, an appropriate mathematical function will allow of an explicit solution with all its advantages. The logarithmic utility function is the oldest, and it is also the simplest one to contain the required characteristic of diminishing marginal utility from infinity to zero, over the whole range of incomes. Assuming this, we have

$$u = \phi(z) = \log(z - \bar{z}),$$

where $\bar{z}$ is the minimum of subsistence, and marginal utility is given by

$$\phi'(z) = 1/(z - \bar{z}).$$

Our solution for the behaviour of $\phi'(z)$ now becomes

$$\frac{1}{z_t - \bar{z}} = \phi_0 \left(\frac{1+\alpha}{1+1/\sigma} \right)^t,$$

or in terms of consumption, with C an arbitrary constant

$$c_t = C(1 + 1/\sigma)^t + \bar{z} l_0 (1+\alpha)^t.$$

If now we substitute this back into our original equation we get

$$-\Delta k + k/\sigma = C(1 + 1/\sigma)^t + \bar{z} l_0 (1+\alpha)^t,$$

the complete solution to which is

$$k_t = (A + Bt)(1 + 1/\sigma)^t + \bar{z} l_0 (1+\alpha)^t.$$

A and B are arbitrary constants with $C = -(1 + 1/\sigma)B$. A may be determined from the initial stock of capital and B from the desired terminal growth rate. If we agree to select the final biennial period, f, by the requirement that the new capital goods must be sufficient to employ the whole population, we have, in effect, a third arbitrary constant and a third equation to determine it. We must determine f simultaneously with A and B, since we cannot determine them until we know it, and it until we know them. This can be done iteratively.

The subsistence minimum, $\bar{z}$, is naturally very important in determining the time required for an optimal change-over. There may be no clearly defined minimum, so $\bar{z}$ cannot be taken as given. In such a case we might make a political decision that the change-over must be accomplished in f years, and from this determine what minimal z is to be specified. Indeed, the strong desire to 'catch up' may legitimately be used as an argument for persuading the present generation to sacrifices it might otherwise violently reject. In the example to be discussed below, if subsistence is 8.95 it will take seventy years to change over, but only forty years if subsistence is 7.50. There are, however, severe limits to the choice, for to get the time down to thirty years would require a subsistence of 3.70, and, at the other end, a subsistence of 9.00 would mean that the change-over could never be completed.

For the second example I shall take the extremely high value of five years for the capital–output ratio, σ. In this way we pose the most severe difficulties for a planned industrialisation, so that any optimism in the result cannot be charged to favourable assumptions. Otherwise all the structural data are as in TABLE 11.1. However, the economy must be more productive initially with relation to the subsistence minimum. Accordingly, $\bar{z}$ is taken to be 7.5 in the second example. The change-over will be approximately completed in forty years, which is, then, the period over which utility is to be maximised. The details of the required behaviour are given in TABLE 11.2 and FIGURE 11.3.

In spite of a completely different kind of utility function and a vastly different situation with regard to available surplus, it will be seen that the qualitative prescriptions for the two cases are the same. Consumption is severely restrained, the savings ratio rises to great heights and income is first accelerated and then decelerated. The quantitative behaviour differs, naturally, in detail because of the great differences in the real structure. In the second example the marginal savings ratio begins much higher, does not need to be pushed quite so high and turns down sooner. Similarly, the savings ratio has a much less sharp peak and somewhat less extreme behaviour than in the previous example. The growth rate begins higher, rises sooner, but therefore does not need pushing to such great heights as in the first case. The wage rate [col. (9)] can be allowed to drift upward more rapidly, but not strikingly so. Altogether this case can take it more easily than the first case because it is richer, as would be made clearer if the subsistence minima were equated, instead of the outputs. Perhaps the most striking uniformity in the ideal policy for these two quite dissimilar countries is the total length of change-over, thirty-eight years in the one and forty years in the other case.

Not only is it possible to analyse the logarithmic utility valuation (and all constant multiples of it), but we can go much further and consider a whole family of skewed logarithmic curves which allow us to consider

TABLE 11.2

t	k (1)	y (2)	c (3)	s (4)	l (5)	v (6)	u (7)	c/l (8)	c/v (9)	s/y (10)	$\Delta s/\Delta y$ (11)	$\Delta y/y$ (12)
0	500	100	77.4	22.7	10.00	6.50	3.50	7.75	11.9	0.227	0.54	0.045
4	600	120	85.8	34.3	10.82	6.66	4.16	7.95	12.9	0.286	0.61	0.057
8	755	151	96.9	54.3	11.70	6.91	4.79	8.25	14.0	0.359	0.66	0.072
12	1004	201	113.1	88.1	12.71	7.31	5.40	8.90	15.5	0.438	0.68	0.088
16	1397	279	137.1	142	13.65	7.93	5.72	10.1	17.3	0.509	0.68	0.102
20	2043	409	179	230	14.79	8.97	5.82	12.1	19.9	0.563	0.66	0.113
24	3066	613	253	360	16.00	10.70	5.30	15.8	23.6	0.588	0.60	0.118
28	4700	940	390	550	17.30	13.22	4.08	22.5	29.4	0.585	0.50	0.117
32	7090	1420	655	765	18.71	17.07	1.64	35.0	38.4	0.539	0.33	0.108
36	10460	2090	1157	935	20.20	20.2	0	57.5	58.2	0.447	−0.09	0.089
40	14060	2810	2124	686	21.90	21.9	0	97.0	97.0	0.244	−1.88	0.049

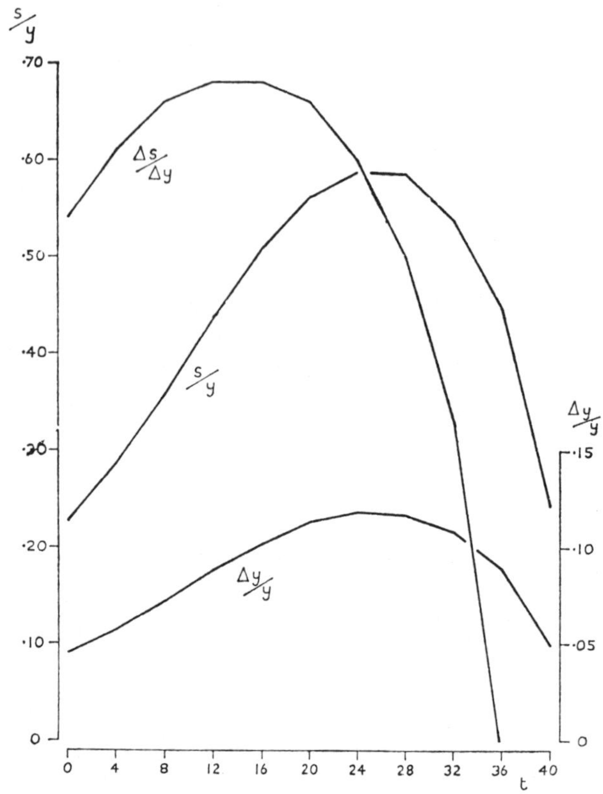

FIGURE 11.3

any degree of fall in the marginal utility of money. Thus we may consider the much more general case of

$$\phi'(z) = \frac{1}{(z-\bar{z})^{\epsilon}},$$

where ϵ is positive but may take on any value from zero to infinity, reducing to our previous result for $\epsilon = 1$. For $\epsilon < 1$, the marginal value of future higher incomes will lie above our previous case, approaching a constant for values near zero. If $\epsilon > 1$, future income is less prized. The solution, which is naturally somewhat more complicated, is

$$k(t) = Ab^t + Bh^t + \frac{\bar{z}l_0}{1/\sigma - \alpha}d^t,$$

where
$$b = 1 + 1/\sigma,$$
$$h = \frac{(1+1/\sigma)^{1/\epsilon}}{(1+\alpha)^{1/\epsilon - 1}},$$
$$d = 1 + \alpha.$$

Also
$$C(t) = (b-h)Bh^t + \bar{z}l_0 d^t.$$

In this way we may investigate a very different valuation curve, given by $\epsilon = \frac{1}{5}$. In this example the marginal utility curve, lies well above that of the last example for most of the range that matters, and that of the first example lies somewhere in between the other two. Thus, we shall have samples of a very wide range of different valuation curves. Otherwise everything is as in the second case except that $\bar{z}$, at 8.75, is taken very near the critical limit of 9.00, above which the change-over cannot be effected. This means that accumulation is painful; on the other hand, it is urgently desirable, since $\epsilon < 1$ means that the gains from postponing consumption are much greater. These two effects seem partially to cancel one another, for we find that the industrialisation will be completed in an optimal way in about forty-one years, almost equal to the second case. The detailed results, given in TABLE 11.3 and FIGURE 11.4, are broadly similar to those of the other two examples, but with important differences of degree. The combination of a high capital requirement and low available surplus with a high psychic value of future high incomes means that the change-over is an extremely difficult affair. Thus the standard of living is scarcely allowed to rise at all until nearly the end of the process (which is not quite terminated by the fortieth year). The severity of the effort required is shown by the fact that in the years 28–30, 95 per cent of the increased output is ploughed back into capital goods [col. (11)]. Unemployment [col. (7)] proves to be more intractable than in the first two examples, becoming nearly as great as employment around the twentieth year. One consequence of the stringency is that the average wage rate [col. (9)] actually declines between the years 20 and 32, though the standard of living does not. This results from the lowering of the burden of parasitic unemployment. No such behaviour occurs in either of the first two cases. However, by comparing FIGURE 11.4 with FIGURES 11.2 and 11.3, we see that this case is qualitatively the same as the others. The specific features of the first two cases are all found here only in more extreme form.

Differing in essential ways, these three different types of model all share the same qualitative policy implications, i.e. extreme constraint on consumption per head in the early years and relaxation in varying

TABLE 11.3

t	k (1)	y (2)	c (3)	s (4)	l (5)	v (6)	u (7)	c/l (8)	c/v (9)	s/y (10)	$\Delta s/\Delta y$ (11)	$\Delta y/y$ (12)
0	500	100	88	12	10.00	6.5	3.5	8.75	13.5	0.125	0.30	0.025
4	554	111	95	16	10.82	6.6	4.2	8.75	14.4	0.144	0.41	0.029
8	622	125	102	22	11.70	6.7	5.0	8.75	15.2	0.178	0.54	0.036
12	723	145	111	34	12.70	6.9	5.8	8.75	16.2	0.231	0.67	0.046
16	869	174	120	55	13.65	7.1	6.6	8.75	16.9	0.314	0.79	0.063
20	1120	224	130	96	14.79	7.5	7.3	8.75	17.3	0.426	0.86	0.085
24	1560	312	140	174	16.00	8.2	7.8	8.75	17.1	0.556	0.91	0.111
28	2368	474	152	325	17.30	9.5	7.8	8.75	16.0	0.686	0.95	0.137
32	3907	783	165	621	18.71	12.0	6.7	8.85	13.7	0.794	0.95	0.159
36	6870	1375	248	1136	20.20	16.7	3.5	12.3	14.8	0.825	0.43	0.165
40	11730	2345	1680	686	21.90	21.9	0	76.8	76.7	0.293	−18.5	0.059

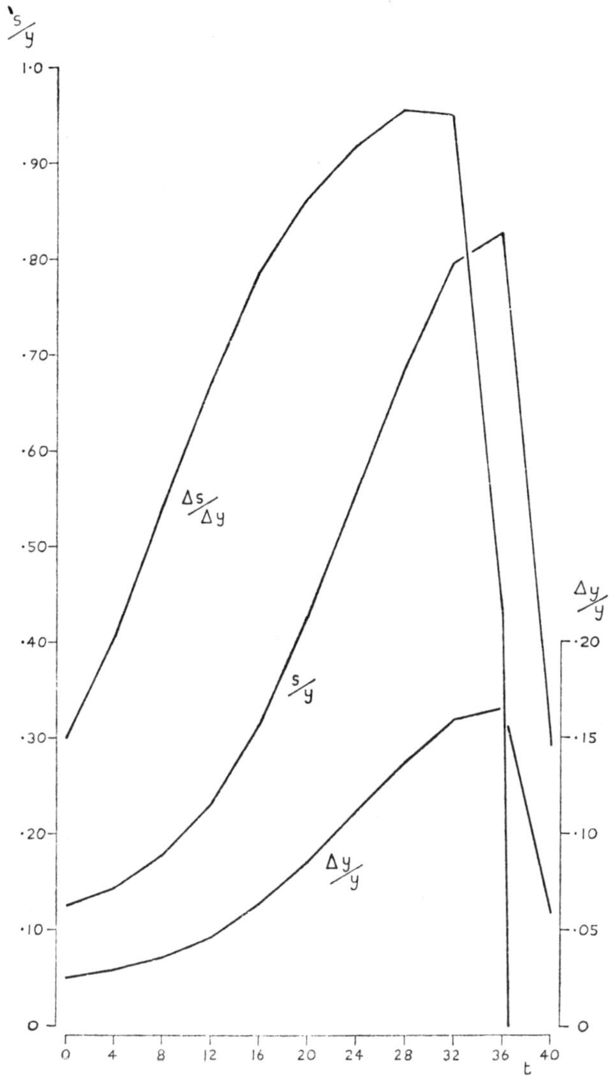

FIGURE 11.4

degrees later. Such unanimity gives support to the supposition that this pattern represents a generally applicable ideal in the direction of which all development policies should be modified. Somewhat less clear are the implications of the fact that all three change-over processes require the same absolute amount of time. It is difficult to know to what extent this is accidental and to what extent there is a kind of rough optimal time-constant for industrialisation. To some extent any monotonically decreasing valuation of increments of income does impose rather severe restrictions on rational policy. There tends to result some uniformity of pattern in accumulation, which, combined with the violence of prolonged exponential growth, does perhaps yield some tendency to a common duration even under rather various circumstances.

The darkest aspect of all this is the basis of the social evaluation of different income levels. Such a comparison cannot be made on any scientific or positivistic basis, but only by an act of political judgement. The difficulties involved are, however, no ground for evading the issue. Any policy, or worse still any lack of policy, involves the most thoroughgoing comparison of the welfares of the living and of the unborn. Failure to pursue a severe rate of accumulation is compromising the welfare of those who have no direct say in current decisions. The difficulty of making these value judgements is vastly increased by ignorance of what are the objective consequences of any action or inaction. Working out the consequences of various marginal valuation functions along the lines of this paper should help in arriving at some more rational basis of policy than at present.

It is urgent to see the problem in its full awkwardness. To justify the robbing of poor now to pay the rich later is not easy, but it is implied by the enormous productivity of modern techniques. It is the instinctive recognition of this fact that makes all the underdeveloped countries so anxious to undertake what can only be an arduous and initially painful process. The basic factors that condition an optimal change-over are the existing achievable output, the minimum level at which consumption standards can be kept and the more or less arbitrary weights attached to the higher levels of consumption whenever achieved. Barring absurdly low values, some violent process of capital accumulation of the type illustrated is the ideal. The simplifications of the model give an unduly sharp outline of the ideal policy, but its general character is surely a sound guide to policy.

IV

Our problem is properly one in the calculus of variations, and may be so treated with a gain in elegance but with a loss of realism. We have to drop the lag between investment and capacity, a matter of great practical importance in planning. Keeping all the other assumptions, the planners must seek, amongst all possible $z(t)$s, the one which will maximise

$$\int_0^f \phi(z)dt$$

But $$z = \frac{y - \sigma\dot{y}}{l(t)} = \psi(y, \dot{y}, t).$$

Therefore they seek that time series, $y(t)$, which, when altered slightly, will leave unaltered the value of

$$\int_0^f \phi[\psi(y, \dot{y}, t)]dt.$$

The necessary and sufficient condition for the stationariness of this expression is given by Euler's equation,

$$\phi'(z)\frac{\partial\psi}{\partial y} = \frac{d}{dt}\phi(z)\frac{\partial\psi}{\partial\dot{y}},$$

which, in this case, reduces to

$$\frac{d\phi'}{dt}\bigg/\phi' = -(1/\sigma - \alpha),$$

which, in slightly different form, I have called Ramsey's Rule.

If we assume a logarithmic weighting function, then

$$\phi(z) = \log(z - \bar{z}),$$

and we seek that $y(t)$ which renders stationary

$$\int_0^f \log\left(\frac{y - \sigma\dot{y}}{l(t)} - \bar{z}\right)dt.$$

Integrating Euler's equation, we get the solution

$$y(t) = (Y_1 + Y_2 t)e^{t/\sigma} + \frac{\bar{z}l_0}{1 - \sigma\alpha}e^{\alpha t},$$

where Y_1 and Y_2 are arbitrary constants to be determined by such boundary conditions as we choose. This is the continuous analogue of the finite difference solutions given above.

To show the similarity with the previous cases, we may construct an example under still more different conditions. Let us assume the following: capital–output ratio $\sigma = 4$ years, the rate of growth of labour force $\alpha = 1$ per cent, $l_0 = 10$, $y_0 = 100$, $\bar{z} = 9$ and the productivity of the old techniques $\epsilon_A = 15.4$ and of the new $\epsilon_N = 333$. Requiring a terminal growth rate of 5 per cent per year, full employment is reached in around twenty-three years and the whole labour force is equipped with the new techniques in between thirty-four and thirty-five years. Taking $f = 34$ years, we may determine our arbitrary constants, giving

$$y(t) = (6.25 - 0.160t)e^{0.25t} + 93.75e^{0.01t}.$$

The details are given in TABLE 11.4. In spite of a population pressure only half as great as the others, 11.4 requires only 4–6 years less to complete change-over. We again find the same patterns of marginal and average saving, the marginal rate beginning at over 50 per cent [col. (7)]. The result again gives support to the view that the general policy prescriptions are not very dependent on the particular assumptions about social valuation, capital–output ratios and the like.

TABLE 11.4

t	y (1)	C (2)	S (3)	l (4)	c/l (5)	s/y (6)	ds/dy (7)	$\dot{y}/y$ (8)
0	100.0	90.6	9.4	10.0	9.06	0.094	0.548	0.023
1	101.8	91.7	10.1	10.1	9.08	0.099	0.588	0.026
2	105.3	92.9	12.4	10.2	9.11	0.118	0.624	0.030
3	108.7	94.1	14.6	10.3	9.14	0.134	0.655	0.034
5	117.6	96.8	20.8	10.5	9.22	0.177	0.710	0.044
10	160.0	107.3	52.7	11.1	9.7	0.330	0.778	0.083
20	566	205	361	12.2	16.8	0.638	0.658	0.159
25	1286	448	838	12.8	35.0	0.653	0.596	0.163
30	2747	1280	1467	13.5	94.8	0.534	0.199	0.132
32	3499	2034	1465	13.8	147.5	0.420	−0.334	0.102
34	4092	3297	795	14.1	234.0	0.195	−3.0	0.048

NOTES

1. The substance of this paper was originally presented to the Oxford–London–Cambridge Seminar on 10 November 1956.
2. E. J. Ramsey, 'A Mathematical Theory of Saving', *Economic Journal*, December 1928.
3. 'A Statistical Method for Measuring "Marginal Utility" and Testing the Justice of a Progressive Income Tax' in *Economic Essays in Honour of John Bates Clark* (New York: 1975) p. 186.

12. A Growth Cycle[1]

SOCIALISM, CAPITALISM AND ECONOMIC GROWTH, 1967, ED. C. H. FEINSTEIN

Presented here is a starkly schematised and hence quite unrealistic model of cycles in growth rates. This type of formulation now seems to me to have better prospects than the more usual treatment of growth theory or of cycle theory, separately or in combination. Many of the bits of reasoning are common to both, but in the present paper they are put together in a different way.

The following assumptions are made for convenience:

(1) Steady technical progress (disembodied);
(2) Steady growth in the labour force;
(3) Only two factors of production, labour and 'capital' (plant and equipment), both homogeneous and non-specific;
(4) All quantities real and net;
(5) All wages consumed, all profits saved and invested.

These assumptions are of a more empirical, and disputable, sort:

(6) A constant capital–output ratio;
(7) A real wage rate which rises in the neighbourhood of full employment.

(5) could be altered to constant proportional savings, thus changing the numbers but not the logic of the system. (6) could be softened but it would mean a serious complicating of the structure of the model.

Symbols used are:

q is output;
k is capital;
w is wage rate;
$a = a_0 e^{\alpha t}$ is labour productivity; α constant;
σ is capital–output ratio (inverse of capital productivity);
w/a is workers' share of product, $(1 - w/a)$ capitalists';

Surplus = profit = savings = investment = $(1-w/a)q = \dot{k}$.
Profit rate = $\dot{k}/k = \dot{q}/q = (1-w/a)/\sigma$.

$n = n_0 e^{\beta t}$ is labour supply, β constant;

$l = q/a$ is employment.

Writing $(\dot{q/l})$ for $d/dt(q/l)$, we have

$$(\dot{q/l})/q/l = \dot{q}/q - \dot{l}/l = \alpha,$$

so that $\dot{l}/l = (1-w/a)/\sigma - \alpha$.

Call $u = w/a, \quad v = l/n,$

so that $\dot{v}/v = (1-u)/\sigma - (\alpha+\beta)$.

Assumption (7) may be written as

$$\dot{w}/w = f(v),$$

as shown in FIGURE 12.1.

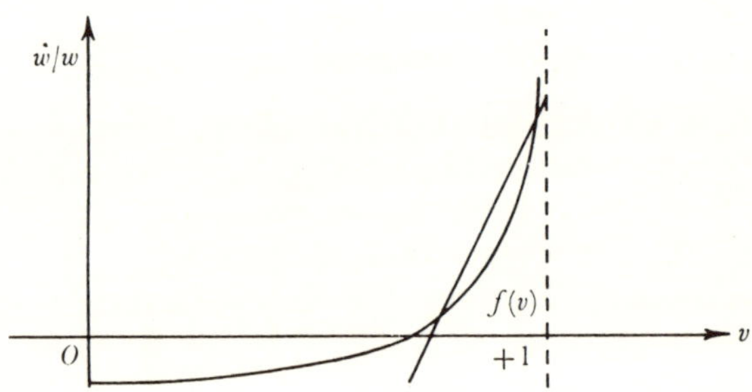

FIGURE 12.1

The following analysis can be carried out using such an $f(v)$, with a change in degree but not in kind of results. Instead, in the interest of lucidity and ease of analysis, I shall take a linear approximation (as shown in FIGURE 12.1),

$$\dot{w}/w = -\gamma + \rho v,$$

and this does quite satisfactorily for moderate movements of v near the point $+1$. Both γ and ρ must be large. Since

$$\dot{u}/u = \dot{w}/w - \alpha, \qquad \dot{u}/u = -(\alpha+\gamma)+\rho v.$$

From this and the equation above for v, we have a convenient statement of our model.

$$\dot{v} = [(1/\sigma - (\alpha + \beta)) - 1/\sigma u]v. \tag{1}$$

$$\dot{u} = [-(\alpha + \gamma) + \rho v]u. \tag{2}$$

In this form we recognise the Volterra case of prey and predator (*Théorie Mathématique de la Lutte pour la Vie*. Paris, 1931). To some extent the similarity is purely formal, but not entirely so. It has long seemed to me that Volterra's problem of the symbiosis of two populations—partly complementary, partly hostile—is helpful in the understanding of the dynamical contradictions of capitalism, especially when stated in a more or less Marxian form.

Eliminating time and performing a first integration we get

$$(1/\sigma)u + \rho v - [1/\sigma - (\alpha + \rho)] \log u - (\gamma + \alpha) \log v = \text{constant}.$$

Letting

$$\theta_1 = 1/\sigma; \quad \eta_1 = 1/\sigma - (\alpha + \beta),$$

$$\theta_2 = \rho; \quad \eta_2 = \gamma + \alpha,$$

we can transform this into

$$\phi(u) = u^{\eta_1} e^{-\theta_1 u} = H v^{-\eta_2} e^{\theta_2 v} = H\psi(v), \tag{3}$$

where H is an arbitrary constant, depending on initial conditions, since $1/\sigma > (\alpha + \beta)$, all coefficients are positive. By differentiating,

$$d\phi/du = (-\theta_1 + \eta_1/u)\phi, \quad d\psi/dv = (\theta_2 - \eta_2/v)\psi,$$

so that we can see that these functions have the sorts of shapes given in FIGURE 12.2.

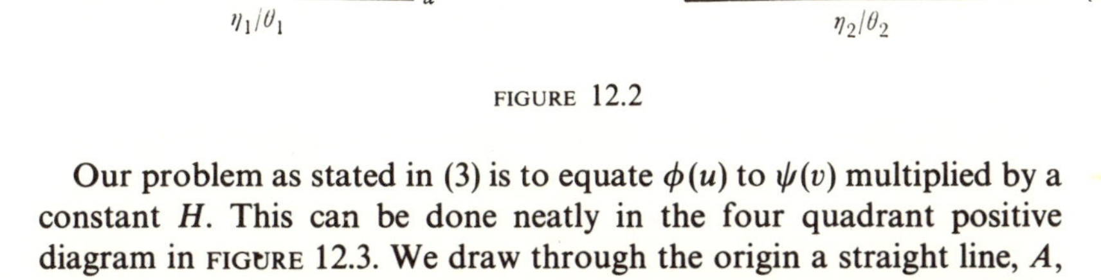

FIGURE 12.2

Our problem as stated in (3) is to equate $\phi(u)$ to $\psi(v)$ multiplied by a constant H. This can be done neatly in the four quadrant positive diagram in FIGURE 12.3. We draw through the origin a straight line, A, with the slope $\phi/\psi = H$ (arbitrary since dependent on the given initial condition). Then in symmetrical quadrants we place the two curves ϕ and

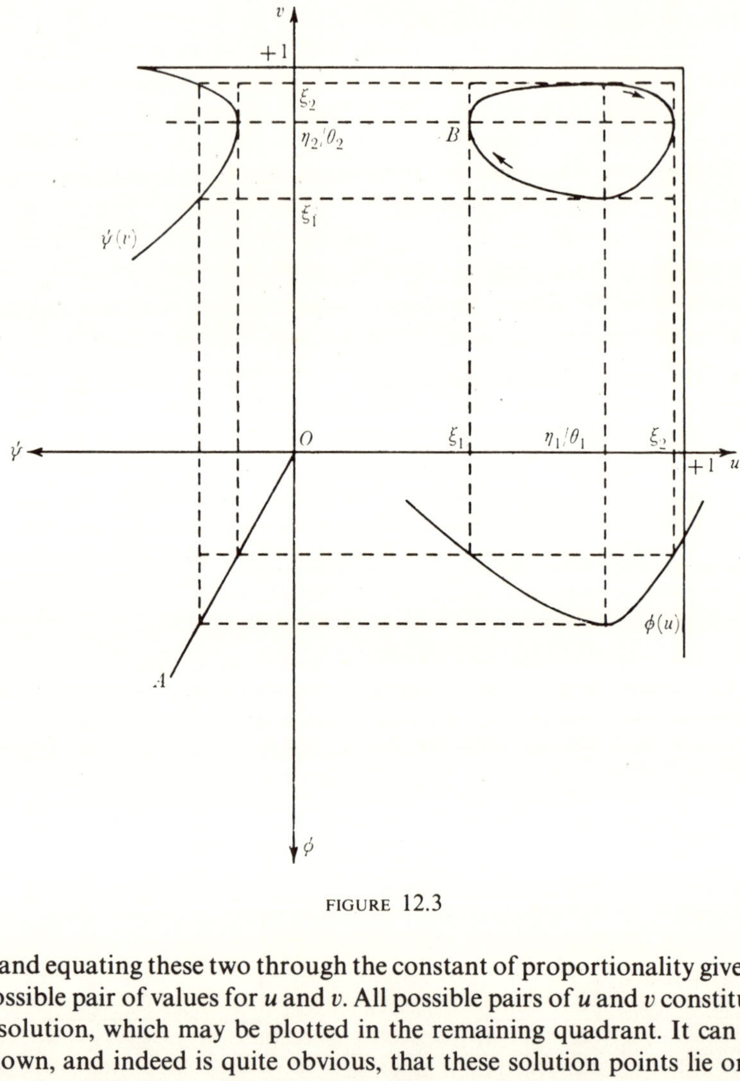

FIGURE 12.3

ψ and equating these two through the constant of proportionality gives a possible pair of values for *u* and *v*. All possible pairs of *u* and *v* constitute a solution, which may be plotted in the remaining quadrant. It can be shown, and indeed is quite obvious, that these solution points lie on a closed, positive curve, *B*, in *u*, *v* space. By going back to equations (1) and (2) we can find in what order the points succeed each other and hence in what direction we traverse curve *B*, as indicated by arrows in FIGURE 12.3. A second integration will yield *u* and *v* as functions of time, thus allowing us to determine the second arbitrary factor, the point on *B* at which we start. By varying the slope of *A* we can generate a family of closed curves broadly similar to *B*, thus yielding all the possible solutions. One initial condition selects the curve, a second fixes the starting point, and then we traverse some particular curve B in the direction of the arrows for ever, in the absence of given outside changes. There remains only to spell out the meaning of the motion.

Hence we may classify our model as a non-linear conservative oscillator of, fortunately, a soluble type. As the representative point travels around the closed curve B, u vibrates between ξ_1 and ξ_2, and v between ζ_1 and ζ_2. Both u and v must be positive and v must, by definition, be less than unity; u normally will be also but may, exceptionally, be greater than unity (wages and consumption greater than total product by virtue of losses and disinvestment). Over the stretch 0 to $+1$ on the u axis, the point u indicates the distribution of income, workers' share to the left, capitalists' to the right. The capitalists' share, multiplied by a constant, $1/\sigma$, gives us the profit rate and the rate of growth in output, $\dot{q}/q$. When profit is greatest, $u = \xi_1$, employment is average, $v = \eta_2\theta_2$, and the high growth rate pushes employment to its maximum ξ_2 which squeezes the profit rate to its average value η_1/θ_1. The deceleration in growth lowers employment (relative) to its average value again, where profit and growth are again at their nadir ξ_2. This low growth rate leads to a fall in output and employment to well below full employment, thus restoring profitability to its average value because productivity is now rising faster than wage rates. This is, I believe, essentially what Marx meant by the contradiction of capitalism and its transitory resolution in booms and slumps. It is, however, un-Marxian in asserting that profitability is restored not (necessarily) by a fall in real wages but rather by their failing to rise with productivity. Real wages must fall in relation to productivity; they may fall absolutely as well, depending on the severity of the cycle. The improved profitability carries the seed of its own destruction by engendering a too vigorous expansion of output and employment, thus destroying the reserve army of labour and strengthening labour's bargaining power. This inherent conflict and complementarity of workers and capitalists is typical of symbiosis.

An undisturbed system has constant average values η_1/θ_1 for u and η_2/θ_2 for v, hence a constant long-run average distribution of income and degree of unemployment. Much more remarkable is the fact that a *disturbed* system still has the same constant long-run values. The time averages of u and of v are independent of initial conditions. We can see this from the fact that a rotation of A (an outside change) will only make the curve B larger or smaller but will not alter its central point. Therefore continual shocks will alter the shape of the cycle but not the long-run average values. Output and employment both will show alternating rates of growth. Whether they actually decrease or merely rise less rapidly will depend on the severity of the cycle. For a mild cycle the growth rate may decrease but never become negative, in other cases there may be a sharp fall. However, the increases must predominate over the decreases, since the time average of $1 - u$ is positive and hence so also is that of $\dot{q}/q$. Likewise employment grows in the long-run at the same rate as labour supply, since the time average of v is constant. Similarly the equality of the growth rate in wages to that in productivity follows from the constancy of u. By contrast the profit rate is equal to $1 - u$ and therefore tends to constancy. We may look at this as standing Ricardo (and Marx) on his head. Progress first accrues as profits but profits lead to expansion and expansion forces wages up and profits down. Therefore we have a Malthusian Iron Law of Profits. This is because of the tendency of capital, though not capitalists, to breed excessively. By contrast labour is something of a rent good since the supply, though variable, does not seem to be a function of wages. Hence it is the sole ultimate beneficiary from technical progress. By now there would, I suppose, be considerable agreement that what happened in history is: wage rates went up; profit rates stayed down. It is to the explanation of this that the present paper is addressed.

NOTES

1. Presented at the First World Congress of the Econometric Society, held in Rome, 1965.

13. Capitalism's Golden Rule

BULLETIN OF THE CONFERENCE OF SOCIALIST ECONOMISTS, 1972

A set of simple, interrelated propositions, based on premises widely accepted by bourgeois economists.

(1) To each profit rate corresponds a set of relative prices. A change in relative prices alters the technique of production chosen by competitive producers.

(2) To any particular growth rate there corresponds an efficient technique, i.e. that collection of production processes which, after allowing for necessary accumulation, yields a greater consumption than any other technique.

(3) This best technique will be chosen by competitive producers if the profit rate on invested capital equals the growth rate.

(4) Any consumption by owners of produced capital goods means that the profit rate is greater than the growth rate. The result is the choice of an inefficient technique, in the sense that both capitalists and workers could consume more had the technique associated with equal growth and profit rates been chosen.

(5) All capitalist economies are inefficient in this sense, since capitalists do in fact consume a part of profits.

(6) Any profit rate greater than growth rate amounts to levying taxes on output for the benefit of a particular class. Like all such taxes they fall unequally on different goods, so that there is an alteration of relative prices which corresponds to no operative aspect of the production process. The result is an inefficient technique and a sub-optimal allocation of resources. This is separate from and additional to the unjustifiable distribution of consumption.

(7) Therefore, optimality requires in effect expropriation of capitalists, since if the owners of capital can never, now or in the future, consume any of the income, the ownership of capital is nominal, its 'fruits' accruing to the whole society.

(8) Just as to each profit and growth rate there corresponds a best technique, so also is there a best technique for the stationary state with zero growth rate. Only a zero profit rate will lead producers to choose that technique.

(9) Therefore, if capitalists cease, either voluntarily or under compulsion, their accumulation, optimality requires the reduction of their revenue to zero in the absence of growth.

(10) Capitalists have been, and still are, engines of growth, however imperfect or wasteful their performance may have been. Consequently, as the industrialised economies gradually but inevitably decelerate, the capitalist loses his function. The determination of the rate of return on capital then becomes a naked struggle over shares in the product. But also the outcome will affect adversely the size of the product to be shared in exactly the same way as monopolistic pricing or excise taxes.

14. Wicksell and the Malthusian Catastrophe

SCANDINAVIAN JOURNAL OF ECONOMICS, 1978

I. Introduction

Wicksell is peculiarly relevant to the agonising reappraisal, now going on, about economic growth. After 200 years of fitful but persistent growth, grave doubts have arisen about its implications for the future. The people want it; politicians preach it and try to practise it; economists could think of nothing else for the last couple of decades. Until the oil crisis, the future apparently worried no one.

Here is where Wicksell is so apposite. After a scientific training, he at one point read and got the Malthusian message. Perceptively he realised that the issues posed required more serious economic analysis than they had received: accordingly he devoted the rest of his life to that task. Thus he soon came under the influence of the new economics—marginalism—and felt it superior to that of Malthus and classical economics generally. It may have been this influence which gradually undermined and ultimately practically eradicated his commitment to neo-Malthusianism. In my view this was a tragedy, and I shall try to explain how and why.

There is the awkward initial question: is neoclassical economic method better than classical? One has to ask: better for what? If I may be dogmatic, I would say that marginalism is, in principle, subtler, more sophisticated and, in a sense, truer than classical analysis. It is vastly more complex and goes into details, into the fine structure of the economy. This gain is achieved, however, at a heavy cost: the broad outlines, the central tendencies, the evolution of the whole, all were lost until Keynes brought something of them back (paying excessive tribute to Malthus in the process).

Wicksell, I feel, sensed that much was being lost and struggled against losing himself in that detail. It was partly for this reason, I think, that, as a student, I preferred him to all other economists. Though he did not shun meticulous logic, he never surrendered to details in the manner of Walras or of Marshall. Nevertheless it is a fact that he did drop the section on demography from the second edition of his final testament, the *Lectures*; he never really carried his analysis of capital beyond the stationary state and simple interest; he relegated the fundamental issue of capital accumulation to a brief and uncharacteristically tentative section of the *Lectures*; and though he remained impressed by Malthus and Ricardo, he seems never to have appreciated the significance of Marx's development of classical economics.

As both Malthus and Wicksell recognised, population is intimately related to production. Demography was and should have remained the province of economists, but they abandoned it, apparently for the simple reason that Malthus's dire predictions were wrong. They failed to notice that the fault lay in the economics more than in the demography. Animal population theory can assume the environment and the availability of food to be essentially constant, as in the classic Reed–Pearl experiment. This will not do for people: Malthus proposed his crude arithmetic–geometric formula. This would not do either, and so we have, at the very least, to progress to Ricardo's declining marginal product of land.

Thus economics became in the early nineteenth century the dismal science because it predicted a homeostatic feedback mechanism for the standard of living: no matter how much technology progressed, the population would increase and swamp the increased product. In the long run the level of consumption had always to be at that level that equated births and deaths. This proposition sounds less than inpressive after 200 years in which they have been unequal: nonetheless it remains true that it is inconceivable to have them indefinitely unequal. However, the precise mechanism by which they are equated and when and at what levels of total world population are matters which have escaped the finest analytic meshes. Of course, Malthus always waits in the wings; if some more gentle mechanism fails, there is the final solution of infinite growth in a finite world.

Malthus's seminal proposition has been falsified for so long because output has been able to keep pace with the population explosion, indeed far to out-pace it in many parts of the world. Ultimately the vital question must be posed: can this be a permanent resolution or has the Malthusian spectre only been postponed? The main reason for renewed doubt springs from the distinction between renewable and non-renewable resources. Malthus thought, quite properly for his time, primarily in terms of agriculture. All things which depend for their source on solar energy may be thought of as eternal for all practical purposes. This leads to the Ricardian theory of rent. By contrast such a theory is totally inapplicable to exhaustible resources such as oil, uranium, iron, copper, etc. They constitute a completely different and disturbingly perverse situation. The urgency springs from two facts. One is that these resources exist in fixed amounts and once used cannot, for the most part, be used again. The second is that so long as only a small part of the globe experienced the great upsurge of production, the problem did not seem pressing. Beginning with the second half of this century, more or less the whole world is aiming to carry out a similar output explosion. It is for this reason that it is necessary to analyse in terms of world output and world population, however unsatisfactory that may be.

The economists abandoned demography to specialist demographers, who have complicated the subject (rightly) without having succeeded in achieving any very satisfactory predictive power. They in turn have abandoned the subject to the historians, which probably is equivalent to giving up hope for a quantitative theory. The historians will no doubt enormously improve the empirical bases of our knowledge of the variety of influences on death and fertility rates, but that any generally valid laws will emerge is open to grave doubt. The defection of economists is to be deplored for the subject really is (apart from the great technical complexities) an economic problem, exactly in the spirit Malthus posed it and Wicksell pursued it. That the problem is one of analysing the nature of the mechanism by which birth and death rates are equalised, has been amply shown in the simpler cases of animal populations.

If one believes, as I do, that there could eventually be some sort of spectacular collapse of our industrial civilisation, then the subject is of great interest, even though it may be remote in time. The fact that the problem is of an intractable complexity does not mean that it will go away. Economists have a bad record here; they have ignored and attacked the assorted scientists, business men, and crackpots who have warned of the danger; they have done so on the sound grounds that no one can predict the economic future (they should know—look at their own disastrous record). But this is a sword that cuts two ways: if we cannot predict disaster, we cannot predict that there will be none. The nineteenth-century belief in perpetual progress appears to have found its last resting place with economists. The multiple disasters of this century, which have cooled the faith in the future, seen only to have awakened it in economists.

What is required is an analysis both qualitative and global—qualitative in not resting on specific, quantitative functions and global in the sense of encompassing large variations in the quantities, and hence not really suitable for linearisation (though I shall have to make use of such for simplicity of analysis). Viewed secularly, our society is in continuous, strong disequilibrium and it will, like all previous societies, disappear in the course of time. A good candidate for analysing this potential decay is demographic analysis which may suggest how and why, though scarcely when, it may disappear. Though we have very little firm empirical knowledge about the factors determining net fertility and death-rates, nonetheless one can reach some global conclusions without any very precise relationships. The most obvious example is that, without knowing anything, one can say that birth- and death-rates cannot be permanently unequal. I shall use the crudest of concepts with the limited aim of getting something like an aerial view of the terrain that lies ahead. This involves using a single world output, a single world natural resource, crude birth- and death-rates, thus ignoring net rates, age composition, dependency and participation rates, national and regional differences. Output per head will be taken to represent standard of living with no regard for the effects of growth rates.

II. Population and Resources: The Prey and the Predator Mechanism

Suppose that, for whatever reason, average birth- and death-rates have been both equal and constant, so that population, x, has, with temporary excursions, remained constant.

$$\dot{x}/x = b - d = 0.$$

If there occurs a small exogenous, parametric change which puts one or the other of b or d above or below the other, then the behaviour of population becomes qualitatively different; in the one case numbers increase without limit; in the other the species disappears. This is to be contrasted with the case in which, with b unequal to d, there is a small change: the behaviour is altered quantitatively but not qualitatively. With b and d equal the system is said to be structurally unstable—to be sharply distinguished from the ordinary dynamical instability. Where such a small parametric change gives rise to a clear bifurcation in behaviour is the simplest example of what René Thom has christened a catastrophe, a designation peculiarly appropriate to population theory.[1]

The case of $b > d$ corresponds to a species newly introduced into an area with a given environment of edible plant life. However, this regime is untenable for any prolonged period: there must be a mechanism for bringing the two rates into equality. With a constant energy source (solar), producing a constant flow of food, there will be a population, $\bar{x}$, which just consumes the annual output of food. Any larger x will lead to over-grazing and a falling per capita food supply, with rising d and possibly falling b. Assuming a linear approximation, the result is the basic population equation, the logistic:

$$\dot{x}/x = A - Bx,$$

giving $x = A/B$ for $\dot{x} = 0$. Though a bit too simple for human populations, this does illustrate the powerful logic of Malthus.

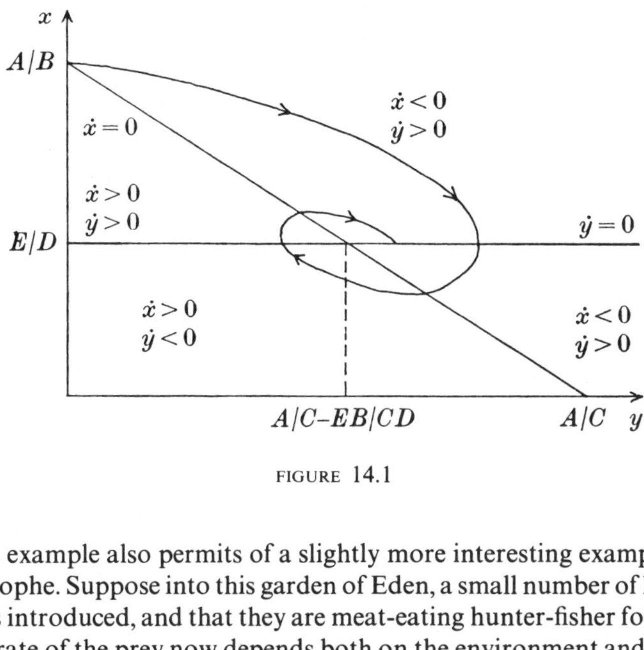

FIGURE 14.1

This example also permits of a slightly more interesting example of a catastrophe. Suppose into this garden of Eden, a small number of human pairs is introduced, and that they are meat-eating hunter-fisher folk. The death-rate of the prey now depends both on the environment and on the number of men, y. x now denotes the stock animals and y the human population. Then, keeping to growth-rate linear relations,

$$\dot{x}/x = A - Bx - Cy,$$

yielding, for $\dot{x} = 0$,

$$x = A/B - (C/B)y.$$

The men have only the prey as food supply, a variable one dependent on their own numbers, hence

$$\dot{y}/y = Dx - E,$$

giving, for $\dot{y} = 0$, $x = E/D$. As shown in the accompanying diagram, the vector field consists of four areas along with the two co-ordinate axes. Prior to the appearance of man, the animal population, however disturbed by, say, climate, is confined to the x axis and will be tending always towards the stable equilibrium point, A/B. The introduction of a small number of human beings constitutes a catastrophe which leads to a completely different behaviour of the animal population. The human population increases rapidly in exceptionally favourable circumstances but gradually decelerates as its own growth reduces its prey. Once the predators numbers have fallen sufficiently, the animals begin again to increase. Thus the two populations, interdependent both complementarily and competitively, oscillate out of phase in decreasing swings towards a stable focus.[2] The result is that a very small initial change causes the animals to move away from the point A/B, never to return. Parallel to this, the human population is launched into a large, unsteady growth towards a new equilibrium level, $(A/C) - (EB/CD)$.

The resulting cyclical behaviour is a variant of the famous prey–predator mechanism investigated and solved by Volterra (and independently by Lotka). The theory was generalised by Kolmogoroff[3] and shown to yield useful qualitative results for general, non-linear functions, i.e.

$$\dot{x}/x = f(x,y)$$
$$\dot{y}/y = g(x,y).$$

Knowing only certain qualitative characteristics of the functions, e.g. slope and position, one can describe the nature of the resulting behaviour.

Pursuing this 'stylised history', man discovers a superior technology for exploiting solar energy by settled agriculture, it being much more efficient to feed on plants than to feed on animals who feed on plants. As the grazing lands are turned to cultivation, the animals partially or totally disappear and man becomes subject to a growth law similar to that previously faced by the animals. There will be a certain population $\bar{y} > (A/C) - (EB/CD)$, which will consume the annual produce, beyond which there will be a falling consumption per head. In linear form,

$$\dot{y}/y = A - By.$$

III. Population and Resources: The Mechanism with Exhaustible Prey

Some such stable situation lasted for a long time, perhaps with a slow rise of A. Then came the industrial revolution of the eighteenth to twentieth centuries. This constituted a catastrophe in the sense that it altered both qualitatively and quantitatively the behaviour and structural relations of population and output. The Malthusian mechanism was only noticed when it ceased to operate; the system changed from dynamical stability to dynamical instability. To put a complex matter simply — the death-rate was reduced whilst the birth-rate was not, thus ending the mechanism which had kept them substantially equal. As is well understood, the same scientific revolution which reduced the death-rate, also led to increased output per head by the use of stored up solar energy to replace human and animal energy, along with the massive use of various minerals. For present purposes the essential feature of this process was the use, on an accelerating scale, of exhaustible resources.

The Malthusian trap has been evaded but only in a manner which carries ominous implications for the future. With a rising standard of living the implacable Malthusian mechanism is simply non-existent. The birth-rate is falling in many countries but the mechanism by which it may ultimately be equated to the death-rate is complex and uncertain, and highly unlikely to behave according to past behaviour. But even if in the course of the next century, the two do come into equality, there will be the enormously swollen population and the still more enormously swollen rate of production which will be sucking up non-renewable, finite resources at a correspondingly gigantic rate. Thus the essential logic of the Malthusian problem is posed in a situation quite different from that of constant resources based on solar energy. This is the prey–predator mechanism with the vital difference that the prey, once consumed will not regenerate, even when the predator population is decimated for lack of sustenance. A simple analogue is provided by the so-called Dutch elm disease. A single shipment of timber introduced into England a small number of the carrier beetles. By now there are thousands of millions of these beetles destroying at an increasing rate the elm population on which they depend. As the elms disappear so also will the beetle that uses them. It is a clear case of a small parametric change leading to total, or near total, disappearance of one population, in parallel with an enormous growth and eventual disappearance of another.

The serious predictions of a difficult future for mankind have thus far come from scientists and an assortment of practical and impractical men.

This is partly because of the irresponsibility of economists, who have ignored the world economic problem and restricted themselves to particular countries. Scientists are accustomed to working with relationships specified by numerically given parameters—parameters which will hold under very diverse circumstances. By contrast, economists have no 'universal' constants. Consequently the efforts at prediction by scientists have been understandably greeted with disbelief. What I want to do is to keep to very simple, non-quantitative assumptions, which are, I hope, empirically valid in a rough way, and then to see if it is not possible to arrive at some substantive conclusions from these very 'weak' assumptions.

Suppose that there is a single entity, resources, which may be divided into renewable, $\bar{n}$, and non-renewable, n, so that the total is $n' = \bar{n}+n$. Assume that the human population can similarly be divided into $y' = \bar{y}+y$. In reality, of course, the two types of productivity and associated populations are thoroughly intermingled. y may be thought of as the difference between the population sustainable by all resources and that sustainable by solar derived sources alone. The Malthusian mechanism applies to $\bar{y}$ and I shall make the heroic assumption that the scientific revolution, which unlocked the riches of the earth's crust, has its full effect on the $\bar{y}$ population from the start. Therefore $\dot{\bar{y}}/\bar{y} = A - B\bar{y}$,

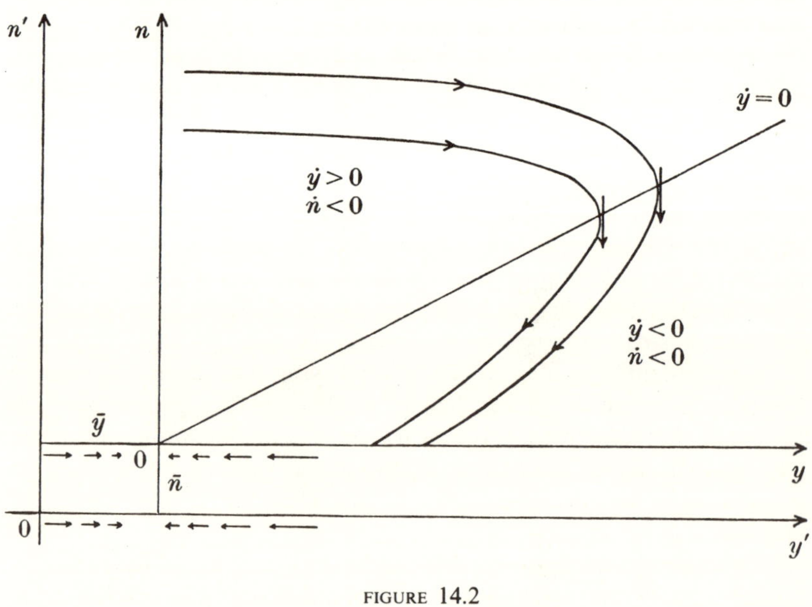

FIGURE 14.2

with its permanent equilibrium level at A/B. The rate of growth of y is taken to be positively related to n and negatively to y. Thus in simple, linear form, $\dot{y}/y = Dn - Ey$, whilst $\dot{n} = -Cy$. Initially y is very small and n very large. By definition both n and y are non-negative. The evolution of such a system can then be represented, with no attempt at accuracy or scale, as in FIGURE 14.2.

Equilibrium states for n and y are given by $n = (E/D)y$ and $y = 0$. The proportional growth of y decelerates from the start but its magnitude first grows and then declines as the size of y begins to have an effect on resources and hence the standard of living. This sequence necessarily continues until $Dn = Ey$ and the population has ceased to grow. At this point, however, the depletion rate of resources is at its maximum. The subsequent decline in y eases the rate of depletion but will not avoid ultimate exhaustion. y then becomes hyper-Malthusian, dying off at an accelerating rate, but this cannot be taken literally; it only points to the unreality of the separation of the two populations as well as of the linearity assumption. The system exhibits global asymptotic stability.

IV. Conclusions

The details of this simple model cannot possibly represent the actual future course of events; it is only meant to reveal clearly certain dominating elements. The assumption of linearity is clearly unsatisfactory and is only defensible in order to make easily intelligible the central features of the process. Secondly, there is almost certain to be hysteresis in the sense that the decline will not obey the same rules as the ascent, for two quite distinct reasons. People do not react symmetrically to rises and to falls. Secondly, the advances in technology, primarily medical, will not entirely be lost in the decline, thus changing the causal relations.

The truly daunting complexity of the problem has the effect that no responsible experts ever face it. The aim of this model, with all its crude oversimplification is to bring out the serious possible consequences of two undeniable facts: the accelerating depletion of a finite stock of resources and the unavoidably huge population dependent on that shrinking stock. No one can say that this debacle must happen but by the same token no one can deny that it may happen. It is possible, but by no means certain, that some remarkable succession of technological advances will continue to circumvent the Malthusian Devil. What is quite certain is that our civilisation will depend increasingly on a technology of an ever more complex and all-embracing sort. This looks like meaning an ever diminishing amount of both freedom and democracy.

In a remarkable paper on Malthus, the British astrophysicist Sir Fred Hoyle argues that the resolution of the population–output explosion will come not through direct impoverishment, but rather as a consequence of the requisite, highly developed technology and organisation. The society, resting on such a complex, delicate structure, becomes increasingly vulnerable to social conflict, violence, pollution and ecological imbalance, with the consequence that '. . . there will be a series of organisational breakdowns, or catastrophes, occasioned by overpopulation.' This would present an alternative, but even more precipitous and drastic, collapse.[4]

Some sort of optimal control of population could conceivably offer a much less disastrous course of events: the obsession of the public, of the politicians, of the economists, with growth makes such a solution unlikely. Moreover the feeble results of such efforts as have been made is not encouraging. As long ago as the turn of the century, Wicksell wrote: 'For my own part I have gradually reached the conviction that this optimum population has already been considerably exceeded in our own country as in all the countries of Europe, so that the road to increased prosperity does not lie in any further increase of population but rather in an energetic reduction of the population, continued through decades.'[5] In view of what we now know of present and projected world population, one wonders what he would have to say now.

NOTES

1. R. Thom, *Structural stability and morphogenesis* (Reading, Mass. 1975).
2. The system can be shown to be globally stable and locally asymptotically stable.
3. A. Kolmogoroff, 'Sulla teoria di volterra della lotta per l'Esistenza', *Giornale dell 'Istituto degli Attuari* (Gennaio, 1936).
4. F. Hoyle, A contradiction in the argument of Malthus, University of Hull, 1963.
5. K. Wicksell, 'The theory of population, its composition and changes'. Translated by Göran Ohlin in *Some Unpublished Works* (Lund, 1977).

Appendix

REPRINTED FROM
INSTITUTE OF RADIO ENGINEERS TRANSACTIONS OF THE
PROFESSIONAL GROUP ON CIRCUIT THEORY, 1960

Two-Stroke Oscillators

P. LE CORBEILLER

I. Introduction

The theory of autonomous, symmetrical oscillators of the second order is now well understood, thanks to the classical paper of van der Pol.[1] One of the variables in the physical system will satisfy either the differential equation given by Lord Rayleigh[2]

$$\ddot{x} - \epsilon\left(\dot{x} - \frac{\dot{x}^3}{3}\right) + x = 0 \qquad (1)$$

or the van der Pol equation

$$\ddot{y} - \epsilon(1 - y^2)\dot{y} + y = 0. \qquad (2)$$

In these equations, x and y are non-dimensional, the independent variable τ is non-dimensional time, and the dots indicate derivation with regard to τ. If we put $y = \dot{x}$, we see that (1) and (2) are mathematically equivalent. Lord Rayleigh considered only the case $\epsilon \ll 1$, where the periodic solution is nearly sinusoidal; van der Pol showed how, as ϵ increases from 0 to $+\infty$, the transients and the periodic solution evolve from the sinusoidal type towards the relaxation type. The curves $x(\tau)$ and $y(\tau)$ are too familiar to be repeated here, as also the corresponding trajectories drawn in the phase-planes (x, y) or $(y, \dot{y})$.[3]

There is some danger that the beauty of these kinematic developments could lead the student or reader into forgetting the physical relationships in the actual *oscillator*, the energy exchanges in particular, as Charles Fabry pointed out to the writer about 1929. In fact two earlier papers were inspired by this remark.[4] It appeared that electrical oscillators of the simplest kind were of two types, dual to each other. In an electrical oscillator of the series type (FIGURE A.1), the energy source is a constant–current generator, in parallel with a current-controlled non-linear diode N and with a *series* combination of inductor L, capacitor C and small resistive load r. In the parallel type (FIGURE A.2) the energy

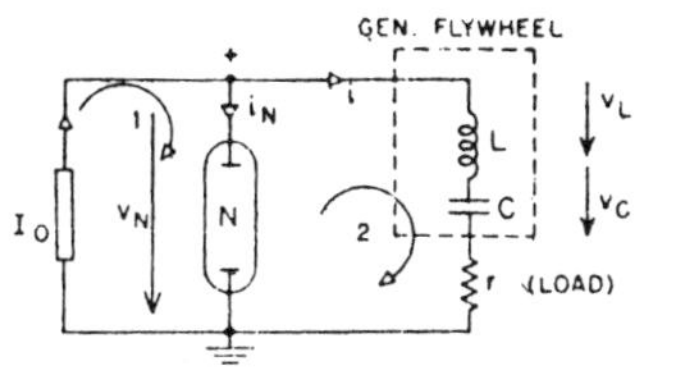

FIGURE A.1 Autonomous oscillator of the second order, series type

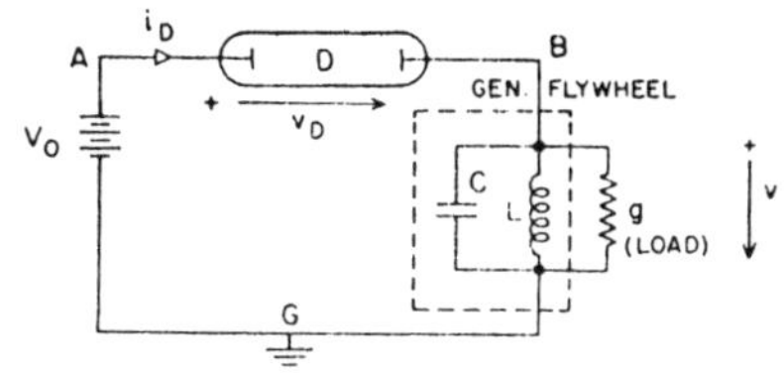

FIGURE A.2 Autonomous oscillator of the second order, parallel type

source is an ideal battery in series with a voltage-controlled non-linear diode D and with a *parallel* combination of linear elements (C, L, g). In FIGURE A.1, mesh 1 carries the constant current I_0, and mesh 2 the oscillating current **i**; in FIGURE A.2, across node-pair AG is the constant voltage V_0, and across node-pair BG the oscillating voltage **v**. The 'characteristic' of diode N is a cubic intersected at its centre of symmetry by the vertical I_0, and the characteristic of diode D is a cubic intersected at its centre by the horizontal V_0 [FIGURES A.3(a) and (b)]. The current **i** through the series triad (L, C, r) and the voltage **v** across the parallel triad (C, L, g), satisfy van der Pol's equation (2). Mechanical oscillators are also of two types, corresponding to the above by mechanical analogy (see Appendix I). In order for any one of these systems to oscillate, the numeric $r/\sqrt{L/C}$ or its analogs must be less than a certain limit.

The pair of conservative elements, inductor and capacitor, of spring and mass, can be called a *generalised flywheel*.[5] In the case of Rayleigh's

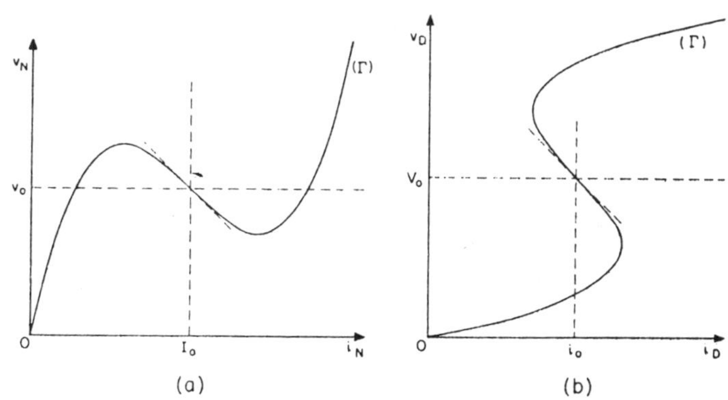

FIGURE A.3 (a) Cubic characteristic for a symmetrical oscillator, series type. (b) Cubic characteristic for a symmetrical oscillator, parallel type

(1), the unique closed trajectory (*limit cycle*) in the (x, y) phase-plane is an oval with the origin as centre. It follows from Liénard's construction[6] that the length of the radius vector oscillates *twice* between a maximum M and a minimum m as the representative point goes once around the oval (FIGURE A.4). Going back from x, y to the corresponding physical quantities one sees that x^2 and y^2 correspond to kinetic energy and potential energy, or vice versa, so that in either case the radius vector squared $(x^2 + y^2)$ corresponds to the total energy stored at time **t** in the generalised flywheel. When the radius vector increases (arcs 1–2, 3–4) the source delivers energy to the load *and* to the generalised flywheel; when the radius vector decreases (arcs 2–3, 4–1) the source *and* the generalised flywheel deliver energy to the load.[7] *The generalised flywheel breathes*, so to speak, *twice within each period*. We shall call oscillators having this property *four-stroke oscillators*. Such are typically the symmetrical oscillators associated with (1) and (2).

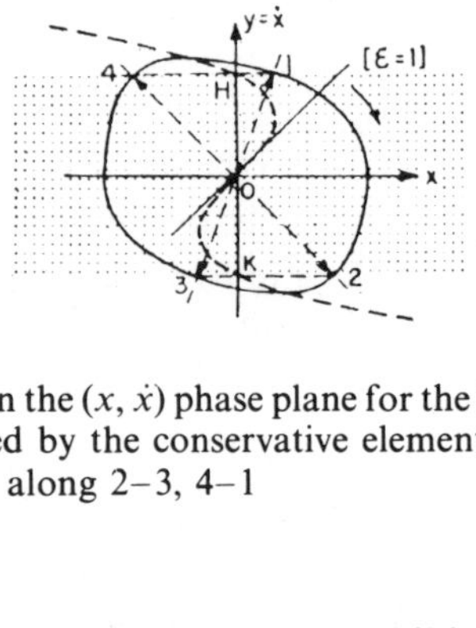

FIGURE A.4 Limit cycle in the $(x, \dot{x})$ phase plane for the Lord Rayleigh equation, $\epsilon = 1$. The energy carried by the conservative elements (L, C) increases along 1–2, 3–4, and decreases along 2–3, 4–1

The object of the present paper is to exhibit several mathematical models of non-symmetrical oscillators, in which the energy stored in the generalised flywheel varies from a minimum to a maximum value and back again *only once per period*. We shall call these oscillators *two-stroke oscillators*. The possibility of their existence tantalised the writer for a long time, since it seemed to him that various biological oscillations, such as breathing, were of that type. The first example of a two-stroke oscillator appeared in the work of an economist, Dr Richard M. Goodwin, who communicated it to the writer in December 1950 (see section V). The presentation which follows consists of a systematic generalisation and justification of Dr Goodwin's original example.

II. Generalisation of Classical Non-linear Equations

We shall first generalise (1) and (2). We shall call a *Lord Rayleigh-type equation* (abbreviated LRT) any equation

$$\ddot{x}+F(\dot{x})+x=0 \tag{3}$$

in which the *characteristic function* $F(x)$ is such that the equation has a unique periodic-solution. (The much over-worked epithet, 'characteristic', is justified below). This equation can also be written

$$\ddot{x}+R(\dot{x})\dot{x}+x=0, \tag{4}$$

and we shall call $R(\dot{x})$ a *velocity-controlled resistance*. This variable resistance must at times be negative, since otherwise there could be no periodic solution.

We shall call a *van der Pol-type equation* (abbreviated VDPT) any equation

$$\ddot{y}+r(y)\dot{y}+y=0 \tag{5}$$

in which the *displacement-controlled resistance* $r(y)$ is such that the equation has a unique periodic solution. This resistance must also at times be negative.

We shall call any solution of (3) or (4) a *Rayleigh function*, and any solution of (5) a *van der Pol function*. We shall say that two specific LRT and VDPT equations form a *pair* if $r(y)$ is the derivative of $F(y)$:

$$r(y)=F'(y)=yR'(y)+R(y). \tag{6}$$

Any van der Pol function is thus the derivative of a Rayleigh function. Note that $r(y)$ is not the derivative of $R(y)$, but of $F(y)$.

III. Construction of the Limit Cycle for a LRT Equation

Let us consider first an electrical, series-type oscillator FIGURE A.1. Let the current-controlled characteristic $(i_N,\ v_N)$ of diode N have the general shape shown in FIGURE A.5, where it was drawn free-hand. The diode current i_N oscillates around I_0, and the diode voltage v_N around v_0 (the ordinate of 0′). Let us put

$$\begin{aligned} i_N &= I_0-i,\\ v_N &= v_0+v,\\ q_C &= q_0+q. \end{aligned} \tag{7}$$

The voltage equation around the oscillatory mesh (L, C, r, N) of FIGURE A.1 is

$$-v + L\frac{di}{dt} + \frac{q}{C} + ri = 0 \tag{8}$$

or

$$v_L + v_C = v - ri = \mathscr{S}(i) \tag{9}$$

where $\mathscr{S}(i)$ is the *stimulance voltage*, a name coined by Professor R. Rüdenberg for the function upon which the whole discussion depends.[8]

We are shortly going to use a graphical construction involving oblique lines perpendicular to each other. This cannot be done with data plotted on i_N, v_N axes, since the current and voltage scales are independent; stretching one scale and not the other would destroy angular relationships.[9] We therefore multiply currents by a constant resistance, say $\sqrt{L/C}$, and put w_N (volt) $= \sqrt{L/C}\, i_N$. Call (N) the characteristic so obtained. Let $w = \sqrt{L/C}\, i$. In FIGURE A.5, $0'v$ is directed vertically upwards and $0'w$ horizontally to the *left*. Let $\overline{QP} = v$, $\overline{0'Q} = w$ at any time t. Draw through $0'$ the line of slope $(-\sqrt{C/L}r)$ (*load-line*). Then $\overline{QR} = ri$. Call M the point such that $\overline{PM} = -L\,di/dt$. We have the vector identity

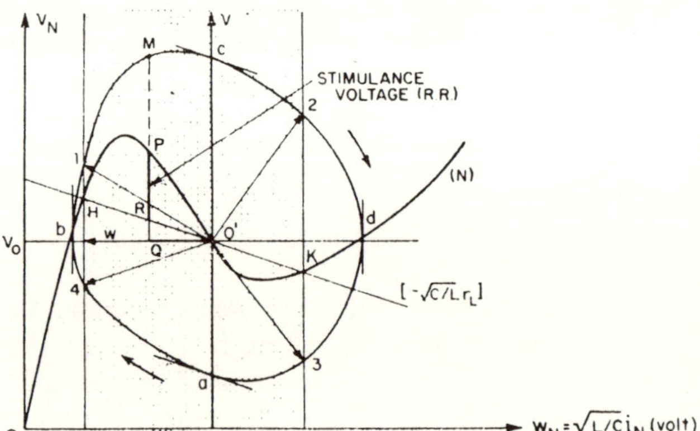

FIGURE A.5 Voltage $v_C + ri = \overline{QM}$, plotted against current i, for the oscillator of FIGURE A.1 in the periodic steady state (closed curve 1–2–3–4–1). Curve (N) is the diode characteristic (not a cubic)

$$\overline{PQ}+\overline{QR}+\overline{RM}+\overline{MP}=0 \tag{10}$$

which corresponds to the voltage equation

$$-v+ri+v_C+v_L=0. \tag{8}$$

Therefore $\mathscr{S}=\overline{RP}=\overline{QP}-\overline{QR}$, the difference between the ordinates of curve (N) and of the load-line.

Let us take $\sqrt{LC}$ for unit of time, and put $t=\sqrt{LC}\,\tau$. We have then

$$w=\sqrt{\frac{L}{C}}\,i=\frac{1}{C}\frac{dq}{d\tau}=\dot{v}_C \tag{11}$$

and

$$v_L=\sqrt{LC}\,\sqrt{\frac{L}{C}}\frac{di}{dt}=\frac{dw}{d\tau}=\ddot{v}_C. \tag{12}$$

Thus, (9) becomes

$$\ddot{v}_C-\mathscr{S}(\dot{v}_C)+v_C=0 \tag{13}$$

an LRT equation.

For a graphical discussion of this equation we turn to the phase-plane (v_C, w) (FIGURE A.6). Equation (13) can be written as

$$\frac{dw}{dv_C}w-\mathscr{S}(w)+v_C=0. \tag{14}$$

Since w is now plotted positively upwards, it is convenient to put $F=-\mathscr{S}$ and to plot F positively to the *left*. Equation (14) then becomes

$$\frac{dw}{dv_C}w+F(w)+v_C=0 \tag{15}$$

or vectorially, $\overline{MP}+\overline{PR}+\overline{RM}=0$.

MP is the length of the 'sub-normal', hence MN is the normal to the locus of M or 'trajectory'. This is Liénard's construction (so named by this writer).

We may call curve $(\mathscr{S})$, which is derived from the physical (i_N, v_N) characteristic by the successive steps we have described, the *reduced characteristic* of the oscillator. If $(\mathscr{S})$ is known, with the help of Liénard's construction we can find the limit cycle $(\mathscr{C})$, when there is one. We note that $(\mathscr{C})$ is entirely determined by the reduced characteristic $(\mathscr{S})$, and vice versa; but no analytic process leading from $(\mathscr{S})$ to $(\mathscr{C})$ is known.

In our example, $(r/\sqrt{L/C})$ is small enough for the load-line to intersect the diode characteristic (N) of FIGURE A.5 in three points. Therefore, the 0w axis intersects curve ($\mathscr{S}$) of FIGURE A.6 in three points H, 0, K, and we can drop four normals from 0 on ($\mathscr{C}$) at points 1, 2, 3, 4 (note the dissymmetry). We are thus dealing with a four-stroke oscillator.

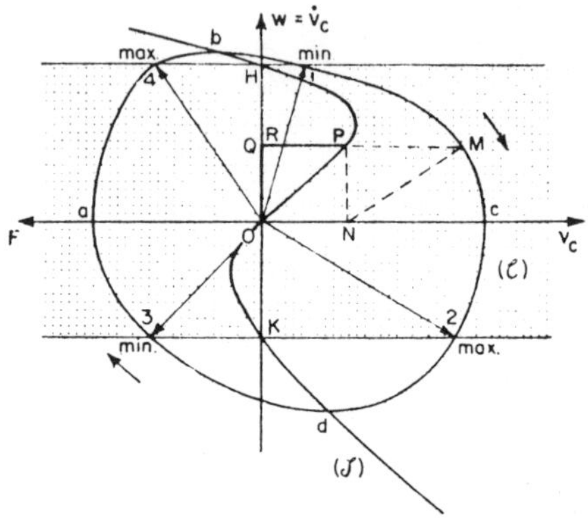

FIGURE A.6 Limit cycle for the oscillator of FIGURE A.1, the diode characteristic being curve (N) of FIGURE A.5. The Liénard graphical construction is shown; curve ($\mathscr{S}$) is the 'reduced characteristic' $\overline{RP} = \mathscr{S}$

We next transfer segment PM from FIGURE A.6 to FIGURE A.5 and we obtain a closed oval, described clockwise, as the locus of point M. At points b and d the tangents are vertical, and at a and c, they are parallel to the load-line. In this oscillator the variable resistance $R(\dot{v}_C) = F(\dot{v}_C)/\dot{v}_C$ is negative between H and K, and positive outside; thus, along the closed curve, positive on 4–1, 2–3, negative on 1–2, 3–4. (In FIGURE A.5, 0′1, 0′2, 0′3, 0′4 are not normals to the closed curve).

The relative values of *all* the currents and voltages in the series oscillator, with a given diode characteristic, are thus known at any moment, for the periodic motion (and also along any transient, if required). The very simple graphical construction above is equivalent to setting up the equation on an analog computer, but can be carried out at one's desk with the simplest equipment, cross-ruled paper and a pair of compasses from Woolworths. Graphical construction of the time-function $v_C(\tau)$ (LRT) is more lengthy (see Appendix II). Current $i(\tau)$ and voltage v_r are van der Pol functions, and v_L is the derivative of a van der

Pol function. Note that the Liénard construction applies to an LRT equation only, and not to the VDP type, unless suitably generalised. (See Appendix III.)

The above discussion was conducted in terms of voltages, v_C, $\dot{v}_C$, etc. using the non-dimensional time variable τ. We may take next any voltage $\mathscr{V}$ as unit, and put $x = v_C/\mathscr{V}$, $y = \dot{v}_C/\mathscr{V}$; the equations shall then have the non-dimensional form of (1) and (2). We shall have occasion later to choose a specific unit $\mathscr{V}$ (sections V and VI).

In a mechanical oscillator of the series type, the analog of v_C is the alternating part of the velocity of mass M (or of the angular velocity of flywheel J) (Appendix I). Thus, the alternating part of the position variable x of M (or θ of J) is the integral of a Rayleigh function, a very smooth curve.

Turning now to a parallel-type oscillator (FIGURE A.2), the characteristic (i_D, v_D) of diode D can be assumed to have the same general shape as that of diode N in a series-type oscillator, simply exchanging the voltage and current axes.[10] This time we shall plot currents along both axes, i_D vertically and $j_D\,(\text{amp}) = \sqrt{C/L}\; v_D$ horizontally. The reader will easily follow our explanations in FIGURES A.5 and A.6, assuming no change in the characteristic or in the two ovals.

The diode voltage v_D oscillates around the battery voltage V_0 and the diode current around i_0 (the ordinate of $0'$). Let us put

$$v_D = V_0 - v \qquad i_D = i_0 + i \tag{17}$$

and

$$\Phi = Li_L = \int v\,dt \tag{18}$$

(from Faraday's law $v = d\Phi/dt$). Let $j\,(\text{amp}) = \sqrt{C/L}\,v$. At any time **t** we have $\overline{QP} = i$ and $\overline{0'Q} = j$ (positive to left). Draw through $0'$ the line of slope $(-\sqrt{L/C}g)$. Then $\overline{QR} = gv$. Put $\overline{PM} = -C dv/dt$. The voltage equation (8) is now replaced by the current equation

$$-i + C\frac{dv}{dt} + \frac{1}{L}\Phi + dv = 0 \tag{19}$$

or

$$i_C + i_L = i - gv = \mathscr{L}_{\text{par}}(v) \tag{20}$$

where $\mathscr{S}_{\text{par}}$ is the *stimulance current*. Taking $\sqrt{LC}$ for unit of time, we find $j = di_L/d\tau$, $i_C = dj/d\tau$. Thus we are led to FIGURE A.6 again, plotting i_L horizontally and j vertically.

In the parallel-type electrical oscillator, $i_L(t)$ is a Rayleigh function, i_0 and v are van der Pol functions and i_C is the derivative of a van der Pol function. In the parallel-type mechanical oscillator, the alternating velocity v of the mass is a van der Pol function, hence the alternating part of the position variable x (or θ) is a Rayleigh function. We observe that in the whole question enter four functions of time:

	Series		*Parallel type*	
	Electrical	*Mechanical*	*Electrical*	*Mechanical*
The integral of a Rayleigh function		x_M or θ		
A Rayleigh function	v_C	v_M	i_L	x, f_K
A van der Pol function	i, v_r	f, v_D	v, v_θ	v, f_D
The derivative of a van der Pol function	v_L	v_K	i_C	f_M

The oscillations of the inertive element, mass or flywheel, are smoother in the series-type than in the parallel-type oscillator, assuming the same characteristics.

IV. Two-Stroke Oscillators, Exponential Types

We now want to build up equations of type (3)–(5) for two-stroke oscillators. The resistance $R(y)$ or $r(y)$ should be negative for $y = 0$, to make the origin unstable. Calling y_0 a positive quantity, the resistance should then be negative for $y < y_0$, positive for $y > y_0$. (This will be our hypothesis from now on; one could just as well take y_0 negative, with the resistance positive on the left of y_0, and negative on the right).

A type of variable resistance which should lead to a unique limit cycle is that of FIGURE A.7, in which the negative resistance goes to zero as $y \to -\infty$. Small oscillations of y around 0 will at first increase in amplitude, and soon become large enough to enter the region where resistance is positive. But the larger the amplitude, the smaller the 'average' negative resistance during a complete oscillation, and the larger the 'average' positive resistance; hence, the amplitudes (greater at left than at right) will gradually reach a limit. A simple analytic expression suitable for either $R(y)$ or $r(y)$ in FIGURE A.7 is $-\rho(1-y)e^y$. If we take $R(y)$ equal to this, we obtain the pair of equations

$$\text{LRT} \quad \ddot{x} - \rho(\dot{x} - \dot{x}^2)e^{\dot{x}} + x = 0, \tag{21}$$

$$\text{VDPT} \quad \ddot{y} - \rho(1 - y - y^2)e^y \dot{y} + y = 0. \tag{22}$$

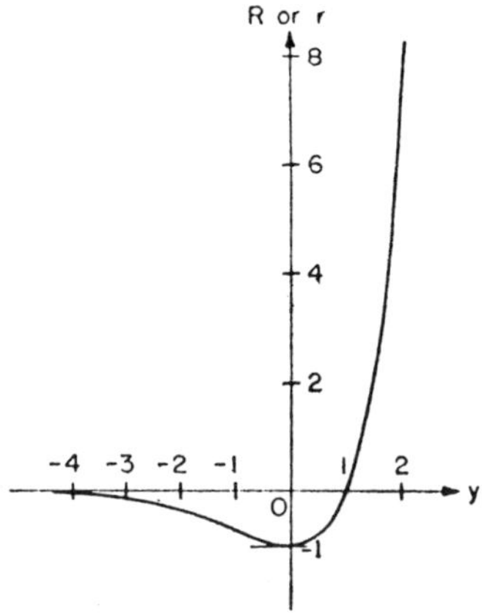

FIGURE A.7 The function R (or r) $= -\rho(1-y)e^{y}$, representing a variable resistance which leads to a two-stroke oscillator with one stable limit cycle, for any positive value of the parameter ρ

If we take the same expression for $r(y)$, we obtain another pair:

LRT $\quad \ddot{x} - \rho[(2-\dot{x})e^{\dot{x}} - 2] + x = 0,$ (23)

VDPT $\quad \ddot{y} - \rho(1-y)e^{y}\dot{y} + y = 0.$ (24)

The advantage of these equations over those which follow is that they have a periodic solution for all positive values of ρ. The limit cycles of (21) and (23) are easy to obtain and are not reproduced here.

The writer has tried out a number of functions, some with one, and some with two exponentials, which lead to two-stroke oscillators. The simplest of all seems to be $\rho(e^{y}-2)$, in which, however, the parameter ρ must be restricted to the domain $0 < \rho < 1$ (FIGURE A.8). Taking $R(y)$ equal to this, we obtain

LRT $\quad \ddot{x} + \rho(e^{\dot{x}} - 2)\dot{x} + x = 0$ (25)

the simplest LRT equation the author has found so far for a two-stroke oscillator, and

VDPT $\quad \ddot{y} + \rho(ye^{y} + y - 2)\dot{y} + y = 0.$ (26)

Using the same expression for $r(y)$ we obtain

LRT $\quad \ddot{x} + \rho(e^{\dot{x}} - 1 - 2\dot{x}) + x = 0,$ (27)

VDPT $\quad \ddot{y} + \rho(e^{y} - 2)\dot{y} + y = 0$ (28)

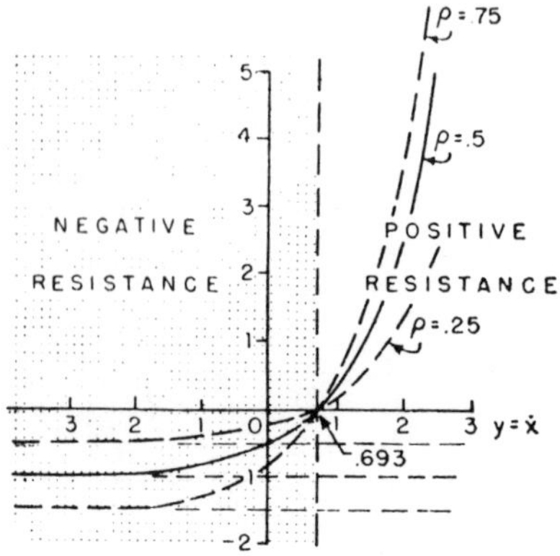

FIGURE A.8 The function R (or r) $= \rho(e^y - 2)$, a type of variable resistance which leads to a stable two-stroke oscillator for any positive value of ρ less than 1

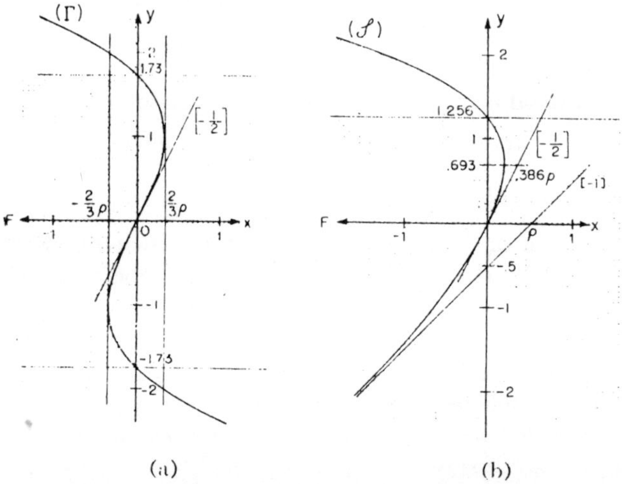

FIGURE A.9 (a) The cubic characteristic of Lord Rayleigh, for $\epsilon = \frac{1}{2}$. (b) The reduced characteristic resulting from the variable resistance of FIGURE A.8, for $\rho = \frac{1}{2}$. The domains of negative $R(\dot{x})$ or $r(y)$, in which the energy in the 'flywheel' (L, C) is increasing, are stippled. Elsewhere, the resistance is positive and the energy in (L, C) is decreasing

the simplest VDPT equation for a two-stroke oscillator. In all four equations, we must take $0 < \rho < 1$.[11]

We have plotted in FIGURE A.9(b) the characteristic ($\mathcal{S}$) of (27), and placed next to it for comparison in FIGURE A.9(a) the familiar cubic

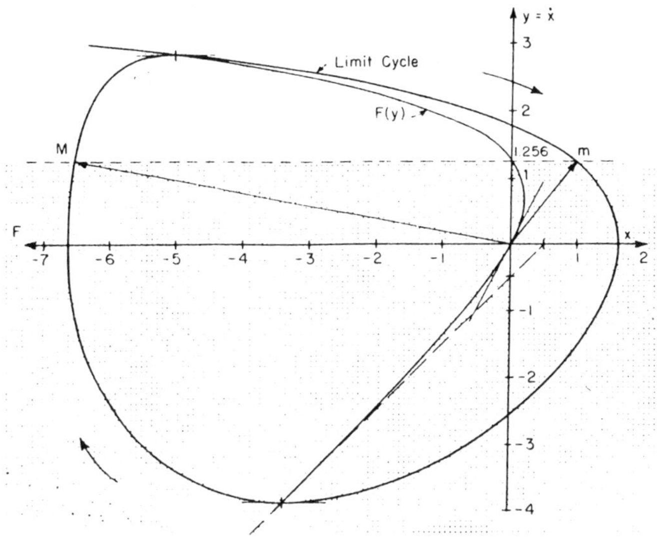

FIGURE A.10 The limit cycle obtained from the reduced characteristic of FIGURE A.9(b)

characteristic (Γ) of Lord Rayleigh, giving to both the slope $(-\frac{1}{2})$ at the origin. It is apparent at a glance that not only is the new characteristic *not* Z-shaped, but it does not even have an inflexion point anywhere. The writer used to believe (and thought it was the general understanding) that a characteristic had to have the general shape of a Z or N or S (or, we might say, had to have *two bends*) in order to produce oscillations, until Dr Goodwin proved to him otherwise.

The limit cycle resulting from the characteristic of FIGURE A.9(b) is shown in FIGURE A.10. The function $F(y)$ has now a single non-zero root, $y = 1.256$; thus, the radius vector of the limit cycle has only one maximum and one minimum. As the representative point (x, y) moves clockwise from **m** to M, the power source delivers energy to the load and to the generalised flywheel (section I); and from M to **m**, the source and the generalised flywheel deliver energy to the load. We have thus obtained from a *one-bend* characteristic, a *two-stroke oscillator*.

The corresponding periodic functions $x(\tau)$ (LRT) and $y(\tau)$ (VDPT), taken from de Figueiredo,[12] are shown in FIGURES A.11(a) and (b).

We have noted that parameter ρ must lie between 0 and 1. FIGURES A.12 and A.13 show the limit-cycle of (27) for the cases $\rho = 0.1$ and ρ

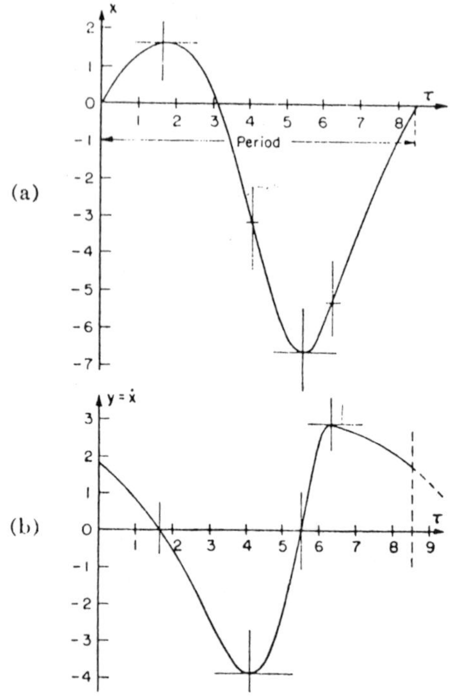

FIGURE A.11 The periodic functions $x(\tau)$, $\dot{x}(\tau)$, obtained from the limit cycle of FIGURE A.10

$= 0.8$. For $\rho = 0.1$, the limit cycle somewhat resembles a circle of radius 2 with its centre at left of 0, but the distortion is much greater than for $\epsilon = 0.1$ in the symmetrical case.[13] For $\rho = 0.8$, the limit-cycle practically coincides with the upper portion of the characteristic, and its lower part approximates a logarithmic spiral. The negative amplitude of y is almost five times the positive amplitude, and therefore the upward stroke of $x(\tau)$ is a small fraction of the period. In the boundary case $\rho = 1$, the lowest point of $(\mathscr{C})$ is at infinity, therefore there is no periodic solution $x(\tau)$.

V. The Goodwin Characteristic

In order to obtain a two-stroke oscillator, we can use a much simpler resistance function $r(y)$ than an exponential one, only it is not analytic.

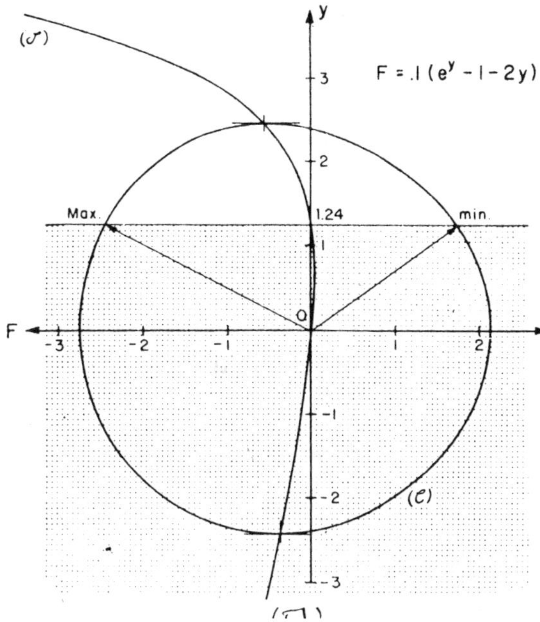

FIGURE A.12 The reduced characteristic ($\mathscr{S}$) and the limit cycle derived from the variable resistance of FIGURE A.8 for $\rho = 0.1$

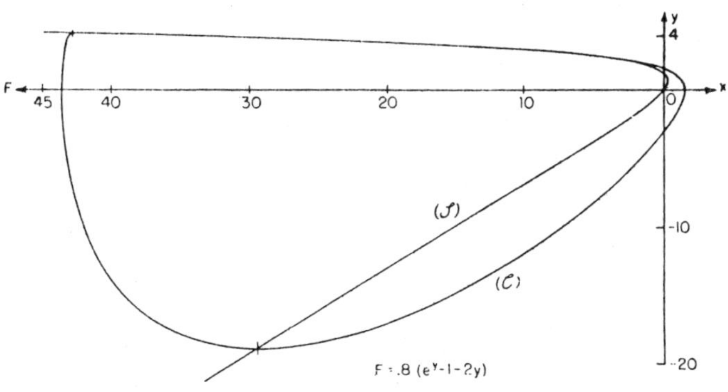

FIGURE A.13 Reduced characteristic and limit cycle for $\rho = 0.8$. Compare FIGURES A.12, A.10 and A.13

Taking as before y_0 positive, at the left of y_0 we assume a constant negative resistance $-\rho_1 > -2$, and at the right a constant positive resistance $\rho_2 > \rho_1$ [FIGURE A.14(c)]. The corresponding differential equations are (3)–(5); $F(y)$ and $R(y)$ are represented in FIGURES A.14(a) and (b).

A characteristic made up of two straight lines, with rounded-off corner, was used by Goodwin in his economic model of 1950 (unpublished); and the characteristic of FIGURE A.14(a), with or without corner, should rightly be called *the Goodwin characteristic.* This two-parameter characteristic could well be taken as canonical for two-stroke oscillators; it is discussed in detail in de Figueiredo's thesis.[12] As a single example, we give here in FIGURES A.15 and A.16 the limit cycle and the functions $x(\tau)$, $y(\tau)$ for the case $\rho = 1$, $\rho_2 = 3$, taken from de

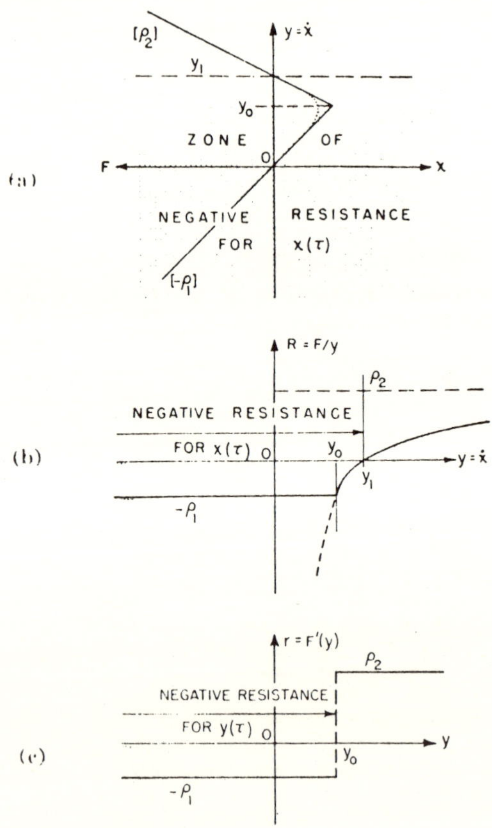

FIGURE A.14 (a) The Goodwin characteristic in the phase-plane $(x, \dot{x})$. (b) The corresponding resistance $R(\dot{x})$ in the LRT equation. (c) The resistance $r(y)$ in the VDPT equation

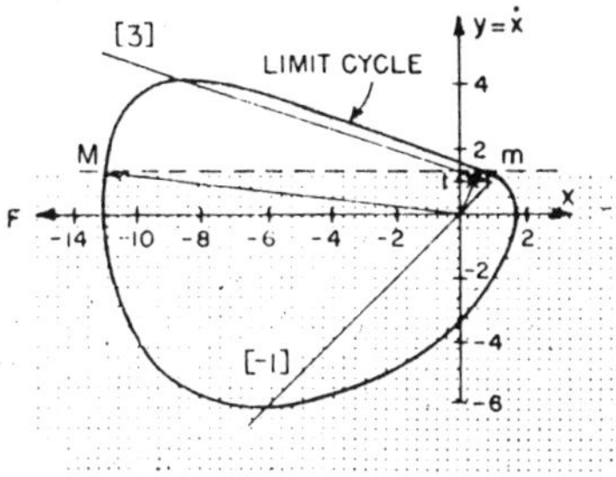

FIGURE A.15 Limit cycle for the Goodwin characteristic, $-\rho_1 = -1$, $\rho_2 = 3$

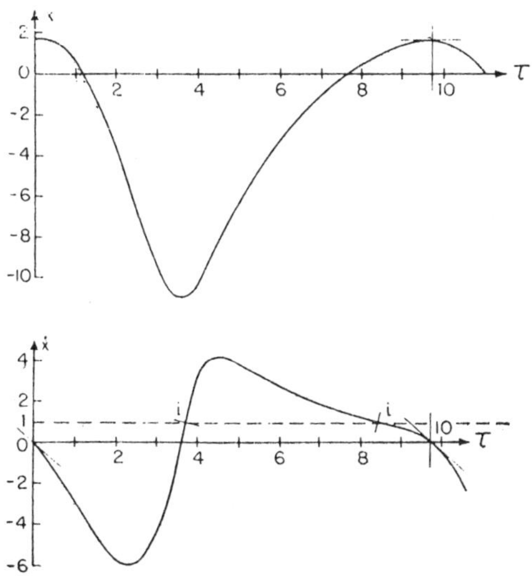

FIGURE A.16 (a) The periodic function $x(\tau)$ derived from the limit cycle of FIGURE A.15 (b) The periodic function $\dot{x}(\tau)$

Figueiredo.[12] By a suitable choice of $\mathscr{V}$ as the unit voltage (section III), it is always possible to assume in FIGURE A.14 $y_0 = 1$.

VI. Cubic Characteristic with High Dissymmetry

As a last example of an analytic characteristic leading to a two-stroke oscillator, we shall present *the cubic characteristic*.

In the symmetrical case, $F = \epsilon(-y + y^3/3)$, a cubic characteristic (Γ) intersects the $0y$-axis in two points, H and K, besides the origin, and we have a four-stroke oscillator [FIGURE A.17(a)]. Actually the distinction, whether the oscillator is four-stroke or two-stroke, does not depend upon the number of points of intersection of the load-line with the diode characteristic; it depends upon whether there are two or one of these points (besides the origin) *inside the limit cycle*. In the present case, if we move the origin of the (x, y) co-ordinates along (Γ), away from the centre of symmetry and towards point C where the slope is infinite, the limit

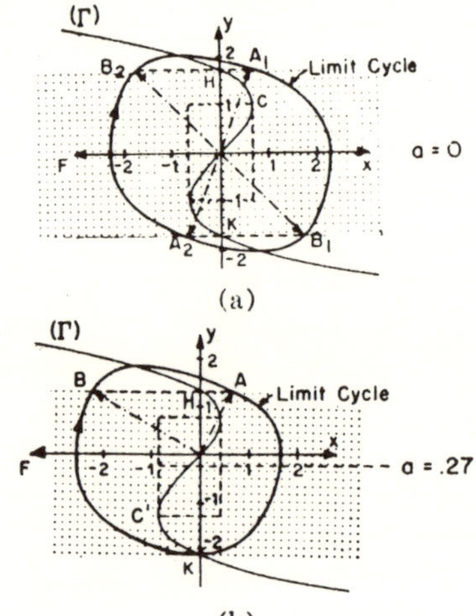

FIGURE A.17 The cubic characteristic and its limit cycle when dissymmetry is increased. (a) Perfect symmetry, origin is inflexion point. Four-stroke symmetrical oscillator. (b) Critical case, ordinate of inflexion point is -0.27, points A_2 and B_1 of FIGURE A.17(a) have merged at K. (c) Dissymmetry greater than critical, radius vector of limit cycle increasing from A to B, decreasing from B to A. Two-stroke oscillator. The Goodwin-type characteristic (Γ′) gives same limit cycle as cubic (Γ)

cycle shrinks and gets closer to point K. For a certain position of the origin, the characteristic, the $0y$-axis and the limit cycle all intersect at K [FIGURE A.17(b)] and for still more eccentric positions of the origin point, K lies *outside the limit-cycle* and we have a two-stroke oscillator [FIGURE A.17(c)]. FIGURE A.17 is taken from de Figueiredo's thesis.

The existence of a limit cycle in FIGURE A.17(c) is not due to the fact that the characteristic Γ is Z-shaped; actually, in this example, the Z-shape is irrelevant, for the following reason. Whenever the limit cycle of an LRT equation surrounds an unstable focus or node, the limit cycle and all the interior trajectories which are asymptotic to it are completely independent of those parts of the characteristic which lie outside the limit cycle. The representative point (x, y), starting from an initial position near the origin, never has a chance during its infinite lifetime to learn anything about them. If, *after* we have obtained the limit cycle ($\mathscr{C}$), we replace the infinite arcs of (Γ) outside of ($\mathscr{C}$) by the tangents to (Γ) (for example), the new characteristic (Γ'), composed of the interior part of (Γ) plus the two tangents, will command exactly the same limit cycle ($\mathscr{C}$) and the same interior trajectories; the exterior trajectories will, however, be different. This procedure still gives a characteristic with two bends, as long as point C' of infinite slope is inside ($\mathscr{C}$); but in FIGURE A.17(c), where C' is outside ($\mathscr{C}$), the new characteristic (Γ') is a Goodwin bilinear characteristic, with its corner rounded off by an arc of a cubic.

FIGURE A.18 shows the functions $x(\tau)$ (LRT) and $y(\tau)$ (VDPT) for FIGURE A.17(c).

We may wish to know under what condition the critical case of FIGURE A.17(b) occurs. We have to decide first on a set of parameters defining the cubic. In FIGURE A.19 let $(-a, b)$ be the co-ordinates of centre C, $(-\epsilon)$ the slope of the cubic at C (same parameter as van der Pol's ϵ), and let $F \sim \gamma y^3/3$ for y very large. The equation of the cubic, referred to axes through centre C, is $F_1 = -\epsilon y_1 + \gamma y_1^3/3$. The maximum and minimum of F_1 lie at the distance $\sqrt{\epsilon/\gamma}$ from C. Let us make this distance equal to 1; this amounts to taking for unit voltage $\mathscr{V}$ (section III) half the difference between the maximum and minimum of v_N on the characteristic (N) of FIGURE A.5. The characteristic function $F(y)$ is then

$$\begin{aligned} F(y) &= b - \epsilon(y+a) + \epsilon(y+a)^3/3 \\ &= -\rho y + \epsilon a y^2 + \epsilon y^3/3 \end{aligned} \tag{29}$$

with

$$b = \epsilon\left(a - \frac{a^3}{3}\right), \quad \rho = \epsilon(1 - a^2), \tag{30}$$

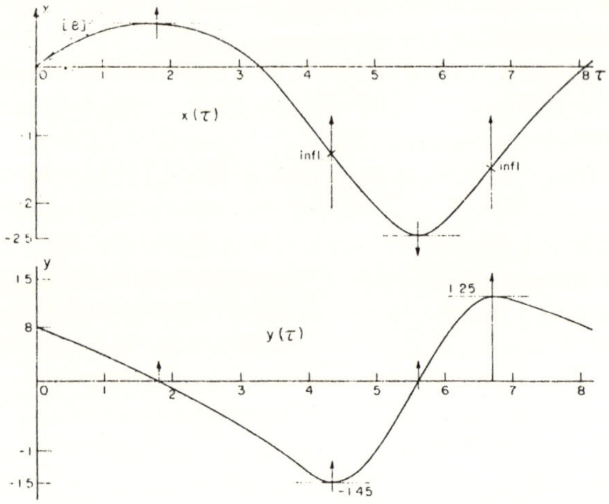

FIGURE A.18 Periodic functions $x(\tau)$ and $\dot{x}(\tau)$ derived from the cubic characteristic of FIGURE A.17(c)

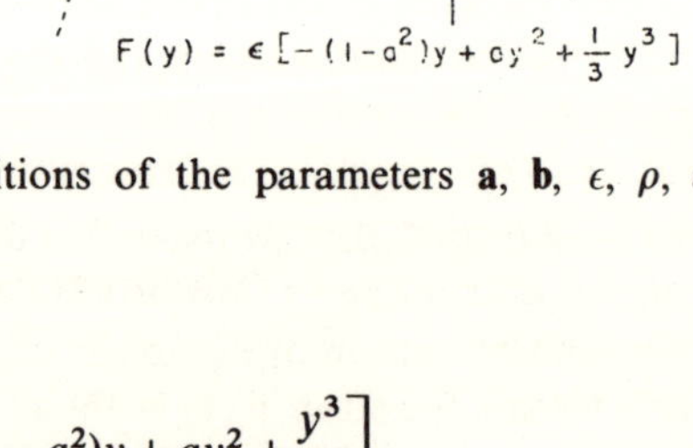

FIGURE A.19 Definitions of the parameters **a**, **b**, ϵ, ρ, attached to a cubic characteristic

or again

$$F(y) = \epsilon\left[-(1-a^2)y + ay^2 + \frac{y^3}{3}\right], \tag{31}$$

which is the standard form adopted by de Figueiredo. While the distinction between sinusoidal and relaxation oscillations is somewhat blurred in the case of two-stroke oscillators, still parameter ϵ tells us whether the cubic we are using is on the sinusoidal or 'soft' side (for $\epsilon < 2$) or on the relaxation or 'hard' side (for $\epsilon > 2$). Parameter **a**, being

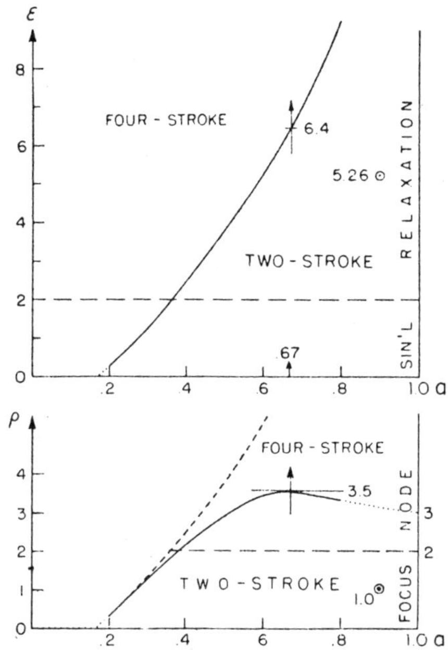

FIGURE A.20 (a) Relation between the parameters **a** and ϵ of FIGURE A.19 when the oscillator is in the critical case FIGURE A.17(b). (b) Relation between parameters **a** and ρ. Points labelled 5.26 in (a) and 1.0 in (b) correspond to the unsymmetrical cubic of FIGURE A.21

the ratio of $A0$ to AB in FIGURE A.19, is a measure of the dissymmetry: for $a = 0$ we have the symmetrical case, for $a = 1$ extreme dissymmetry.

The curve in FIGURE A.20, obtained by de Figueiredo, connects the values of the parameters ϵ and **a** of (31) for the critical case which separates four-stroke and two-stroke oscillators [FIGURE A.17(b)]. We see from this curve that it is always possible for any given ϵ to obtain two-stroke oscillators, but that the minimum dissymmetry required increases with ϵ. The relation between the slope $(-\rho)$ at the origin and the dissymmetry **a**, (30), is shown for the critical case on FIGURE 20(b). We note that ρ must always be less than ϵ, and that the maximum of ρ for the critical case is 3.5; it is thus possible for two-stroke limit cycles to be built around an unstable node ($\rho > 2$). For values of **a** greater than 0.9, putting $a = 1 - \eta$, the relations

$$\rho \sim 3 + 20\eta^2, \quad \epsilon \sim \frac{3}{2\eta} + \frac{3}{4} + \frac{83}{8}\eta \tag{32}$$

seem to be good approximations for the critical case.

FIGURES A.21 and A.22 are an example of two-stroke relaxation oscillations ($\epsilon = 5.6$) with large dissymmetry ($a = 0.9$). Negative resistance at origin is $\rho = 1$. FIGURE A.21 shows the limit cycle and FIGURE A.22(a) and (b), the LR function $x(\tau)$ and the VDP function $y(\tau)$ (see Appendix II).

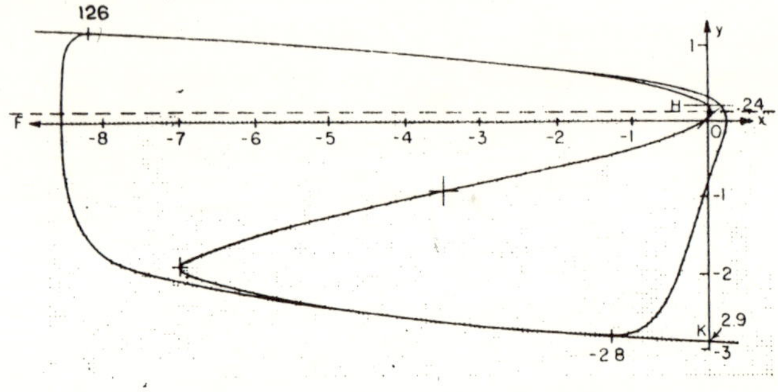

FIGURE A.21 Unsymmetrical cubic and the corresponding limit cycle for large dissymmetry, $a = 0.9$

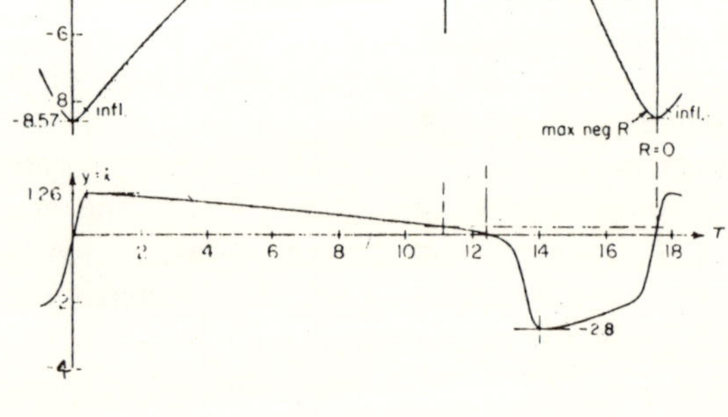

FIGURE A.22 Periodic functions $x(\tau)$ and $\dot{x}(\tau)$ derived from the cubic characteristic of FIGURE A.23. W. Nijenhuis has shown that the ratio of extreme positive and negative amplitudes of the van der Pol function $y(\tau)$ is always less than 3

Dr de Figueiredo has given in his thesis expressions for the van der Pol function $y(\tau)$ derived from a dissymmetrical cubic, for ϵ small and ϵ large. For ϵ small, his expression of $y(\tau)$ consists of eight terms, up to $\cos 4\omega_0 t$, and his expression for ω_0 contains three corrective terms of the order of ϵ^2. For ϵ infinite the van der Pol function has two discontinuities; de Figueiredo gives approximate expressions for the two continuous arcs, for ϵ large but finite and an arbitrary dissymmetry, and also an approximate expression for the period.

Nijenhuis has given approximations to all four parts of the van der Pol function $y(\tau)$, for ϵ (his ϵ') very large and arbitrary dissymmetry.[18]

The case of a cubic characteristic is thus particularly interesting in that it shows the passage from a four-stroke to a two-stroke oscillation. If some parameter λ of a physical oscillator is varied continuously, the reduced characteristic ($\mathscr{S}$) of FIGURE A.6 will in general vary; if it may be assumed that it remains of the third order, the parameters ϵ and **a** will vary as functions of λ, and the (ϵ, a) representative point will describe a certain path in FIGURE A.20(a), by which the transition from four-stroke to two-stroke will be illustrated.

VII. Dr de Figueiredo's Theory of Lord Rayleigh-Type Equations

The reader will certainly have noticed the lack of any mathematical proof in our presentation. So far, statements relating to periodic solutions were supported only by the graphical construction of the corresponding limit cycle. This was done in order to separate clearly this author's work from that of de Figueiredo.

When the characteristic of the non-linear element in the oscillator (section I) is continuous and has a continuous derivative, sufficient conditions are known for the existence and for the unicity of periodic solutions. They are based upon classical papers by Poincaré (1882) and Bendixson (1901). The subject has been advanced since that time by several workers, and the field reviewed recently by two leading contributors, Coddington and Levinson.[17]

The bilinear Goodwin characteristic $F(y)$ differed in two ways from the characteristics which had been considered before; for $|y|$ large, F was positive instead of having the sign of y; and the derivative of $F(y)$, $r(y) = F'(y)$, was discontinuous at $y = y_0$ (section V).

The equation

$$\ddot{x} + F(\dot{x}) + x = 0 \qquad (33)$$

is equivalent to the system

$$\frac{dy}{dx}y+F(y)+x=0, \tag{34a}$$

$$\dot{x}=y, \tag{34b}$$

in which the second equation is of the general type

$$\frac{dy}{dx}=f(x,y) \tag{35}$$

with

$$f(x,y)=\frac{-F(y)-x}{y}. \tag{36}$$

Let us assume that F is the Goodwin characteristic of FIGURE A.14(a), with $\rho_1 = -1$, $\rho_2 = 2$ as an example. Four curves of the family $f(x, y) = m$, with $m = -1, 0, 1, 2$, are shown in FIGURE A.23. It is clear that the function $f(x, y)$ is continuous everywhere, but that its partial derivatives f_x and f_y are discontinuous across the line $y = 1$.

Still stronger discontinuities may have to be considered. Let $F(y)$ be the characteristic shown in FIGURE A.24; the corresponding system (34), introduced by de Figueiredo and called by him 'the auxiliary system', plays an important role in his theory. Four curves of the family $f(x, y) = m$ are shown in FIGURE A.25. Here $f(x, y)$ is continuous everywhere, except across the line $y = 0$.

In Chapter II of his thesis, de Figueiredo has shown that if $f(x, y)$ is

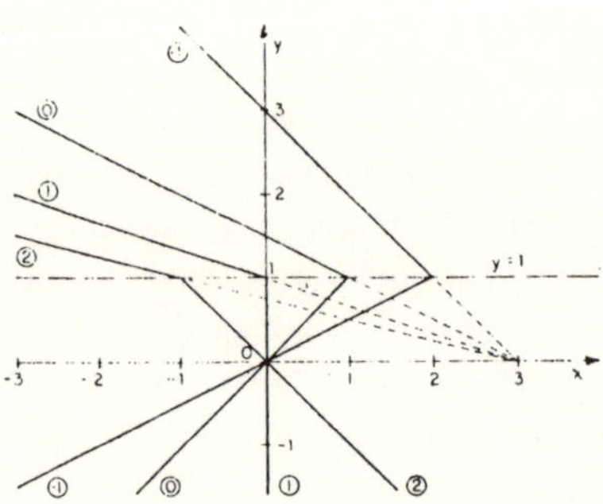

FIGURE A.23 Contour curves of the function $f(x, y) = k$ for the Goodwin characteristic of FIGURE A.14(a), $-\rho_1 = -1$, $\rho_2 = 2$.

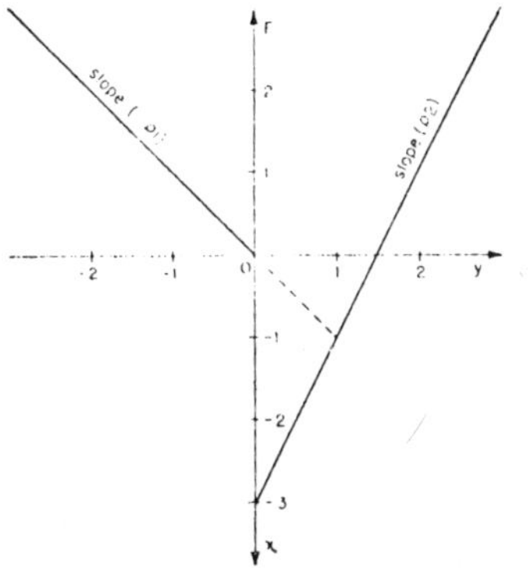

FIGURE A.24 Discontinuous characteristics $F(y)$ used by de Figueiredo in the proof of his existence theorem (Existence and Uniqueness, Chapter IV)

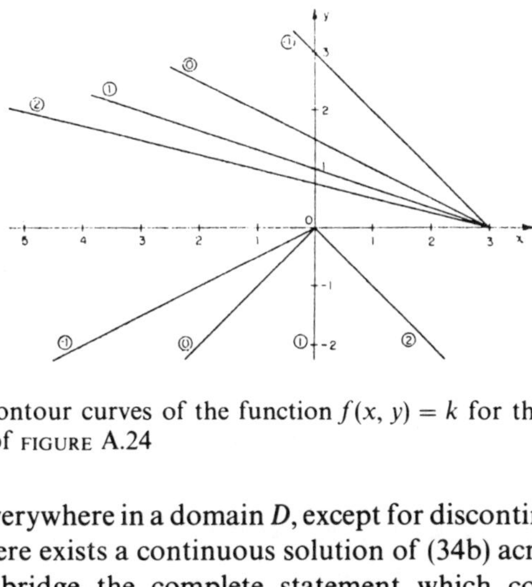

FIGURE A.25 Contour curves of the function $f(x, y) = k$ for the de Figueiredo characteristic of FIGURE A.24

continuous everywhere in a domain D, except for discontinuities across a curve Λ_{12}, there exists a continuous solution of (34b) across Λ_{12} at any point. (We abridge the complete statement which contains several qualifications, in order to bring out the result more clearly). The five-step proof of this theorem introduces several original tools. The theorem covers *a fortiori* the case of an angular characteristic.

In Chapter IV, de Figueiredo gives sufficient conditions for the existence of at least one periodic solution of (33), one of which is that the derivative of $F(y)$—which is $r(y)$ in (5) and (6)—should remain greater than -2 in a region $-\infty < y \leqq y_1$ (-2 is the critical value of ϵ which separates unstable foci and nodes in the equation $\ddot{x} + \epsilon\dot{x} + x = 0$). This is the decisive step which allows us to introduce two-stroke characteristics such as those of sections IV–VI.

In Chapter V, de Figueiredo gives sufficient conditions for the unicity of the periodic solution of an equation which already satisfies the conditions of the theorem of Chapter IV. The main one concerns the comparison of $R'(y)$ with R/y, sufficiently far out at left and at right. All the characteristics used in the present paper satisfy the sufficient conditions for unicity.

Summing up, de Figueiredo has found sufficient conditions for (33) to have a unique periodic solution (to be an LRT equation, section II), and those include the possibility of $f(x, y)$ being discontinuous across a line of the (x, y) plane. This is a notable advance beyond what was previously known. This author's contribution to it consisted in pointing out the problem to a young researcher and giving him quasi-periodic encouragement.

VIII. Conclusion

A four-stroke oscillator, whether symmetrical or moderately dissymmetrical, is one in which the linear, conservative elements receive energy from the source two times per period; such are typically a Class A vacuum tube oscillator, a Class C push–pull oscillator, or a clock with anchor escapement. This paper has presented a number of non-linear, second-order differential equations, which correspond to two-stroke oscillators in which the source is active or strongly active only once per period; such as a Class C oscillator. It is hoped that this second type will lead to a better understanding of a number of oscillations which it has not been possible to interpret so far by means of the four-stroke model.

Appendix I. Electromechanical Analogies

The following is a condensed account of the system of analogies first advocated in the U.S. in 1933 by Dr Floyd A. Firestone and used in the present paper.

The current **i** in a conductor is measured at any one point by an ammeter inserted in series; the tension **f** in a rope is measured at any point by a dynamometer or spring balance inserted in series. Such physical variables are called *through* variables or 1-*point* variables. Current **i** and force **f** are chosen as reciprocal electro-mechanical analogs.

The voltage **v** across a pair of terminals is measured by a voltmeter connected to these terminals. The distance **x** between two points is read from a yardstick placed alongside these two points, or by a caliper or micrometer contacting these two points. Such physical variables are called *across* variables, or 2-*point* variables. The relative velocity of two particles, $v = dx/dt$, (distance **dx** divided by the scalar **dt**) is also a 2-point variable. It is convenient to choose voltage **v** and velocity **v** as electromechanical analogs, because the products **i v** and **f v** represent instantaneous electrical and mechanical power and are measured in the MKS system by the same unit (newton-metre/second = watt).

A capacitance C is defined by the relation $g = Cv$, and the current through it is $i_C = dq/dt = Cdv/dt$; its mechanical analog is a mass M defined by the relation $f_M = Mdv/dt$. An inductance L can be defined by $v_L = Ldi/dt$; its mechanical analog is the reciprocal of a spring stiffness K, defined by $f_K = Kx$, hence $v_K = K^{-1}\,df/dt$. A resistance R satisfies $v_R = Ri$; its mechanical analog is the reciprocal of the viscosity constant D of a dashpot, which satisfies $v_D = D^{-1}f$. (The electrical analog of D is a conductance G).

If three electrical elements (L, G, C) are connected in parallel, the same voltage **v** exists across all three, and the total current $\mathbf{i} = i_L + i_G + i_C$ is given by

$$\mathbf{i} = \frac{1}{L}\int v\,dt + Gv + C\frac{dv}{dt}. \tag{37}$$

Its mechanical analog consists of a spring, a dashpot and a mass connected in parallel, for, calling **v** the relative velocity of their two common nodes, the total force $\mathbf{f} = f_K + f_D + f_M$ is given by

$$f = Kx + Dv + M\frac{dv}{dt}. \tag{38}$$

The reader will easily write down the equations for the two analog series triads (L, R, C) and (K^{-1}, D^{-1}, M); as also the equations for a series or a parallel rotational mechanical system, in which angle replaces distance, angular velocity replaces linear velocity, and torque replaces force.

Appendix II. Graphical Construction of the Periodic Function of Time Satisfying a Lord Rayleigh-Type Equation

We have seen how the limit-cycle of an LRT equation can be obtained in the phase-plane (v_C, $w = \dot{v}_C$) by the Liénard method (section III). We now want to obtain a graph of the periodic function $v_C(\tau)$ (τ = non-dimensional time $\tau/\sqrt{LC}$). The following procedure will give us at the same time a graph of its time-derivative $w(\tau)$, a van der Pol function.

The limit cycle of the LRT equation, shown in FIGURE A.6, gives us two values of w for each value of v_C within the cycle; let us choose the positive one first. In the (v_C, τ) plane, across a horizontal of arbitrary ordinate v_C, we draw a number of small parallel segments of slope $w = dv_C/dt$. We repeat this construction for all suitable values of v_C; next we draw free-hand an arc of curve having at every point the prescribed slope, as in the method of isoclines (the horizontals are the isoclines). This gives us the greater part of the rising branch of $v_C(\tau)$, crossing the 0τ axis at an arbitrary time.

Repeating this construction, further out at right along 0τ, we obtain separately the greater part of the falling branch of $v_C(\tau)$. However, it is not possible to connect these two branches with precision, because the points where v_C reaches a maximum or a minimum are very ill-defined.

A simple way out of this difficulty is as follows. After we have sketched the rising branch of v_C we can, choosing an arbitrary vertical scale for $w = dv_C/d\tau$, plot for each abscissa the point of positive ordinate w which corresponds to v_C. Joining these points by a smooth curve, we obtain an arc of $w(\tau)$, concave downwards, and it is easy to prolong this arc or arch until the points where it meets 0τ. We thus obtain a point τ_1 where v_C is minimum, and a point τ_2 where v_C is maximum.

Repeating this construction on that part of our sheet where we sketched the falling branch of v_C, we obtain an arc of $w(\tau)$, negative and concave upwards, which we prolong until the points where it meets 0τ. We thus obtain a point τ_3 where v_C is maximum, and a point τ_4 where v_C is minimum.

Tracing all four arcs on one sheet of paper, making τ_2 and τ_3 coincide, we obtain, on the same diagram, the periodic curves $v_C(\tau)$ and $w(\tau)$. The same process applied to a VDPT equation of which the limit cycle is known will give us the periodic curves $w(\tau)$ and $\dot{w}(\tau)$.

Appendix III. Generalisation of Liénard's Construction to a Broad Class of Second-Order Differential Equations

Liénard's graphical construction (section III) is only applicable to an LRT equation

$$\ddot{x} + F(\dot{x}) + x = 0.$$

One advantage of this method, when applicable, is the quickness with which small elements of trajectories are obtained by means of a pair of compasses, keeping the dry point fixed and using a number of arbitrary radii.

This advantage can be retained while extending the Liénard method to the following, broader class of equations

$$\ddot{x} + F(x, \dot{x}) + x = 0 \tag{39}$$

or, putting $\dot{x} = y$

$$\frac{dy}{dx} y + F(x, y) + x = 0. \tag{40}$$

The problem is again, given an arbitrary point M in the phase-plane (x, y), to find the point N where the normal MN to the trajectory going through M crosses the $0x$ axis.

First we sketch on the phase-plane a few curves of equation $F(x, y) = k$, giving to k successive values $\ldots -2, -1, 0, 1, 2, \ldots$. Next we mark off on the $0x$ axis the points N_k of abscissa $(-k)$ FIGURE A.26.

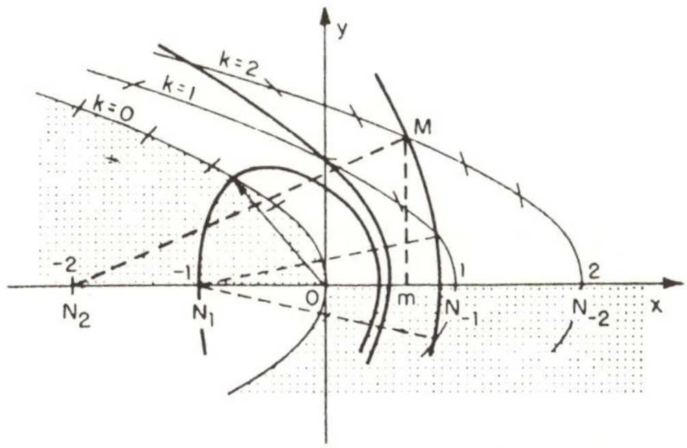

FIGURE A.26 Generalised Liénard construction, on the example of the equation $\ddot{x} + (\dot{x})^2 + 2x = 0$, $F(x, y) = y^2 + x = k$. The equation is explicitly integrable once: $(y^2 + 2x - 1)e^{2x} = C$. The trajectory $C = 0$ (shown) separates closed from open trajectories. In the stippled regions, the radius vector increases

Taking $k = 2$ as an example, consider any point M on the curve $F(x, y) = 2$. The normal to the trajectory going through M is MN_2. For we have, calling m the projection of M on $0x$,

$$\overline{mN_2} + \overline{N_2 0} + \overline{0m} = 0, \tag{41}$$

or

$$\overline{mN_2} + k + x = 0, \tag{42}$$

hence, from (40), $\overline{mN_2} = y\,dy/dx$, the sub-normal.

The construction of the trajectories of (40) follows, the curves $F(x, y) = k$ playing the role of the horizontals in Liénard's method. Among the trajectories there may or may not be closed ones (limit cycles).

The reader may find it interesting to compare this method with the method of isoclines by applying both of them to van der Pol's equation,

$$\ddot{x} - \epsilon(1 - x^2)\dot{x} + x = 0. \tag{43}$$

Equation (40) is equivalent to

$$\frac{dy}{dx} = \frac{-F(x, y) - x}{y} = f(x, y). \tag{44}$$

Going back to section VII, it is clear that a discontinuity of $f(x, y)$ along a curve Λ_{12} means that the variable x receives a (generalised) impulse whenever $(x, \dot{x})$ crosses Λ_{12}. Dr de Figueiredo's theorem 2.5 in Chapter II of his thesis, and the present graphical construction, thus enable us to analyse a class of oscillators with different constraints in regions 1 and 2 of the phase-plane. If, for instance, $F_2(x, y) = F_1(x, y) + y$, the slope of any trajectory will decrease by 1 at the crossing of Λ_{12} in one direction, and increase by 1 in the other direction.

The maxima and minima of the radius vector squared, $(x^2 + y^2)$, for any trajectory, lie on the locus $yF(x, y) = 0$. Regions where the radius vector is increasing are shown stippled on FIGURE A.26.

NOTES

1. B. van der Pol, 'On relaxation oscillations', *Philosophical Magazine*, vol. 2, 1926, p. 978.
2. Lord Rayleigh, 'On maintained vibrations', *Philosophical Magazine*, vol. 15, 1883, p. 229; also *Theory of Sound* (New York: Dover Publications, Inc., 1945) vol. 1, p. 682.
3. P. Le Corbeiller, *Self-Maintained Systems and Relaxation Oscillations* (Paris: Hermann, 1931) (in French); van der Pol, op. cit.
4. Le Corbeiller, op. cit.; P. Le Corbeiller, 'The non-linear theory of the maintenance of oscillations', *Journal of the Institute of Electrical Engineers*, vol. 79, 1936, p. 361.
5. Le Corbeiller, 'The non-linear theory of the maintenance of oscillations', op. cit.

6. A. Liénard, 'Study of maintained oscillations', *Rev. gen. elect.*, vol. 23, 1928, pp. 901–46 (in French); Le Corbeiller, *Self-Maintained Systems and Relaxation Oscillations*, op. cit.; Le Corbeiller, 'The non-linear theory of the maintenance of oscillations', op. cit.
7. P. Le Corbeiller, 'The non-linear theory of the maintenance of oscillations', op. cit.
8. R. Rudenberg, *Transient Performance of Electric Power Systems* (New York: McGraw-Hill Book Co., Inc., 1950) Chapter 36.
9. L. Brillouin, *Tensors* (Paris: Masson, 1938) (in French); (New York: Dover Publications, Inc., 1946), Chapter 1, p. viii.
10. P. Le Corbeiller, *Self-Maintained Systems and Relaxation Oscillations*, op. cit.
11. Equation (25) was discussed by the writer at a Harvard colloquium on 4 October 1957 and in an invited lecture at Rensselaer Polytechnic Institute on 27 March 1958. The pair (27), (28) was later suggested to him by Dr van der Pol and by Dr de Figueiredo, independently.
12. R. J. P. de Figueiredo, 'Existence and Uniqueness of Periodic Solutions in Autonomous Oscillators', Ph.D. thesis, Harvard University, Cambridge, Mass., December 1958.
13. See FIGURE 8 of Le Corbeiller, 'The non-linear theory of the maintenance of oscillations', op. cit.
14. R. J. P. de Figueiredo, 'Existence and Uniqueness of Periodic Solutions in Autonomous Oscillators', Ph.D. thesis, Harvard University, Cambridge, Mass., December 1958.
15. Ibid.
16. W. Nijenhuis, 'A note on a generalized van der Pol equation', *Philips Research Reports.*, vol. 4, 1949, p. 401.
17. E. A. Coddington and N. Levinson, *Theory of Ordinary Differential Equations* (New York: McGraw-Hill Book Co., Inc., 1955).
18. F. A. Firestone, 'A new analogy between electrical and mechanical systems', *Journal of the Acoustical Society of America*, vol. 4, 1933, p. 249.

Index

Page numbers in *italics* refer to tables.